Women in the Third World

We want a world where inequality based on class, gender and race is absent from every country, and from the relationships among countries. We want a world where basic needs become basic rights and where poverty and all forms of violence are eliminated. Each person will have the opportunity to develop her or his full potential and creativity, and women's values of nurturance and solidarity will characterize human relationships. In such a world women's reproductive role will be redefined: child care will be shared by men, women and society as a whole. We want a world where the massive resources now used in the production of the means of destruction will be diverted to areas where they will help to relieve oppression both inside and outside the home. This technological revolution will eliminate disease and hunger, and give women means for the safe control of their fertility. We want a world where all institutions are open to participatory democratic processes, where women share in determining priorities and making decisions.

Gita Sen and Caren Grown for
Development Alternatives with
Women for a New Era (DAWN)
Development, Crises and Alternative Visions
(Earthscan: London, 1988, pp. 80–1)

Women in the Third World

Gender Issues in Rural and Urban Areas

Lynne Brydon

Sylvia Chant

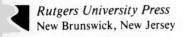

Rutgers University Press
New Brunswick, New Jersey

Second paperback printing, 1993

First published in the United States of America in cloth and paperback by
Rutgers University Press, 1989
First published in cloth and paperback in the United Kingdom by Edward
Elgar Publishing Limited, 1989

Library of Congress Cataloging-in-Publication Data
Brydon, Lynne
  Women in the Third World: gender issues in rural and urban areas
  Lynne Brydon and Sylvia Chant.
    p. cm.
  Bibliography: p.
  ISBN 0-8135-1470-3 – ISBN 0-8135-1471-1 (pbk.)
  1. Women – Developing countries – Social conditions. 2. Women in
development – Developing countries. 3. Sex role – Developing countries.
  I. Chant, Sylvia H.   II. Title.
  HQ1870.9.B79 1989
  305.4′09172′4 – dc20
                                                              89-8119
                                                              CIP

84

Contents

Preface

This book developed from a joint proposal to teach a course called 'Women in the Third World' to final-year social science students in the University of Liverpool.* When the proposal was first made, there were several excellent texts and collections available for teaching purposes, but we felt that none was broad enough on its own to serve as background for a substantial part of the course: if a broad range of issues was discussed, then the geographical focus was not particularly wide; regional at best. On the other hand, studies dealing with a number of countries or regions tended to focus on one issue, or at most a narrow range of related issues. So we decided to produce a book of our own to use as background and source material and which, we felt, gave the necessary comparative overview.

The size of our bibliography attests to the enormous amount of work on women's issues in the Third World, and we should emphasize here that we have merely scraped the surface: omissions are due to logistics rather than any lack of relevance. We should like to put on record our sincere gratitude to our colleagues and students in the Geography and Sociology Departments and the Institute of Latin American Studies in the University of Liverpool for their valuable comments, suggestions and support. In particular we extend our thanks to Anne Rowland in the Inter-Library Loan office in the Sydney Jones Library, to Sandra Mather in the Drawing Office, and to Tina Benson and Tricia McMillan in the Sociology Department. Sylvia Chant would also like to acknowledge a debt to Caroline Moser of the Department of Social Science and Administration at the London School of Economics (this is set out specifically in Chapter 9).

*The writing of this book was carried out entirely in Liverpool before Sylvia Chant left her joint lectureship in Geography and Latin American Studies to take up her present appointment at the London School of Economics.

Finally we have to thank each other and our respective partners for forebearance and calm tolerance of intermittent crises which necessitated long phone calls and interrupted weekends.

Lynne Brydon
Sylvia Chant
Liverpool, July 1988

1 Introduction: Women in the Third World: An Overview

INTRODUCTION

This book provides an overview of women's roles and status in the contemporary developing world. By roles we refer to the manifold activities carried out by Third World women, such as child-care, housework, subsistence farming, remunerated employment and health care. By status we refer to the value and meaning given to these activities by wider society, which in turn both reflect and influence the general rubric of gender relations. Barbara Rogers (1980) points out that the phrase 'status of women' often carries a rather 'pejorative tone' and suggests that 'Judgements made by anthropologists and sociologists alike about the "status of women" in other societies may tell us more about those who are making these judgements than about their subjects' (ibid, p.33). Rogers also argues that status is essentially a static concept and observes that the 'status of men' is rarely, if ever, a subject for study. However, we use the term with no derogatory overtones, and recognize that 'status' should be construed as a dynamic concept, with the implication of change over time.[1] We also try, as far as possible, to avoid ethnocentric value-judgements.

In what follows we explore major aspects of women's lives in Third World countries, and, more specifically, look at the extent to which 'gender inequality' is incorporated into development, both ideologically and practically. Where possible we draw upon studies based upon the subjective experiences of Third World women, rather than secondary sources such as government statistical reports or census data. These latter kinds of material not only say little about the meaning of women's lives, but are also prone to gross inaccuracies, often under-recording women's activities or even excluding them altogether.[2]

Although the book's primary concern is to detail and analyse

1

various aspects of *women's* lives in Third World societies, we attempt to do so with consistent reference to the overall context of gender relations; thus we examine issues affecting women in relation to the experience of their male counterparts. Any analysis of the situation of women which ignores this broader canvas is likely only 'to distort the reality we are trying to understand' (Fortes, 1980. p.363).

Where reference to women's and men's roles and interrelations is made, we use the term 'gender' rather than 'sex' since the latter only describes biological characteristics, whereas the former encompasses socially constructed categories of gender (Mackintosh, 1981). An exception here is the phrase 'sexual division of labour'. This we use as a commonplace shorthand version of what Mackintosh more correctly identifies as a 'division of labour along gender lines' (ibid. p.2), that is, a division of labour between men and women deriving from the social framework of gender relations.

The women we discuss in this book are mainly low-income women for two main reasons: first, because poverty is the condition of the vast majority of people in the Third World, and second, because far more has been written about poor women than those belonging to middle- or upper-income groups. This is not to imply that the situations of middle-class and elite women are not in themselves problematic, nor that they do not merit enquiry. Indeed, it has often been pointed out that while membership of a higher class (here equated with income) may improve the material aspects of women's lives and raise their overall 'status' in society, they continue none the less to suffer from gender subordination (Fernandez-Kelly, 1981; Oppong, 1974). Gender relations obviously have repercussions on the lives of all women, and at apposite points in the text we make reference to higher-income women whose experiences of subordination shed light upon the overall position of women in society. However, there are sound academic reasons for confining our analysis primarily to lower-income groups. Although gender subordination frequently transcends class barriers, class as a factor in itself also plays a major role in determining the specific nature of gender inequality. Evidence from Latin America and the Caribbean has shown this to be the case (e.g. LACWC, 1980; Deere and Leon de Leal, 1982). The women of the Latin American and Caribbean Women's Collective (1980) go as far as to say that the conditions of middle- and working-class women are often so divergent that 'The differences between women in many ways are more relevant than the similarities between them' (LACWC, 1980, p. 10).

For historical and scholarly reasons, 'class' in the literature is much less contentious in Latin America than in Africa and Asia. In Asia, class analyses are complicated by ideological considerations of caste and religion, while in Africa, where the vast majority of women reside in rural areas, the debate continues over the relevance of class as an analytical concept, let alone what 'class', if any, women might be members of.[3]

ORGANIZATION OF THE BOOK

The Rationale for Rural and Urban Sections

We have divided the text into two major sections. The first looks at women's positions in rural areas, the second examines their conditions in towns and cities. There are several reasons for this division, one of the most important, and pragmatic, being that the bulk of the literature on women in development tends to concentrate on one or other area only. With the exception of national or regional overviews of gender, or analyses of particular topics such as migration (and concomitant rural–urban linkages), most detailed case studies are based on research carried out in *either* rural *or* urban areas, often in a single village or city, and have rarely spanned the rural–urban divide.

Before going on to identify other reasons for our chosen division, we must point out that there are problems with the definition of 'urban', and more particularly with the definition of 'urbanization'. For census purposes, arbitrary cut-off points are established between communities with a given number of inhabitants (conventionally 5000 or 20,000), the larger communities thus designated being labelled 'urban'. But it is obvious when we come to consider 'urbanization' that such kinds of arbitrary definition are often irrelevant. What is crucial here is not so much the actual numbers of inhabitants in towns or cities, but rather the range and kinds of employment (and training) opportunities available, the distance of the town from a rural 'home' area (in the case of migrants), and the status of the city (whether it is a national or administrative capital, a major port, and so on). For example, until the early 1970s when the effects of Nigeria's oil boom permeated the economy, Kano, a northern city with a population of around 100,000, had few employment opportunities in the 'modern' industrial sector, and was scarcely distinguishable from much smaller settlements nearby. External factors have since meant that Kano's economy has become much more differentiated than those of smaller local settlements, and as a result the city now offers a much wider range of employment opportunities and socio-economic conditions. Being 'urban' or becoming 'urbanized' therefore, has less to do directly with settlement size, and more to do with access to productive (and reproductive) resources.

Bearing these problems in mind, we do feel there is a positive pedagogic justification for making a rural–urban distinction in analytic terms. First, adopting a thematic approach (pp.8–13) and subdividing the relevant empirical material according to rural or urban residence allows us to avoid a narrow particularistic focus on individual countries and to present a broader comparative overview of women in the Third World. Second, such a division permits us to group various kinds of factors according to whether they are associated with long-standing social customs or more recent processes arising from the imposition of colonial rule, incorporation into the world capitalist system, and 'economic development'. Many authors have noted that the lives of urban women are currently undergoing different types and degrees of change from those of their rural counterparts. For example, in cities women are either dependent upon their husbands for maintenance or must seek remunerated employment on their own account. In rural areas, by contrast, women may still have to rely upon marriage to gain access to productive resources, but as an additional option to selling their labour, may also draw upon support from kin and acquire land through inheritance (see Chapter 2). Of course, the range of opportunities for women to earn a cash income is usually much wider in towns than in the countryside. Our objective is emphatically *not* to demonstrate or even to broach the issue of whether women's general status is 'worse' or 'better' in urban or rural areas. Not only does a wide range of conflicting evidence imply that comparisons cannot be given generalized treatment, but the controversial issue of selecting universal standards by which one would assess the relative status of women in different areas demonstrates the pointlessness of mounting such a task at the outset. However, by emphasizing 'long-standing social customs' more in the 'rural' section of the book, and then dealing with the impact of colonial rule and subsequent developments in both sections, we feel we are adding a sense of actual history.

It is vitally important to note that our emphasis on traditional practices in the 'rural' section in no way implies acceptance of, or adherence to, the work of the 'modernization' theorists of the 1960s and 1970s; this school took 'urbanization' as a *sine qua non* of economic development, and a proxy for the 'modernization' of attitudes (e.g. Germani, 1970, 1981; Gugler and Flanagan, 1978; Harkess, 1973; Kahl, 1968). 'Modernization's' Western-biased view of the kinds of values appropriate to economic progress dictated that the process of becoming 'urban' would necessarily involve the rejection of traditional (and, by implication, 'obsolete') values. As stated previously, we feel that 'urbanization' is essentially a *demographic* phenomenon, which above all affects *access to resources*. We in no way imply that urban is 'advanced' and rural 'backward'. Everywhere, whether rural or urban, Third World women live in the late twentieth century.

Having argued that there are various reasons for dealing with various issues in terms of their association with a rural or urban setting, we would also like to draw attention to the fact that in certain cases we have included 'rural' examples in our 'urban' chapters and vice versa in order to illustrate specific points. We do this in order to avoid needless repetition, and besides, several processes affecting women are similar, regardless of residence. More specific justification of where we have taken up certain themes for detailed analysis in different sections are identified below.

As a footnote to this sub-section, we emphasize that as far as possible, the book should be considered as an integrated whole. Neither of us feels that 'rural' and 'urban' issues can or should be separated in any comprehensive analysis of the Third World, and we stress again that the main rationale behind the division is to make the most appropriate use of available material. We hope that our repeated attempts to identify linkages in the substantive chapters and conclusion will help the reader gain a fairly general and informed impression of gender issues in the contemporary Third World.

APPROACHES TO GENDER AND DEVELOPMENT

Theoretical Orientations in Development Studies

Broadly speaking we can divide approaches to 'development' into two: conservative 'modernization' approaches, and radical 'dependency/underdevelopment' approaches (see Blomström and Hettne, 1984; Hoogvelt, 1976; Webster, 1984, for general discussions of development theories). Those subscribing to the former assume that the model for development is that followed by Western Europe through the Industrial Revolution and subsequently. Thus it is believed that with a certain level of industrial production, of education, and a certain proportion of the population in towns to supply labour, then Third World countries will 'take off' into sustained economic growth (Rostow, 1960). Thereafter they will be able to compete in world markets with the advanced economies. As economic development proceeds, as we discussed in the previous section, then 'values' and 'attitudes' become 'modern'. This is thought to happen most effectively in urban areas, and that over time the effects would 'trickle down' into the 'backward' rural regions.

Modernization theses have been largely discredited within the contemporary development literature for a number of very sound reasons. Approaches with an underlying 'dependency' or 'underdevelopment' orientation have much more current credibility. These see the situation of contemporary Third World states as one of structural dependency: Third World states rely on First World markets to buy their produce (mainly primary or agricultural products) in order to buy foreign exchange to finance projects concerned with providing the infrastructure and services necessary for development, such as schools, transport networks, and so on. Because of the need to secure hard currency, Third World states are usually in competition with one another over the sale of their produce and therefore do not form cartels to help 'fix' the price of their export products. The Organization of Petroleum Exporting Countries (OPEC) was a notable exception to this general rule, but even then its hold on the world oil market has been progressively undermined by internal competition. (See Rees and Odell, 1987, for an up-to-date review of the international oil industry.) More cynical commentators argue that First World governments make sure that competition between developing countries remains in order to tighten their economic stranglehold.

Both these sets of approaches are essentially 'top-down' views of development; they look at the general situation of Third World countries and their relations with the advanced economies and try to adduce the factors bringing about change, or not, as the case may be.

What is particularly striking about them from our point of view is that they have little or no place for women. Women are either assumed to be attached to men, or are ignored altogether; that is they are not analysed as a social group in their own right. Those who suggest that women's status improves with economic development, frequently fail to take into account the widespread structures of patriarchy which keep women in subordinate positions. A more recent approach to development advocating a 'bottom-up' strategy is that of 'basic needs' (Webster, 1984; Stewart, 1985), but here again there is inadequate recognition of patriarchy and other ideological structures as they influence the position and 'needs' of Third World women. Clearly, conventional development theories are inadequate in terms of providing us with a basic framework within which to explore issues affecting Third World women. However, the same is more or less true for theories which have come to the fore in the analysis of gender.

Theoretical Orientations in Gender Studies

Most theoretical advances in the study of women and gender relations have been formulated on the basis of historical and contemporary studies of women in the First World, particularly North-West Europe and the United States (Benería and Sen, 1981). As such, few of the precepts apply in their entirety to Third World countries. Pepe Roberts (1984), for example, describes the limitations of mainstream feminist theory in terms of its relevance to Africa. Existing theories about women and gender also range widely; not only is there a considerable divergence in overall approach (especially in terms of whether 'patriarchy' as a catch-all for male domination of women should be seen as independent of, interactive with or determined by the mode of production (especially capitalism) (e.g. Adlam, 1979; Beechey, 1979; Eisenstein, 1979; Ennew, 1979), but there is also a considerable lack of consensus *within* the various strands of analysis. Feminist debates can be extremely confusing: Marxist-feminism for example, contains a plethora of different points of view, leading Michèle Barrett (1986, p.8) to conclude that much of the work generated within this theoretical framework remains 'fragmentary and contradictory'.

Given these numerous standpoints, and particularly because they

are so often tied to the historical experience of Europe and North
America, we do not include a detailed overview of current theoretical approaches to gender here, nor, in the course of the book, do we
draw upon one conceptual framework in particular. Instead we have
tried to use as much empirical evidence as possible, and to synthesize
the interpretations and arguments used by a wide range of authors
working from different theoretical perspectives. If anything, however, our overall approach is pinned to the feminist paradigm
outlined by Lourdes Benería and Gita Sen (1981) in their review of a
decade of research on women and development following the
publication of Ester Boserup's seminal work *Woman's Role in
Economic Development*. Here they argue that the roots of women's
oppression must be sought not only within the sphere of production,
but also reproduction, not only in economic structures, but also in
social and cultural structures, and that women's frequent loss of
status in the course of economic development must be conceived in
the context of an 'interweaving of class relations and gender relations' (ibid., p.288). This view is at one and the same time precise
enough and broad enough to permit us to organize and interpret a
wide range of material relating to gender issues in the Third World
today.

MAJOR THEMES

We have focused on four major themes which have relevance for
'gender questions' in less-developed countries: the household,
reproduction, production and policy (Chapters 2–4 and 6–9).
Chapter 5 deals with a fifth theme, migration, to bridge the rural-
urban divide. We recognise that these themes interact and are
structurally interdependent, but again for analytic purposes it is
useful to break them down into their component parts.

The Household

The household, however we define it, is a fairly common form of
social organization in most regions of the developing world, and
often represents the primary site for the structuring of gender
relations and women's specific experience (Harris, 1981). Janet

Townsend and Janet Momsen (1987, p.40) arguing from a feminist perspective identify the household as an 'arena of subordination'.

A household is usually defined as a residential unit whose members share 'domestic' functions and activities — a group of people who 'eat out of the same pot' (Mackintosh, 1979) or who 'share the same bowl' (Robertson, 1984a). Although members of a household often share the same residence, this is not always the case, nor do they necessarily share consumption. However, Olivia Harris (1981, p.52) observes generally and in relation to women that:

The English term household denotes an institution whose primary feature is co-residence; it is overwhelmingly assumed that people who live within a single space, however that is socially defined, share in the tasks of day-to-day servicing of human beings, including consumption, and organise the reproduction of the next generation. Co-residence implies a special intimacy, a fusing of physiological functions, or a real distinction from other types of social relations which can be portrayed as more amenable to analysis. It is undoubtedly the case that whether or not it coincides with a family of procreation, household organisation is fundamental to ideologies of womanhood, and that households are in material terms the context for much of women's lives.

Although membership of a household implies at least a minimal degree of interaction with others in the unit, it cannot be assumed that such interaction entails equality or even cooperation among individuals (Harris, 1981; Murray, 1987; Roberts, n.d.). Frequently there are considerable disparities in terms of the inputs, benefits and activities of various household members, with age and sex often being critical variables in the equation (Kabeer, 1985; see also Chapters 2, 3 and 6).

It is also important to point out that while most 'households' consist of kin (either affinal, consanguineal or both), it is also wrong to assume *ipso facto* that 'households' may be equated with residential 'family' units.[4] Unrelated household members may sometimes be co-opted as 'fictive' kin through ritual practices such as 'godparenthood' or *compadrazgo* (Goody, 1971), but equally they may retain their non-kin status. Households may not be visible entities in terms of buildings or sets of rooms within residential units, but isolable only in terms of specific functions such as cooking or the pooling of finance; on the other hand, there may be active inter-household networks of reciprocity and exchange which are regular features of multi-family compounds and low-income neighbourhoods (Arizpe, 1977; Kemper, 1977; Lomnitz, 1977; Sharma, 1986). We must therefore ask the question: 'Is the concept of the household a relevant one at all?' We feel it is, primarily because it is both the point of origin and destination for the labour and resources of its component members, the household is the point at which reproductive and productive relations meet. As Marianne Schmink (1986, p.40) suggests:

The boundaries and functions of domestic units vary across societies and through time. In some cases coresidence is coterminous with kinship relationships. Domestic units may also be the principal locus of production and/or of biological reproduction. In many cases coresidence defines the unit of most forms of consumption, where a *final* pooling and redistribution of resources to individuals takes place (our emphasis).

The 'household' is critical for the analysis of gender roles and relations, and is usually the focal point of the sexual division of labour.

The forms and functions of rural households are dealt with in Chapter 2, and an outline is provided of the primary features of kinship systems in various regions of the developing world. Critical issues here are women's status and roles both in the household and in the wider community. In our parallel analysis of these themes in the urban section, Chapter 6 identifies some of the most important changes taking place in household form and functions with urbanization. What implications do processes such as migration and changing access to material resources in towns and cities have for the sexual division of labour, gender relations and the lives of 'urban' women?

Reproduction

Our second major theme, 'reproduction', has a wide variety of connotations, ranging from the process of 'biological' reproduction at one end of the spectrum to the process of 'social' reproduction at the other. 'Biological' reproduction comprises child-birth and lactation; 'physical' reproduction involves the daily regeneration of the wage labour force through cooking, cleaning, washing and so on; and 'social' reproduction, an all-embracing category, refers to the maintenance of ideological conditions which reproduce class relations and uphold the social and economic status quo (Barrett, 1986; Edholm, Harris and Young, 1977, 1982; Mackintosh, 1981).

Reproduction encompasses various individual and collective forms of consumption and therefore can also be used to describe the transformation of goods and services for household use and welfare. In most societies reproductive activities tend to fall upon the shoulders of women, and to remain outside the domain of public life and politics. In recent years, however, the bureaucratic 'state' in many Third World countries has become involved in various aspects of the reproductive process, particularly in cities, thereby forging new and more visible relations with women.

In Chapter 2 we consider various aspects of reproduction in rural communities; this involves discussion of household 'welfare' functions, kin groups and women's reproductive activities in both the household and local community. In Chapter 8 we examine urban women's role in areas of reproduction in which the state has become progressively involved, notably family planning, health-care, urban housing and services. Obviously birth control and health are issues which also concern rural areas, and evidence is drawn from rural case studies in order to exemplify specific points, however we have chosen to deal with these issues in the urban section because medical and contraception programmes have often been directed, initially at any rate, at urban populations, for administrative convenience.

Production

Our third major theme, 'production', has different possible meanings in urban and rural contexts. In urban areas, production is usually defined (and defined for our purposes here) as all activities which directly generate income. Nevertheless, this classification is not entirely satisfactory. Many Marxist-Feminists argue that activities spanning the entire spectrum of reproduction and production create value, and are therefore potentially 'income-generating'. Merely because 'domestic' tasks such as housework and child-care are unwaged in virtually all societies does not mean that these activities are 'unproductive', and still less that they do not constitute a category of 'work'. Several domestic-based activities contribute income to the household unit in the form of saving, budgeting or the provision of unpaid services.

The problems of defining the boundaries between production and reproduction in rural environments are complicated by the existence of an intermediate category of activity, subsistence farming. Subsistence farming is essentially production for *use* (and in this sense akin to reproduction), yet in content it displays similarities to income-generating rural activities, and in times of surplus may itself (in part) become production for *exchange*. In view of this, we might well ask whether drawing a rather arbitrary divide between 'productive' and 'reproductive' labour is valid, let alone necessary. Again, we argue its worth in analytical terms. In most parts of the world, involvement in 'production', or recognizable income-generating activities (the creation of 'exchange values'), is accorded greater value than involvement in the subsistence or reproductive sphere (the creation of 'use values'); the former is usually dominated by men and the latter tends to be the domain of women. The overall status and material benefits of those engaged in wage-earning, self-employment, cash-cropping and so on tends in general to be higher than those confined to the domestic sector.

Chapter 3 on gender and rural production contains a detailed examination of women's roles in various types of rural production, as well as reminding us of the problems of separating 'production' from 'reproduction' in rural contexts. Chapter 7 on gender and urban production considers the position of women in urban labour markets and attempts to explain their low status in the employment hierarchy.

Policy and Planning

The twin theme of policy and planning is more easily defined than the preceding concepts, primarily because it is linked to the direct actions of Third World governments, international aid and development agencies, charities and non-governmental organizations on rural and urban communities. In Chapter 4 we consider the effect on women of various agricultural and rural development schemes, including large-scale land reform. We are also concerned in this chapter to look at the bases for enumeration and evaluation of women and women's work by governments and development agencies. In Chapter 9 we examine policy and planning initiatives in the urban context, including housing programmes, service provision, and general community development projects. Here we also concentrate specifically on the ideology of self-help and community participation (a 'bottom-up' orientation), drawing on evidence from both urban and rural examples. Policy issues are extremely relevant in any contemporary analysis of gender given that the recent United Nations Decade for Women (1975–85) marked a significant step forward in recognizing women's critical role in Third World development (see Chapter 10).

Migration

Our final theme, migration, is dealt with in Chapter 5, and here we aim to show some of the linkages between rural and urban areas. The main focus is upon the migration process itself, its relationship to changing patterns of rural development, regional variations in sex- and skill-selectivity of migrants, the effects on rural areas of out-migration, and the relationships maintained between those in the countryside and those in the town. This sets the scene for the analysis of gender roles and relations in urban environments in Chapters 6–9.

Having outlined the scope of the book, we now provide brief descriptions of the major characteristics of women's roles and status in the major Third World regions from which we shall be drawing substantive examples in the course of the text.

OUTLINE OF WOMEN AND GENDER RELATIONS IN MAJOR THIRD WORLD REGIONS

In attempting to present an overview of women in major regions of the developing world, we realize we risk running into dangerous levels of generalization. Within the broad areas specified (see below) there are not only several intra-regional and inter-community differences on the basis of religion, culture, political ideology and so on, but also significant variations in women's status according to their position in the class hierarchy. Although we attempt to highlight the most prominent variations in each major area, given limitations of space, we confine our descriptions mainly to dominant characteristics at the regional or continental scale. Obviously with such a task it is also necessary to simplify some very complex issues and we urge the reader to supplement the text where possible with the references cited.

Our 'regions' are primarily geographical: Latin America, the Caribbean, Sub-Saharan Africa, South Asia and Southeast Asia (see Figure 1.1). The Middle East and North Africa are dealt with as a single entity due to their common experience of Islam, a religious ideology which has had a marked effect on gender relations throughout the area. As far as possible we try to include at least some information on all nations in each region. However, certain countries are omitted from the analysis for the simple reason that we have found little material about them: one such group is Oceania which comprises several small islands such as Vanuatu, New Guinea, Tonga, Fiji, Samoa and Guam. Another 'group' includes islands such as the Seychelles and the Maldives in the Indian Ocean. Two major countries are also omitted, not because of lack of material in this case, but rather because they are markedly 'atypical' in terms of general 'Third World' characteristics: the People's Republic of China and the Republic of South Africa. We hope we do not offend specialists in any of the above areas by excluding them from the text.

The broad issues covered in the following vignettes of women's condition include historical development, contemporary economic and demographic characteristics, religion, 'culture' and the family. We intend this overview to inform the reader about the general situation of gender in the regions identified, thereby providing him or her with some kind of contextual framework against which the specific examples we draw upon later in the book may be better understood.

Women and Gender in Latin America

At a distance, and sometimes even at close quarters, there appears to be a remarkable degree of cultural, religious and linguistic uniformity for a continent the size of Latin America. Much of this is due to the active nature of the colonization process embarked upon by the Spanish in particular during three centuries of direct rule from the end of the fifteenth century onwards.[5] Despite the fact that there were several well-established indigenous civilizations on the continent before the conquest, including the Maya, Aztec and Inca

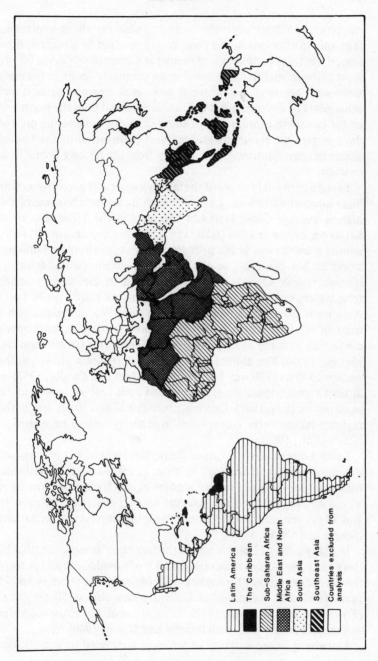

Figure 1.   Guide to Major Third World Regions

empires, the vigour with which the colonists set about implanting Hispanic institutions in the New World resulted in a marked dilution, if not total decimation, of many pre-Columbian ways of life. In most cases formal ties with the Iberian peninsula broke in the early nineteenth century, but informal links with Spain, Portugal and other parts of Europe, notably France, persisted until the beginning of the twentieth century and in some cases continue to the present day, despite the economic and cultural penetration of the United States into the continent, particularly from the Second World War onwards.

In spite of the debt crises of the last five years and notwithstanding huge internal variations, Latin America as a whole has one of the highest average Gross National Products in the Third World: at $2160 per capita in 1986 (IDB, 1987). During the decade 1971–80, annual growth rates in the primary sector (agriculture and mining) stood at 3.4 per cent; in the secondary sector (manufacturing, transport, and so on) at 7 per cent; and in the tertiary sector (commerce, services, and so on) at 6.5 per cent (IDB, 1987). Latin America is the most 'urbanized' of the Third World regions with a total of 42.5 per cent of the population residing in settlements containing as many as 100,000 or more inhabitants (Armstrong and McGee, 1985). The annual rate of urban population growth in the decade 1970 to 1980 was 3.8 per cent (Gilbert and Gugler, 1982) as against a total population growth rate of 2 per cent per annum in the same period (UN, 1981). Currently between 25 and 30 per cent of the region's labour force is employed in industry-related occupations. (Crow et al., 1983).

Latin America also has one of the highest rates of women engaged in waged work and trading; in most countries of the continent, between 26 and 45 per cent of women aged 15 years or more have waged employment, and on average women constitute between 16 and 35 per cent of the total labour force in Latin American nations (Seager and Olson, 1986).

In many parts of Latin America the 'sex ratio' is feminine (that is, there are more women than men per 1000 of population) and average female life expectancy throughout the continent is between 60 and 75 years (with the exception of Bolivia where this is 50–59 years) (Townsend and Momsen, 1987). In most Latin American countries women live longer than men (Seager and Olson, 1986).

Machismo, a term rightly or wrongly attributed to a particular

Hispanic–New World form of patriarchy, is often cited as the hallmark of gender relations in Latin America. Explanations and characterizations of *machismo* vary; the term derives from the Spanish word *macho* meaning male, and is often associated with male control (both ideological and physical) of women (Cubitt, 1988; LACWC, 1980; Pescatello, 1976). Also embodied in the concept is the idea of virility, sexual prowess, courage and competition between men (Cubitt, 1988). Manifestations of *machismo* include male domination of household and other familial decision-making, along with the imposition of restrictions on women's social, sexual and economic freedom. *Machismo* is also frequently invoked as a cultural legitimation of violence against women (Arizpe, 1982; Stevens, 1973), and even among the poorest strata of society, the ideology is argued to reproduce male privilege (Zabaleta, 1986).

Some trace this pattern of gender relations, in Spanish America at least, to the colonial period, during which time the Crown and the Roman Catholic Church colluded to promote both a patrilineal kinship system and an ideology of female chastity, fidelity and subservience (Scott, 1986a). Concepts of honour and shame tied to the morality of women had their roots in many circum-Mediterranean countries, but they flourished to an even greater degree in the New World (Cubitt, 1988). Downgrading of female status also reached unprecedented levels in the Americas: not only was womanhood denigrated to the point that the Iberian law codes identified woman as *imbecilitus sexus* (an imbecile by nature) (Pescatello, 1976), but racism towards indigenous New World populations combined with sexism to produce a situation in which women came to be seen both as sexual *and* social inferiors (Elmendorf, 1977; Youssef, 1972). This early racial–sexual association has been argued to have profoundly influenced the subsequent development of gender relations in the continent. As Tessa Cubitt (1988, pp.103–4) notes of *machismo*:

Since its early expression was in the form of sexual relations between conquering white soldiers and dominated Indian women, it has taken on a distinctly aggressive element which can emerge in the form of violence.

Cubitt goes on to add that, as such, *Machismo* is far more characteristic of *mestizo* (people of mixed Spanish and Indian descent) than indigenous communities; the latter arguably display greater degrees of egalitarianism and complementarity between the sexes (see also

Buenaventura-Posso and Brown, 1987; Scott, 1986a; and Wolf, 1959).

The Roman Catholic Church has played a major role in reinforcing and perpetuating the subordinate position of women. In census data most of the Latin American population is registered as Catholic, and even if church attendance is irregular, the general precepts of the faith are widely held.[6] The major aspects of Catholicism affecting women include a glorification of motherhood and female suffering, personified in the image of the Virgin Mary, and an encouragement to accept one's lot on earth in preparation for a better life in heaven (Arnold, 1978). Stoic behaviour is expected of women as guardians of faith, virtue and the moral order, and includes amongst other things, the silent endurance of unhappy marriages and financial penury. Only in a few Catholic countries is formal divorce readily permitted (Lewenhak, 1980). The Church actively advises women against using artificial birth-control methods, thereby reducing their chances to gain control over their own fertility (Cubitt, 1988). Women are encouraged to be good wives, and above all to be 'good' mothers – 'good' in this case meaning the demonstration of self-denial, passivity and resignation (Arizpe, 1982; LACWC, 1980; Pescatello, 1976; Stevens, 1973). As Escobar, González and Roberts (1987, p.60) point out for Mexico: 'The long-suffering mother, mainstay of the family, is a cultural heroine . . .'

Within both home and family there is a marked sexual division of labour and a strict normative gender role system such that Latin American women often have little power to exercise choice over their lifestyles. Most are brought up with the idea that their main role in life is to become mothers, and to give birth to large numbers of children usually all those that 'God wills'. The fact of having several children is not in itself problematic, and indeed Lourdes Arizpe (1982, p.80) suggests that Latin American women often gain a social centrality and an emotional power through motherhood that Western women lack. However, the status trappings of motherhood *are* problematic for those who are unable or unwilling to conceive. Unmarried or childless women tend to be seen as 'deviant' and are often subjected to pressures from kin to validate their 'true' gender role by fostering a sister's or a cousin's child. Quasi-parental responsibilities not only ensure that single women fulfil themselves as *women*, but also provide them with 'respectability' in a society where the control of female sexuality is paramount. Thus fertile or infertile, willing or not, for the majority of Latin American women, all roads ultimately lead to 'motherhood'.

Generally there is a low emotional content to a husband–wife relationship compared to that between a mother and son (Lomnitz, 1977). Men hold their mothers in far higher esteem than their wives, primarily because they do not have a sexual relationship with the former. This state of affairs has sometimes been explained in terms of the contradictory ideals set up for women via Catholicism's reverence of the Virgin Mary and its insistence on the Immaculate Conception.

As the Catholic symbol of the perfect woman, the Virgin Mary presents a definition that is, in the end, damaging to women. The twin ideal of mother and virgin is impossible for a woman to achieve. The destiny and purpose that this myth establishes for women (i.e. motherhood) is then also devalued – since sex is necessary for a woman to fulfill her destiny. A symbol of renunciation, the Virgin puts the female believer in a position of acknowledged inferiority and so underlines the dangers of sex, the fear of corruption and her sense of sin. (Deighton et al, 1983, p.146)

The nuclear patriarchal family is the norm in Latin America today, despite the massive growth of women-headed households in the last ten to twenty years (Nash, 1980). Even among relatively isolated cultural groups such as the Bari of Colombia where there has long been a custom of egalitarianism between the sexes and communal forms of living, 'development' and contact with the rest of Colombian society has led to a shift towards the nuclear family and a consequent isolation of women (Buenaventura-Posso and Brown, 1987). The sexual division of labour is possibly at its most marked within the family unit and this plays a major role in determining women's involvement in wider aspects of social and economic life.

In parts of Latin America which have undergone social and political revolution, such as Nicaragua and Cuba, it is proving extremely hard to wrench men and women away from stereotypical views and attitudes, despite state and judicial exhortations to the contrary. For example in Cuba the Family Code stresses that the socialist family, as the 'elementary cell of society', should be an egalitarian institution meeting 'deep-rooted human needs in the social field and in the field of affection for the individual' (Stone, 1981, p.140). Chapter Two, Section One of the Code, concerning the relationship between husband and wife states that marriage is established with equal rights and duties for both partners, that spouses must 'live together, be loyal, considerate, respectful and mutually helpful to each other', and that they must participate in the care of children resulting from the marriage and in the running of the home *'to the extent of their capacity or possibilities'* (ibid., p.146; our emphasis). Suffice to say that these egalitarian principles are rarely observed in practice; after thirty years of socialism, men are still the primary breadwinners, occupy posts of greater public prestige, and leave women to carry out the bulk of child-care and domestic labour. (See also Chapter 4.)

Maria Patricia Fernandez-Kelly (1981, p.275) argues that socialist governments have often intensified rather than diminished women's burden', by encouraging them to take on a greater share of economic activity. Nevertheless, these outcomes should not be viewed as intended, and at least some socialist governments in Latin America have tried to promote an ideal of marriage and family life founded on love, affection, cooperation and equality, rather than on imperatives of financial need or property. In Cuba, for example, women do not need to get married in order to obtain social 'status' or access to physical means of survival such as housing and employment. Furthermore, marriages may easily be dissolved by both parties if there is no longer any love between the couple.

This situation contrasts starkly with non-socialist Latin American countries such as El Salvador. Article 265 of the Salvadorean Penal Code for example, condemns a married woman who has 'carnal access to any man other than her husband' to between six months and two years' imprisonment, whereas this only applies to a man where he attempts to *keep* a concubine, and through the resultant costs, fails to meet his family obligations (Thomson, 1986, p.30).

Most Latin American women are married or have children by the time they are in their mid-twenties, and between 10 and 25 per cent of girls in the age group 15–19 are or have been officially married, compared to an average figure of under 10 per cent for most of the developed world (Seager and Olson, 1986). In most Latin American countries women bear between four and six children, and in Ecuador, Bolivia, Honduras and Nicaragua the average is over six (Seager and Olson, 1986). The crude birth-rate in Latin America as a whole was projected at 32.3 per 1000 in 1980–85 (UN, 1981).

Summing up the overall situation of women in Latin America, their position is one of pressure to conform to ideals of motherhood and domesticity, backed by a cultural system legitimizing male superiority and the Roman Catholic Church. Despite the fact that many Latin American women have paid work, especially in urban areas, and that they often head their own households, real independence is difficult to achieve in an overall context of gender discrimination. As such, many women are effectively forced to attach themselves to a man, often within the context of a patriarchal nuclear household. This reinforces still further their isolation from wider social, political and economic life.

Women and Gender in the Caribbean

The Caribbean region is often dealt with as an appendage to Latin America, because of its geographical location and certain structural similarities in historical evolution and contemporary economic development, particularly its involvement with the United States. However, in terms of gender, there are several reasons for treating the region independently. The first concerns the racial and cultural heritage of Caribbean women, the majority of whom are of African descent, with another major group originating in the East Indies. The second is the fact that Caribbean women arguably have a greater degree of social and economic autonomy than their Latin American counterparts (Ellis, 1986).

The Caribbean region includes major islands such as Jamaica, the Dominican Republic, Haiti, Trinidad and Tobago; several smaller islands such as Grenada, St Lucia, Barbados, St Vincent, Antigua, Barbuda and Guadelupe, and also the Guyanas on the northern tip of mainland South America. Per capita GNP varies greatly among the constituent countries; in 1985, for example, it was $7070 US in the Bahamas and only $940 US in Jamaica. Countries such as Haiti are among the poorest in the world with a per capita GNP of only $310 US dollars (World Bank, 1987).

Historically the Caribbean basin was a major locus of the international slave trade; many of the islands were transferred from Spanish to British rule during the course of the seventeenth and eighteenth centuries. The main period of independence from Britain occurred as late as the 1960s–1980s, and since this time there has been increasing influence from North America (Ellis, 1986). Recent intervention by the United States in Grenada's political affairs testifies to the significance of external pressures (see, for example, Latin America Bureau, 1983).

Caribbean states are typical of many others in the developing world in that their economies are overwhelmingly dependent on agricultural exports, many of which are cultivated on a plantation basis – a major legacy of the colonial period. Less than one quarter of the labour force is employed in industry (Crow et al., 1983). Periodic employment shortages mean that many of the islands are points of departure for a great deal of permanent and seasonal migration, both on an intra- and an inter-regional basis. The bulk of this migration is male which is one major factor accounting for the long-term rather unique situation of Caribbean women, one of relative independence in the management of household life (Laguerre, 1978; Massiah, 1986b). Around one-third of all households are headed by women who provide the bulk of economic support for their dependants (Barrow, 1986).

Caribbean women aged 15 years or over display an average rate of participation in trade and waged employment of between 45 and 65 per cent, which is among the highest for the developing world as a whole and on a par with the most industrialized countries of Southeast Asia (Seager and Olson, 1986). Despite the periodic outmigration of men from rural areas, overall there are similar numbers of men and women in the Caribbean region and female life expectancy is between 60 and 75 years (Townsend and Momsen, 1987). In general Caribbean women also live longer than men (Seager and Olson, 1986).

In considering gender relations in the Caribbean and the popular stereotype of the prominent roles of women, Pat Ellis (1986) argues that a wide variety of factors has to be taken into account; slavery and the long period of economic and political dependence upon Britain, the present involvement of North America in the region, and the unique Creole culture of Caribbean society. With respect to Ellis's first point, it is often argued that slavery accustomed Caribbean women to work; at the same time, since men and women were often kept in separate living quarters, it was women who became responsible both for the economic and domestic welfare of their children (Blumberg and García, 1977). The second relates largely to the post-war industrialization of the region. During the 1960s and 1970s in particular, several North American companies established offshore manufacturing plants in the Caribbean and many of them employ women. Women have thus been able to continue their roles of household support dating from the slavery period (Ellis, 1986; IBG, 1984; Safa, 1981).

When we consider the racial and cultural heritage of Caribbean people, black and East Indian women need to be analysed separately. Cheryl Williams (1986) argues that up to the end of the nineteenth century women of African descent were extremely important as bearers of tradition, especially since so many of them were in charge of their own households. Indeed, the phenomenon of matrifocality itself has been interpreted by some as reflecting the survival of the matrilineal societies of West Africa in the New World (Blumberg and García, 1977; Gerber and Rasmussen, 1978; Solien de Gonzales, 1965).[7] However, after 1900, a progressive anglicization of Caribbean society together with the rise of Calypso and the steel band (male-dominated cultural activities), caused women's position to deteriorate. East Indian women by contrast, have always tended to occupy a less independent role than their black counterparts (Williams, 1986).

Christianity is the dominant faith in the Caribbean (primarily Anglican, Presbyterian and Baptist). Most groups of East Indian descent are Hindu. Christianity carries with it a patriarchal ideology, but the material conditions of Caribbean women have permitted them to resist many of the doctrinal influences which in other areas have downgraded the status of women and encouraged the ideal of female domesticity.

There is a wide diversity of family types in the area, the main ones being the 'European' nuclear family, the 'African' matrifocal or mother-centred household and the 'East Indian' extended family group (Ellis, 1986). Legal marriage is regarded as the ideal, but 'free unions' (common-law marriages) are also widespread, especially among the black population. There are also a number of 'visiting unions' where women do not reside with their partners nor have any legal attachment to them (Powell, 1986). Between 10 and 25 per cent of all girls aged 15–19 years are or have been officially married (Seager and Olson, 1986). However, far more important than marriage is motherhood; 75 per cent of Caribbean women have children, the average being 4.5 (Ellis, 1986). In many of the constituent countries, the average is over six (Seager and Olson, 1986). Around two-thirds of all births take place outside an official marriage (Powell, 1986), and in some islands, such as Antigua and St

Lucia, this proportion is as high as 77 and 87 per cent respectively
(Seager and Olson, 1986). The crude birth-rate in the Caribbean as a
whole was projected at 27 per 1000 in 1980–85 and the annual
population growth rate at 1.7 per cent in the same period (UN, 1981).

In spite of the authority and respect accruing to Caribbean women
from motherhood and economic power, they are still subject to a
number of expressions of male dominance common throughout the
world, such as domestic violence (Kamugisha, 1986). This is a
phenomenon from which many women could conceivably escape
since economic independence allows them to establish their own
households. However women achieve still more status if they have a
man attached permanently to them (Ellis, 1986). In part this derives
from the fact that religious and social ideology encourages people to
think that marriage is the proper condition for parenthood (Powell,
1986). In part it is profoundly pragmatic: men not only have access
to better jobs than women both within and outside the region, but it
is also increasingly difficult for contemporary Caribbean households to survive on one income alone (Bolles, 1986).

To summarize, the position of Caribbean women, especially those
of African descent, is curiously ambivalent. On the one hand they
have a long tradition of economic independence and authority
within the household, helping to explain in part why female-headed
households are more numerous here than in any other region of the
Third World. However, on the other hand, they still have secondary
status within society at large, and have to contend with several
problems arising from sexual discrimination in the labour force and
violence from men. Nevertheless, common stereotypes of female
subordination perhaps apply less to this region than in many others
and in general terms Caribbean women are relatively freer from male
control than their counterparts elsewhere.

Women in the Middle East and North Africa

The reason for dealing with Middle Eastern and North African
countries in one section is that they cover a relatively contiguous
geographical area bordering the southern and eastern Mediterranean, and display considerable social and cultural similarities as a
result of common historical experiences, in particular, the imprint of
Islam. This is not to suggest that Islam has the same face in all areas.

Indeed there are two main doctrinal schools: Sunni and Shia, of which Sunni, the 'orthodox' form, has more adherents, and is predominant throughout the region except in Iran, Syria, Iraq and Afghanistan (Minces, 1982; El Saadawi, 1980).[8] Nevertheless, the basic beliefs and practices are similar, especially as they affect women. We have also included three countries of the eastern Sahelian belt of Africa in this section, namely the Sudan, Somalia and Ethiopia; the populations of the former two are predominantly Muslim, and the latter has pockets of Islam interspersed with Christianity.

Many Middle Eastern countries are dependent on the export of oil and are very wealthy; however, despite high per capita GNPs (16,000 US dollars per annum in Saudi Arabia and 19,870 in Kuwait (Crow et al., 1983)), inequality is rife and widespread poverty exists. Corresponding per capita GNPs in poorer North African states are 870 US dollars in Morocco and 690 US dollars in Egypt (Crow et al., 1983). The oil-rich industrial economies of the Middle East and North Africa have supported generally higher levels of urbanization than those countries in the region where people depend primarily on agriculture. For example, 67 per cent of Saudi Arabia's population and 72 per cent of Iraqis were urban in 1980, compared with only 41 per cent in Morocco and under 10 per cent in the Yemen Arab Republic (Gilbert and Gugler, 1982, pp.6–7). Population growth in North Africa in 1980–85 was projected at 2.6 per cent per annum, and in the Middle East (defined by the UN as 'Arab countries'), 3.3 per cent (UN, 1981).

Women in the Middle East and North Africa have the lowest rates of labour force participation in the world (Townsend and Momsen, 1987). Usually less than one quarter of women aged 15 or more are engaged in waged work or trade, and in many countries, notably Syria, Algeria, Saudi Arabia, Libya and Egypt, this figure is below 10 per cent; on average less than 15 per cent of the total labour force in the region is made up of women (Seager and Olson, 1986).

In much of the Middle East and North Africa men far outnumber women and the sex ratio may therefore be described as highly masculine (Harriss and Watson, 1987). Female life expectancy is between 60 and 69 years across most of the area, and between 50 and 59 years in Saudi Arabia, Sudan and Oman (Townsend and Momsen, 1987). Given that other things being equal, women should expect to live longer than men on account of inherent biological hardiness, masculine sex ratios indicate the degree to which the cultural under-valuation of women results in a disproportionate number of female deaths, especially during infancy and childbirth.

The division of gender roles is extremely pronounced in most Islamic countries of North Africa and the Middle East. Women are not only segregated from men, but are also frequently subject to seclusion or *purdah*. Fatima Mernissi (1985) suggests that rigid control of Muslim women stems from a conception of women that is markedly different from that of the West. In the West, women's 'inferiority' has been tied to an idea that they are sexually passive, physically weak and in need of protection from men. While these ideas are also found in Islamic society, Mernissi suggests that the fundamental rationale behind female subordination is that *men* are seen to need protection from *women*. Muslim women are regarded as extremely powerful, capable of making men lose their reason through *fitna* (disorder or chaos provoked by sexual attraction) and threatening in terms of their potential to divert men's devotion from Allah. Women in North Africa and the Middle East are thus possibly subject to greater constraints than their counterparts in many other developing societies.

Despite the fact that the *Qu'ran* (the holy book containing the word of Allah as told to the Prophet Mohammed) and the *hadiths* (interpretive moral codes based on the sayings of Mohammed) contain numerous references to gender equality (Ingrams, 1983; El Saadawi, 1980), and while women are required to submit to the will of Allah just as much as men and to observe Muslim teachings, they are rarely allowed to attend religious gatherings, enter a mosque, or assist at public meetings and festivities. The *umma*, or community of believers, is an all-male community (Mernissi, 1985).

According to Islamic faith, marriage is compulsory. Polygamy (up to four wives) is permitted and practised in many Muslim societies, albeit with the proviso that a man treats his wives equally (Afshar, 1987; Ingrams, 1983; Tessler et al., 1978). Polygamy is an extremely significant variable in the equation of female subordination and male privilege: married women often see their co-wives as rivals thus preventing the development of any genuine female solidarity. Polygamy also allows a man to fulfill his sexual appetite, at the same time as detracting from the formation of strong conjugal bonds with individual women (Mernissi, 1985).

Inequality within Islamic marriage is institutionalized by law. In the Moroccan Family Code, for example, there are separate articles for a man's rights *vis-à-vis* his wife and a wife's rights *vis-à-vis* her husband. On marriage a man has the right to total fidelity from his wife, obedience, the performance of domestic labour, breast-feeding of children and the right to command his wife's deference towards his parents and close relatives. A wife, on the other hand, cannot expect her husband to be faithful, obedient or to show respect to her own relatives, even though she can legitimately demand financial support, the right to be treated equally with other wives, permission to visit her parents and the prerogative of disposing freely of her own possessions (Mernissi, 1985, p.110). As Mernissi notes, Moroccan husbands owe no moral duties to their wives and the alleged rights of women are in fact restrictions on their freedom. The clause on female deference towards her husband's immediate relatives opens a door onto one of the key characteristics of the Islamic family – the importance of a woman's *hma* (mother-in-law).

Muslim mothers-in-law usually play a significant part in arranging the marriage of their sons, particularly in the selection of a bride, and thereafter exercise a major influence over the nature of the couple's relationship. Wives often go to live with their husbands in their family homes (Mernissi, 1985; Chapter 2). This continued close contact with the husband's mother inhibits the couple's potential for intimacy and thus drives a wedge between them. As Magida Salman (1987, p.8) points out: 'The mother of a male child will often interfere to prevent the appearance and growth of love and companionship between her son and daughter-in-law'. Filial bonds take precedence over conjugal bonds and reduce scope for the development of joint interests between husbands and wives, thereby exacerbating women's oppression. Men's mothers act as moral watchdogs and often burden their daughters-in-law with a huge range of domestic chores. The only compensation for young women in such positions is to look forward to the future when, if they bear sons, they in turn will achieve seniority and status. Age is also associated with greater spatial and social freedom; post-menopausal women are no longer an object of sexual desire and as such cannot bring shame upon their families by appearing in public places (Mernissi, 1985; Salman, 1987).

Between 25 and 50 per cent of women aged 15 to 19 years in the Middle East and North Africa are or have been officially married

(Seager and Olson, 1986). Only a very few remain unmarried by the age of 30 (Minces, 1982). Youthful marriages ensure that women's sexual behaviour is controlled and therefore that they do not bring dishonour upon their male kin. However, as much as marriage is an almost inevitable event in Muslim women's lives, the spectre of involuntary divorce is never far away. Although women themselves have increasingly obtained the courage and/or right to divorce their husbands in many Islamic countries, they remain extremely vulnerable to the threat of repudiation. One of the most common forms this takes is the *talaq al bid 'a* or 'innovatory divorce' where the husband merely repeats a repudiation statement three times before a witness (Coulson and Hinchcliffe, 1978; Minces, 1982). Infertility, or failure to bear sons, both of which are blamed on women, frequently provide grounds for men to divorce their wives. Nevertheless, if a husband so decides, he can take his wife back within the first three months following the divorce during which time she legally remains his property (El Saadawi, 1980).

The fate of divorced women is hard; it is difficult for a 'used' (non-virginal) woman to remarry, and the family's need to protect her honour while unattached means that she will probably have to return to live as an appendage in her paternal or fraternal home (Youssef, 1972). Children from a broken marriage eventually come under the guardianship of their legal father, defined as the man to whom the woman was married at the time of the birth, irrespective of whether or not he is the natural parent (Coulson and Hinchcliffe, 1978; Minces, 1982). Even where children stay with their mother because the father is deemed 'unfit', as is sometimes the case in Qatar, it remains the man's duty to make financial provision for the food, clothing, shelter and education of his offspring (Abu Saud, 1984).

Given the pressure on women to bear sons, fertility is high in Islamic countries, although birth control is not expressly forbidden by the *Qu'ran*, and certain countries such as Egypt, Algeria, Tunisia and South Lebanon have instigated family planning programmes (Minces, 1982; Salman, 1987). On average, women in North Africa and the Middle East give birth to at least six children (Seager and Olson, 1986), and crude birth-rates were projected at between 41 and 44.5 per 1000 in the period 1980–85 (UN, 1981).

Aside from general considerations of women's vulnerability and subordinate position within the family, there are two further aspects of gender inequality in Islamic societies which have been interpreted as reinforcing male control and women's secondary status: seclusion and 'circumcision'. It is important to note that although they *occur* in Islamic societies, they should not be construed as *Islamic customs*. They are by no means known in all Muslim countries, and are often found in non-Muslim countries as well. Nevertheless, they are most common in the Middle East and North Africa where Islam is the religion of rule.

Aside from restricting women's mobility, as we observed earlier, seclusion (*purdah*) involves the wearing of long concealing garments and/or a veil. The degree to which Muslim women are covered varies considerably from place to place (Minces, 1982). In eastern areas of Algeria for example, a long cloak and black veil cover the entire face and body except for one eye, whereas in Tunisia women may go unveiled. Qatari women have traditionally worn a *batula*, a kind of face mask with two slits for the eyes, although this is now dying out among the younger generation (Abu Saud, 1984). The primary function of the veil is to ensure modesty and to limit women's contact with all men other than their own husbands or male kin (Katib-Chahidi, 1981). The veil also symbolizes the invisibility of women in 'male spaces' such as the street or public places (Mernissi, 1985). In some cases *purdah* can also signify social status; some argue that only rich men can afford to seclude their wives. Nevertheless, there are also pragmatic reasons why women wear *purdah*. In Iraq, for example, Doreen Ingrams (1983) points out that the *abaya* (a voluminous black garment covering everything except the face and hands) is sometimes worn by poor women to hide their old clothes. Having said this, all Iraqi women put on an *abaya* to enter the mosque, as a sign of decorum and respect (Ingrams, 1983).

The other practice, which has become equated in the West with Islam, but which is by no means a Muslim institution, is female 'circumcision' (Thiam, 1986). Termed by some 'genital mutilation', circumcision is often argued to reduce women's sexual desires, thereby ensuring pre-marital chastity and conjugal fidelity. However, there are severe doubts about its effectiveness, as Scilla McLean (1985, p.7) points out:

Although the intention of the operation may be to diminish a woman's desire, the facts, from a medical point of view, are that the excision of the clitoris reduces *sensitivity*, but it cannot reduce desire, which is a psychological attribute (her emphasis).

Other reasons for circumcision include the idea that it is more hygienic, more aesthetic, or that it constitutes a critical *rite de passage* for female adulthood (McLean, 1985).

There are three main types of circumcision. The mildest, and least common, is 'Sunna' circumcision. This involves the cutting of the prepuce or clitoral hood, and as such need not physically impair a woman's sex life, although sometimes it is associated with psychological trauma. The term 'Sunna' imbues it with an authenticity under Islamic orthodoxy and no doubt encourages its practice by Muslim followers, although in no part of the *Qu'ran* is it advocated (McLean, 1985; WHO, 1979). The second type is 'excision' where the clitoral glans or even whole clitoris and surrounding tissue is removed. The third and most radical type of 'social surgery' is known as 'infibulation' where, along with the clitoris, the labia minora and majora are removed, and the two parts of the vulva then sewn together leaving only a tiny orifice for the passage of urine and menstrual blood (McLean, 1985; WHO, 1979). On a girl's wedding night the orifice is widened with a razor, dagger or scalpel (Minces, 1982). This last type of circumcision is especially common in southern Egypt, the Sudan, and the Eastern Horn of Africa and is also known as 'Pharaonic' circumcision since it preceded the arrival of Islam (Cloudsley, 1981; WHO, 1979).

Nawal El Saadawi's research in Egypt demonstrates that the majority of families 'still impose upon young female children the barbaric and cruel operation of circumcision' (in this case excision) even though education and social change appear to be sensitizing people to the medical, if not psychological, harm done by the custom (El Saadawi, 1980, p. 34). In most cases excision and infibulation are performed on girls of between 5 and 8 years old, often by an older woman, and may result in a whole series of short- and long-term medical problems (McLean, 1985; WHO, 1979). Immediate effects include shock, haemorrhaging, retention of urine, damage to the urethra or anus, and a series of bacterial infections; longer-term gynaecological and genito-urinary complications include abscess-ridden dermoid cysts, chronic pelvic infection, infertility and difficulties in childbirth (WHO, 1979). In most cases, 'genital mutilation' persists, despite the attempts of so-called progressive states to adopt a more humanitarian approach to the issue. So far only one country, the Sudan, has officially made excision and infibulation illegal (Thiam, 1986), but even so, something like 80 per cent of

Sudanese women are still infibulated (McLean, 1985), and because it has been made a criminal offence, few people seek hospital treatment for resultant infections (WHO, 1979). The practices of excision and infibulation are less common in the Middle East and other parts of North Africa.

One of the few countries in the region which has attempted to 'raise the status' of women is Tunisia, which after independence in 1956 and under President Habib Bourguiba, introduced a Personal Status Code to replace *Qu'ranic* law in the fields of marriage, divorce and children's rights. The Code forbade polygamy, instigated court proceedings for divorce, granted universal suffrage and established a minimum age for marriage (15 for girls, 18 for boys) (Durrani, 1976; Huston, 1979; Tessler et al., 1978). However, in the late 1960s and early 1970s, partly due to Bourguiba's repeated bouts of illness, and partly due to the rise of Islamic fundamentalism, the position of women once again showed signs of becoming more constrained (Tessler et al., 1978).

Another country in which Muslim women have undergone dramatic and fluctuating changes in terms of their legal and social position is Iran, where in 1936 women were compulsorily unveiled, making it one of the first countries officially to outlaw the veiling of women (Jayawardena, 1986; Pakizegi, 1978). The Shah felt that the seclusion of women resulted in a waste of half the country's productive resources and called for the participation of women in wider social and economic life; this began a long process of relaxation in some of the major constraints and restrictions placed on Iranian women (Jayawardena, 1986). For example, the Family Protection Law of 1967 prohibited men from taking multiple wives, and stipulated that they had to obtain permission from a court of law if they wished to take a second wife. The court was obliged to consult the first wife for evidence of her husband's economic capacity to support another woman; the law also granted women the right to ask for a divorce in the event of their husbands bringing another woman into the home (Pakizegi, 1978). However, the social position of Iranian women consistently lagged behind changes in their legal status, and women could still, for example, be prevented from working by their husbands if their employment threatened to disrupt the smooth running of the family home (Pakizegi, 1978). Furthermore, as the London Iranian Women's Liberation Group (1983) point out, women's emancipation under the Shah was foisted on them 'top-down' to suit the needs of the regime and not out of any genuine concern for women *per se*.

Gender inequalities have intensified since the revolution of 1978–79 where emphasis on Islamic fundamentalism has meant that women have returned to wearing the veil (*chador*) and given up a number of freedoms. In addition, some women under Khomeini have been executed for adultery and prostitution (LIWLG, 1983). As Haleh Afshar (1987: 83) points out:

The Islamic Republic in Iran has created two classes of citizen; the male who benefits from the provisions of Islamic law and justice, and the female who does not. With the sole exception of the right to vote, Iranian women are in all other respects formally recognised as second-class citizens who have no place in the public arena and no security in the domestic sphere. The husband has become an absolute ruler, entitled to exercise the power of life and death in his own home . . . Iranian women have little to lose and everything to gain by opposing the regime and its dicta concerning women.

To summarize, women in the Middle East and North Africa are forced to conform not only to the roles of wife and mother, but also to bear additional burdens such as obligatory deference to their mothers-in-law and restrictions on their freedom of movement and association. Women's place in the extended or joint household renders them particularly vulnerable to control and domination. While in other societies the nuclear family may give women little freedom and autonomy, several writers on the Islamic world see it as an important vehicle for female emancipation.

Women and Gender in Sub-Saharan Africa

Sub-Saharan Africa, by which is usually meant those states bordering on the southern edge of the Sahara desert (including the Sahel) and those further to the south, is characterized by extreme ethnic, religious, linguistic, political and historical diversity. It is also the largest Third World region in terms of numbers of countries. In the literature a division is often made between West Africa (including the states of Mauritania, Senegal, Gambia, Mali, Guinea, Guinea-Bissau, Sierra Leone, Liberia, Ivory Coast, Burkina Faso, Ghana, Togo, Niger, Chad, Benin, Nigeria, Equatorial Guinea, Gabon, Cameroon and Sao Tome and Principe), East Africa (including Kenya, Uganda, Tanzania, Zanzibar, Mauritius and the Malagasy

Republic), Central Africa (Zaire, the People's Republic of the Congo, the Central African Republic, Rwanda, Burundi, Zambia and Malawi) and the states of the southern African periphery, the 'Front-Line States' (Zimbabwe, Angola, Mozambique and Botswana). Lesotho is completely surrounded by the Republic of South Africa, a fact which has drastically altered the course of its development over the last century (see, for example, Murray, 1981), as is Swaziland, and Namibia is still under the control of South Africa, although there has been increasing pressure over the past 20 years for its independence. Thus set out, the task of summarising information on women and women's status in a necessarily brief introductory overview is extremely difficult. Nevertheless we do our best to present a broad outline of dominant regional characteristics at the same time pointing to some of the more prominent aspects of intra-regional diversity.

With the exception of Liberia, all states in sub-Saharan Africa have been colonies; in most cases the period of 'formal' colonial rule lasted from around 1880 initiated by the European 'Scramble for Africa', to about 1960. The major colonial powers were Britain, France and Portugal, although Belgium, Spain and Germany also exercised influence at one time or another. France's main sphere of influence was in West Africa where her former territories were contiguous with the French colonies of the Maghreb and North Africa. Britain had strong coastal interests in West Africa, but a much larger area under British rule was in East and Central Africa, embracing Kenya, Uganda, Tanzania, Zambia, Malawi and Zimbabwe. The Portuguese colonies were a legacy of Portugal's historical significance as a maritime power, growing up around ports (for replenishment of ships) on trading routes to the East.

There were major differences in the nature of colonial rule by different metropolitan powers, but the effects can, nevertheless, be generally summarized. Alien government meant the increasingly widespread penetration of capitalism and capitalist relations of production, an increasing monetization of local economies and the beginnings of commoditization of productive resources such as land. In addition, new 'state' boundaries were created causing problems particularly for ethnic groups who suddenly found themselves divided by an externally-imposed international frontier. Christian missionaries came as European military and trading posts were established, bringing with them not only religion, but education, thus training lower-level functionaries for the local state bureaucracy, the commercial sector and industry. With the imposition of colonial rule we therefore have the foundations laid for 'peasantization' of the indigenous population (Freund, 1984; Rodney, 1972, but see also Hyden, 1980, 1986a). In the climatically more favourable areas (the Kenyan highlands and Zimbabwe) European settler populations were enthusiastically encouraged, and in the mineral (copper) rich areas of Zambia, large-scale mining enterprises were established.

In addition to the influences of colonial rule, Islam also had its influences south of the Sahara, and in most cases pre-dated Christianity. In the Sahel, Islamicisation was the result of the *Jihads* (Holy Wars, ostensibly with the aim of conversion) from the fifteenth century onwards, and on the East African coast Islamic influence spread as a result of trading with Arab merchants. Although many Africans are either Christian or Muslim, there is a wide range of subsects including apostolic churches, healing/spiritualist churches and sufistic cults. Traditional religions also still survive and have often become incorporated into the world religions; as a result both Christian and Muslim women in sub-Saharan Africa often escape some of the more oppressive aspects of their faiths.

Such is the particular history of Africa, its relative isolation until a late stage in terms of European history, its systems of extensive agriculture, the high proportion of its women involved in agriculture, for example, that one eminent commentator has argued that in general terms of 'development', Africa is unlike any other area (see Goran Hyden, 1986b).

In considering statistical measures of 'economic development' in sub-Saharan Africa, it is important to bear in mind that there are serious inadequacies in information for many of its states. Nigeria, for example, a giant in economic and demographic terms, has not had a validated population census since 1960, and countries such as Angola and Mozambique, in the throes of what are proving to be long-term military struggles, can provide only rough estimates of economic performance. Nevertheless, a key feature of African economies is their diversity. For example, in 1985 per capita GNP ranged from 1110 US dollars in the Congo and $1090 in Mauritius, to $840 in Botswana, $810 in Cameroon and $800 in Nigeria, to $420 in Mauritania, $370 in Senegal, $230 in Togo, and as little as $150 in Burkina Faso and Mali (World Bank, 1987).

The overall percentage of urban residents in sub-Saharan Africa was only 23 per cent in 1980 (this figure also includes the Sudan and Ethiopia), one of the lowest figures in all Third World regions, but again masks huge internal variation. For example, the most 'urbanized' countries were Zambia and the Ivory Coast where 38 per cent of the population was urban, and Ghana with 36 per cent. Senegal had an urban population of 25 per cent, and Zimbabwe, 23 per cent. In contrast, 14 per cent of Kenya's population resided in urban areas, and 12 per cent in Tanzania and Uganda. In Mozambique, Burkina Faso and Malawi only 9 per cent of the population was classified as urban (Gilbert and Gugler, 1982, pp.6–7).

Rates of female labour force participation also vary widely. In some countries such as Tanzania, Mozambique, Burkina Faso, Senegal, Gambia, Rwanda and Burundi it is estimated that over 65 per cent of women aged 15 years or more work for wages or trade, and in most of these countries women constitute over 45 per cent of the total labour force; on the other hand, middling levels of female activity rates of between 26 and 45 per cent are recorded in Zambia, Kenya, Zimbabwe, Botswana, Sierra Leone, the Congo and Liberia, here women constitute between one-quarter and one-third of the labour force; finally in predominantly Islamic countries such as Mali and Niger only 11–25 per cent of women aged 15 years or more have waged work and in both cases women represent less than 25 per cent of the national labour force (Seager and Olson, 1986). However, as we noted earlier in the chapter, women's participation in agriculture is often ignored (see Dixon-Mueller, 1985; and Chapter 3).

Female life expectancy in the early 1980s was between 50 and 59 years across most of sub-Saharan Africa, but less than 50 in Mauritania, Mali, Burkina Faso, Niger, Chad, Angola and Senegal (Townsend and Momsen, 1987). Generally, however, female life expectancy is higher than that of men (Seager and Olson, 1986). The sub-Saharan sex ratio is feminine, with an average of only 980 men for every 1000 women throughout the region (Harriss and Watson, 1987).

Because of these wide disparities in a number of general indicators of 'economic development', kinship systems, women's activities and colonial heritage, it is extremely difficult to generalize about gender relations and 'the African family', except to say that African women are probably under slightly less pressure than their counterparts in other Third World regions (with the possible exception of the

Caribbean) to conform to a full-time mothering role and marital relationship in the context of a male-dominated household. Indeed, matrifocal households are known throughout the continent, albeit for different reasons in different areas.

In many parts of West Africa, for example, the tradition of women living with their female kin persists (Etienne, 1983; Sanjek, 1983; Robertson, 1984a). In southern African countries such as Botswana and Lesotho, women also frequently head their own households, although here the reason is not so much because of matrilineal traditions, but because their husbands are forced to migrate to South Africa to find work (Molapo, 1987; Wilkinson, 1987). In parts of East Africa, such as Mafia island in Tanzania, 'families' are again fairly fluid (indeed there is no Swahili word to describe 'household'), and women have a good deal of autonomy because of their traditional rights to own land (Caplan, 1981, 1984). High numbers of women-headed households on the East African coast are also attributable to locally high divorce rates (Caplan, 1984). Divorce is also common in West Africa, for example among the Kpelle of Liberia (Bledsoe, 1980). When Kpelle divorce cases are brought to court, men are usually found guilty on the grounds of domestic violence or failure to provide adequate financial support for their dependants, whereas women are found guilty of adultery or failure to carry out domestic tasks such as cooking. Nevertheless, even when women are found guilty, which happens in most cases, they usually get custody of their children and are thus able to apportion major items of conjugal property (ibid.). The above evidence indicates that the patriarchal household is by no means the norm in sub-Saharan Africa. Indeed Maria Rosa Cutrufelli (1983) notes that the nuclear family is only likely to be found in large numbers in areas which have been subject to intense colonial pressures, 'development' and the penetration of capitalism.

According to Seager and Olson's (1986) calculations, between 25 and 50 per cent of girls aged between 15 and 19 years in most African countries are or have been officially married, and in the Central African Republic, the Congo and most of West Africa, the figure is over 50 per cent. Whether or not women choose to establish a permanent conjugal union with a man, let alone reside with him, birth rates in sub-Saharan Africa are also high. In Chad, Niger, Gabon, Guinea Bissau and the Congo, women give birth to between four and six children, and in all the other countries of the region, the figure is over six (Seager and Olson, 1986). Crude birth rates in sub-Saharan Africa were projected at between 38.6 and 48.7 per 1000 in 1980–85, and annual population growth at between 2.6 and 3.1 per cent (UN, 1981). One of the major problems faced by African women, in part because of their relative autonomy, is that of obtaining financial support from their children's fathers, and on this front several African states have tried to legislate for at least minimal provision for wives.

In Ghana, for example, a Maintenance of Children Act was passed in 1965, but despite successive updates in the legislation as governments have changed, women still find it difficult in law to take their ex-husbands to court for maintenance. In addition, Article 32 of the suspended 1979 Constitution recognized that every wife was entitled to maintenance from her husband's estate, whether or not he made a will. Although the present PNDC (Provisional National Defence Council) government has also recognized this provision, it is still difficult for women to press such claims, both because of pressure from their husbands' families and because of the legal costs involved (ECA, 1984). Although the Marriage Ordinance Act specifies that a man may only have one wife, the vast majority of marriages in Ghana (94 per cent) are not contracted under the Ordinance (ECA, 1984). Hence both formal polygamy is widespread and also the practice, even for those married under the Ordinance, of keeping 'outside wives' (mistresses) or girlfriends (Dinan, 1983).

As we might expect, Africa's socialist states tend to have most legislation aimed at maintaining and improving women's lot. Nevertheless, as we have noted for the case of Latin America, legislation itself is often unworkable in practice. Ruth Weiss's (1986) account of women in Zimbabwe describes not only the struggle that women had as part of the ZANU (Zimbabwean African National Union) and ZAPU (Zimbabwean African People's Union) armies, but also their subsequent battles with Zimbabwean men to recognize their rights to be independent adults: only in December 1984 was the legal minority status of women abolished in Zimbabwe.

The Organization of Angolan Women (1984) have also described their struggles, not only against the legacy of patriarchal colonial rule, but also against, what they term, the *machismo* of Angolan men. Although special rights are granted for working women under the General Labour Law, such as maternity leave, time off for breastfeeding and taking a child to the doctor, these rights, they

claim, are not widely respected, and legislation in Angola has yet to
tackle the problems of the 'double burden' (OAW, 1984; see also
Chapter 4).

We began this section by recognizing the diversity of African
women's condition, and pinpointing some of this diversity in the
overview. In summary, we can perhaps say that although African
women, as indeed Caribbean women, appear to face fewer constraints than their counterparts elsewhere as a result of *de facto*
independence in the management of household life, they are none
the less subject to many pressures. Even if African women are not
necessarily forced to become wives, motherhood is an important
component of female status and the necessity of caring for young
children inevitably impinges to some degree on their spatial mobility
(IBG, 1984). Women are also frequently in the position of providing
sole financial support for their offspring, which obviously exacer-
bates hardship. Finally, the fact that many women in Africa still
reside in rural areas makes it very difficult for governments or
agencies to address their problems (of education, health, basic
services, and so on), let alone alleviate them.

Women and Gender in South Asia

South Asia, by which we refer to India, Nepal, Pakistan, Bangladesh
and Sri Lanka, is also an extremely diverse region and as such
difficult to outline in general terms. One factor contributing to this
diversity is the area's wide range of religious faiths including Islam,
Hindu, Buddhist, Jain and Sikh, the first three being numerically the
most important. Since we have already outlined the main tenets of
Islam (the state religion of both Pakistan and Bangladesh) in
previous sections, we shall focus our discussion of religious
influences on gender in the South Asian region most closely on
countries where Hinduism and Buddhism are strongest, namely
India, Sri Lanka and Nepal.

Historically most of the Indian sub-continent came under the
influence of British colonial rule. The British withdrew in 1947
partitioning the continent along crudely-drawn religious lines, leaving a legacy of political strife, displaced persons and economic chaos
(Liddle and Joshi, 1986). India itself has undergone a series of
profound social and economic changes since Independence and its

urban population has grown dramatically: during the decade 1961 to 1971 alone, the overall rate of urban population growth was 37.8 per cent (Sarin, 1979). Currently between 16 and 30 per cent of most South Asians reside in urban areas, although Nepal and Bangladesh have urban populations of less than 15 per cent (Drakakis-Smith, 1987).

Around two-thirds of the South Asian population depend directly on agriculture for survival and GNP per capita in 1985 was only 380 US dollars in Sri Lanka and Pakistan, 270 in India, and as low as 160 in Nepal and 150 in Bangladesh (World Bank, 1987). Between 26 and 45 per cent of all Nepalese, Indian and Sri Lankan women aged 15 or over are engaged in waged work or trade, and represent between 26 and 35 per cent of their countries' national labour forces; corresponding figures are far lower for the Islamic states of Pakistan and Bangladesh where less than 25 per cent of women aged 15 years or more have waged work. In Pakistan less than 15 per cent of the total labour force is made up of women (Seager and Olson, 1986).

The sex ratio in South Asia is highly masculine, ranging from 1040 males per 1000 females in Sri Lanka, 1049 in Nepal, 1067 in Bangladesh, 1073 in India, and 1078 in Pakistan; these disparities have increased steadily during the course of the twentieth century (Harriss and Watson, 1987). Masculinization of the sex ratio is usually attributed to the comparatively poor nutrition of young girls, and the fact that they are far less likely to receive medical treatment than their brothers (Horowitz and Kishwar, 1984; Chapter 8). In India, female life expectancy at birth is 50 years for women and 51.2 years for men, in Nepal, 78.6 and 72.1 years respectively, in Sri Lanka, 66.5 and 63.5, in Pakistan 70.9 and 67.6, and in Bangladesh as low as 46.1 and 47.1 years (Seager and Olson, 1986).

We have already seen that Islam assigns women a low status, a trait which is also apparent in the other religions of the subcontinent. Maitrayee Mukhopadhyay (1984, p.19) maintains that the Hindu religion, for example, has a 'curiously ambivalent attitude towards women', with the dominant ethos being 'derogatory and unjust – women have absolutely no worth in themselves'. The reason for this ambivalence derives on the one hand from the fact that Hindus even deify and worship the Female Principle (*Shakti*), but on the other, despise the 'real flesh and blood woman'.

The Hindu faith is predicated on an elaborate caste structure which requires one to act according to one's status at birth in order to be rewarded in a subsequent life. Castes are, at their most basic, occupational and status groups, but in addition Hinduism is pervaded by notions of purity and pollution. Not only are members of lower castes polluting to higher-caste groups, but also women of all castes are seen as inferior in the sense of being more 'unclean' than men. Hindu women are not allowed to study the *Vedas* (holy scriptures) or to perform any religious sacrifices (Mukhopadhyay, 1984). As elsewhere in the world, commonplace female biological events such as menstruation and childbirth are regarded as key sources of pollution and during these times women are strictly segregated (APHD, 1985; Pearson, 1987).

The Hindu religion dictates that women should never be allowed to have independent lives and always to come under the jurisdiction of a man. Women are supposed to be so devoted to their husbands that until its formal abolition in the colonial period, *sati*, a custom whereby widows were required to throw themselves upon their husband's funeral pyre, was widely practised (APHD, 1985). Accordingly widowhood also has unclean status (contaminated by death pollution) (Parry, 1980). However, as Liddle and Joshi (1986) point out, the abolition of *sati* and other discriminatory practices such as female infanticide were not due to real concern about women's emancipation on the part of the British, but instead derived from first, a sense of moral outrage, and second, the need to find political ammunition for their refusal to grant India's right to self-rule. This is borne out by the fact that in certain areas such as land reform and personal law, British actions had very deleterious effects on women, such as the effective destruction of matriliny among the Nayars of Kerala (Fuller, 1976; Liddle and Joshi, 1986; Wilson, 1985).

Although *sati* has virtually died out, once widowed a woman's life is still severely restricted. Widows are expected to sacrifice all pleasure and to refrain from adorning themselves (APHD, 1985). In Nepal they are also forbidden from remarrying (Pearson, 1987). In India the remarriage of widows is gradually increasing, although religious rites may not be performed at a woman's second marriage; men on the other hand are allowed as many religious ceremonies as the virgins they marry (Mukhopadhyay, 1984).

Widowhood is not the only difficulty for Hindu women, however, marriage too is highly problematic. In recent years, for example, there has been a massive increase in bride deaths both in South Asia itself and amongst Hindu communities abroad (Sharma, 1984). Bride deaths occur when a girl's parents cannot or will not meet the dowry payments required by the groom's family. Dowry is usually negotiated around the period of betrothal, but many authors have noted that there is an upward spiral of demands over time, reflecting the fact that wives are eminently dispensable and easily replaced. Sometimes brides are murdered by their in-laws, and sometimes they commit suicide in the face of systematic physical violence or verbal abuse (Kishwar and Vanita, 1984; Manushi, 1983; Mukhopadhyay, 1984). Despite the fact that an Act of 1961 made dowry transactions a criminal offence, official action is rarely taken to protect women in these circumstances and police officers are wont to ignore even blatant incidences of violence (Kishwar and Vanita, 1984; Manushi, 1983).

In Buddhism, there is no caste structure. Buddhists believe in respect for all living things and the religion is ostensibly far more egalitarian than either Hinduism or Islam, in both social and sexual terms. Lord Buddha himself proclaimed a belief in the equal status of men and women (APHD, 1985). In contrast to Hindus and Muslims, Buddhists since early times have admitted women into the ranks of the clergy (Jayawardena, 1986). However, feminity is seen to act as a hindrance to women's attainment of *nirvana* (blessedness or enlightenment) and the *Bhikunni* (nun) is accorded lower status than her male counterpart, the *Bhiku* (monk) (Mukhopadhyay, 1984).

As in other areas of the Third World, the kinship system exerts an extremely important influence on women's lives. The typical South Asian family is patriarchal and extended, despite the fact that increasing numbers of young couples wish for personal reasons to establish independent households (Sharma, 1986). In India, Nepal and Bangladesh more than 50 per cent of young girls aged between 15 and 19 years are or have been officially married and the most common nuptial age for women in 1980 was 9 as against a legal minimum age of 18 (Seager and Olson, 1986). Marriages are usually arranged and brides must be virgins. The primary goal for South Asian women is motherhood, and in Hindu and Muslim society alike, to give birth to boys (Mukhopadhyay, 1984). In India and Sri Lanka women have an average of between four and six children, and in Nepal, Pakistan and Bangladesh the average is over six (Seager and Olson, 1986). In South Asia as a whole the crude birth-rate was projected at 38.5 per 1000 in 1980–85, and overall population growth at 2.14 per cent per annum (UN, 1981).

South Asian women in general are subject to considerable pressure to conform to the domestic roles of wife and mother, and are subject to religious ideology which places a heavy emphasis on female inferiority. Arranged marriages, the dowry system and status problems of widows reinforce the social and economic dependence of women. The fact that the sex-ratio is highly masculine in the region is a pertinent reminder of the fact that women are generally held in very low esteem.

Women and Gender in Southeast Asia

Southeast Asia is another region containing a large diversity of religions, cultures and economies. For the purposes of convenience we include the Indonesian islands in this section, along with the Philippines and mainland Southeast Asia which comprises Taiwan, Malaysia, Singapore, Thailand, Laos, Kampuchea, Vietnam, Burma and the Koreas to the north.

One reason for diversity is the region's varied colonial history; the British ruled Malaysia and Singapore, the Dutch, Indonesia, the Spanish and Americans, the Philippines, while the French occupied Laos, Kampuchea and Vietnam. Thailand, Burma and the Koreas have never been 'colonies' in the sense that political control was exercised from a European state. It is a moot point whether we consider the economic relations many of these states presently have with the First World as constituting a form of 'neo-imperialism'.

The region also displays vast disparities in types and levels of economic development. Malaysia, Taiwan, South Korea and Singapore stand out as highly industrialized countries where per capita GNP ranges between 1800 and 5910 US dollars, whereas countries such as Thailand which relies on agriculture and services has a per capita GNP of only 790 US dollars (Crow et al., 1983). An average of 31.5 per cent of the East Asian population resides in cities of 100,000 or more inhabitants (Armstrong and McGee, 1985). The rate of overall population growth in the region between 1980 and 1985 was 2.05 per cent per annum (UN, 1981).

The industrialized countries of mainland Southeast Asia and the Philippines are the locus of a considerable amount of export-processing manufacture, where multinational firms have relocated assembly operations to tariff-free production zones. High numbers of multinational 'world market factories' (plants which are 100 per cent foreign-owned and specialize in assembly for export) and a preference for hiring female labour (on account of its relatively low cost), mean that rates of female employment in Southeast Asia are among the highest in the Third World. For example, in no one country in Southeast Asia do women constitute less than 26 per cent of the labour force, and in the Philippines, Laos, Burma and South Korea, the figure is between 36 and 45 per cent (Seager and Olson, 1986). As Townsend and Momsen (1987) point out, female activity rates are high in both rural *and* urban areas in Southeast Asia, unlike any other part of the Third World. Sex ratios in most of Southeast Asia tend to be slightly feminine, with only 990 men for every 1000 women (Harriss and Watson, 1987); but in only a few cases is female life expectancy over 50 years (Townsend and Momsen, 1987).

Despite a feminine sex ratio and high rates of female labour force participation, women's 'status' in Southeast Asia is not necessarily 'better' than in regions where their involvement in remunerated work is lower, since many of the activities engaging women are those which reinforce patriarchal power structures, such as prostitution and sexual services in Thailand and the Philippines (Heyzer, 1986; Phongpaichit, 1984).

The dominant religions in Southeast Asia are Buddhism and Islam, with pockets of Christianity, Hinduism, Shintoism and Confucianism (Crow et al., 1983). Shintoism is a Japanese religion which reveres ancestors and nature spirits. Confucianism is based upon the teachings of the sage, Confucius, and embodies the dualistic Yin–Yang cosmology of traditional Chinese culture. This ideology views male and female as opposite poles: the female element (yin) is dark, weak and passive, whereas the male principle (yang) is bright, strong and active (Heyzer, 1986). All the major world religions therefore legitimize patriarchy to varying degrees. In Singapore, for example, Aline Wong (1981, p.449) observes:

The traditional religiocultural systems of Confucianism, Hinduism and Islam prescribed a subordinate status to women within the household. Whether born Chinese, Indian or Malay, a woman was socialised from a young age to play the roles of wife, mother and daughter-in-law, and to lead a secluded life.

In Taiwan, for example, traditional Chinese cultural norms dictate that women are inferior to men, and the ideal family type is the patrilocal joint family with several generations and married couples living under one roof (Lu, 1984). Under Confucianism women are subject to 'Three Obediences' (meaning they must defer to their fathers, husbands and sons at all times), and to attend to their 'proper' wifely duties within the home (Jayawardena, 1986). In Malaysia, where Islam dominates, despite women's increasing participation in the wage labour force, the 'ideal' role of women is still that of wife and mother (Young and Salih, 1987). In Thailand, which is predominantly Buddhist, it was not until 1976 that the Civil and Commercial Amendment Act permitted women the same rights as men to petition for a divorce (Thitsa, 1980).

It is only really in socialist countries in Southeast Asia, such as Vietnam, where major steps have been taken to improve the position of women both within and outside the family. For example, since the revolution, legislation outlawing polygamy has been passed, as well as the elimination of bride-price payments (White, 1981).

Although evidence shows that female waged employment is tending to raise the marrying age for women, in Indonesia and Singapore 25–50 per cent of girls aged between 15 and 19 years are or have been officially married; this figure is 10–25 per cent in Thailand, Burma, Malaysia and the Philippines, and only in South Korea and Taiwan is the rate below 10 per cent (Seager and Olson, 1986).[9] On average Southeast Asian women give birth to between four and six children (Seager and Olson, 1986). The crude birth-rate in the region between 1980 and 1985 was projected at 32.4 per 1000 (UN, 1981).

To summarize, in spite of high rates of remunerated employment among women in Southeast Asia, religious and cultural ideals emphasize that their primary responsibility is to home and family. Economic development has had an equally important role to play in reinforcing women's secondary status; when they move into the labour force their work is often of a highly exploitative nature, be this in a world market factory or a house of prostitution. As such the women of Southeast Asia face similar constraints and problems to their counterparts in most of the other regions of the developing world.

In the following chapters we turn to look at some of these problems in more depth.

NOTES

1. The measurement of women's 'status' in developing countries has long been a subject of controversy – basically in terms of the indicators selected to represent the 'status' of women, and the standards chosen by which those indicators should be judged. For example, Joni Seager and Ann Olson (1986) have mapped women's 'status' for the world as a whole, using a compound index comprising women's literacy, suffrage, contraceptive use, paid work and life expectancy on a scale of 0–100. However, indicators such as contraceptive use, for example, are arguably very Western-centred, and besides are not necessarily a 'good thing' for women. In turn, life expectancy is as much a function of poverty as it is of women's status and as such cannot be employed meaningfully in any comparative analysis. Given the problems associated with the idea of universal indices, we basically confine our analysis of women's positions to the general context of the countries to which they belong, and make few attempts at cross-cultural comparisons. The problems of evaluating 'status' will be elaborated upon further in the substantive chapters.
2. See, for example, Ruth Dixon-Mueller (1985) for a wide-ranging discussion of the inadequacies of conventional data sources for the analysis of women's work.
3. The problem of 'class' as an analytical category in pre-capitalist modes of production is discussed in terms of a Marxist debate by Molyneux (1977), Rey (1979) and Terray (1972, 1975, 1979). See also Hyden (1986a) for a more general discussion of the applicability of the term 'class' in Africa.
4. 'Affinal' means related by marriage – 'in-law' is the English equivalent. 'Consanguineal' means related by blood.
5. The Portuguese were far less concerned than the Spanish about imposing their culture and religion upon the indigenous population of South America.
6. The exact form of Catholicism, whether 'pure' or embracing elements of indigenous belief systems, varies from place to place throughout the Latin American continent.
7. Matrifocality does not always mean that a household is woman-*headed* in the sense that there is no resident male, and is more commonly used to describe households which are mother-*centred*. Matrifocality may therefore be associated with households in which the man is only present on a temporary basis, or where the woman plays the dominant role psychologically (Solien de Gonzales, 1965). Matriliny means descent through the female line and is discussed in more detail in Chapter 2.
8. Sunni Islam, to which the majority of Muslims subscribe, and Shia

Islam, differ in a number of ways. Crudely speaking, the minority Shi'ites declare that the Sunnis killed the rightful heir to Mohammed and believe in the coming of another great leader. The Sunnis, on the other hand, believe there is only one prophet.

9. Fertility data for the socialist countries of Southeast Asia are not included in Seager and Olson's (1986) map of motherhood.

2 Gender, Households and Rural Communities

The next three chapters can in many ways be considered parts of a whole. In addition to the range and variety of social settings in which women live (Chapter 2), and a discussion of work and its social context (Chapter 3), the theme of women's status also runs through the first two chapters and is the focus of key questions in Chapter 4. But these chapters are also linked historically. This chapter is concerned primarily with the range of social organization which constrains or otherwise affects women's roles and status, both at the household and community levels. While emphasizing that these forms of social structure exist and are influential today, the discussion is also intended to serve as a background matrix for the subsequent chapters, which deal with changes in rural women's roles and status in colonial and post-colonial capitalist societies (Chapter 3) and changes resulting specifically from socialist policies and 'conventional' development schemes (Chapter 4).

After the discussion in Chapter 1 on the nature and significance of the household, it is easy to understand why we begin the substantive part of the book with an analysis of rural households: the household, whether defined as unit of residence or domestic consumption is a crucial feature in rural social organization, whatever form it takes. A further reason for the central role of a household is its multiplicity of function: it is the site of biological and social reproduction, of socialization, of nurturing and of fundamental decision-making. However, although we argued the case for using 'household' as an analytical construct in Chapter 1, we must also be aware of the problems surrounding its translation to an empirical context in rural areas. These problems can be roughly divided into two:

1. Problems about the nature of 'work', 'production' and 'reproduction'.

2.   Regional empirical variations, both in 'traditional' social organization and in different experiences of colonialism and incorporation into the world capitalist system.

It is when we come to consider rural areas in particular that we
become aware of the fact that what goes on in households cannot be
relegated simply to the sphere of reproduction, as in conventional
Marxist analyses, and left un-analysed, as non-work, or at least, not
productive work. Indeed, Veronika Bennholdt-Thomsen (1981)
argues the case for analysing not only the labour of Third World
peasant producers in subsistence production as 'productive work',
but also the work done by housewives in capitalist societies. It is
because Marx himself and the early Marxists assumed that a division
of labour into productive and domestic relations, with women
predominating in the latter, was 'natural' and therefore outside of
the parameters of any social analysis, that categories of domestic
reproductive work and subsistence production have largely
been ignored (Bennholdt-Thomsen, 1981; see also Harris, 1980;
Guyer, 1984b; Babb, 1986). Thus, again for analytical purposes
only, we make a division between reproductive and productive
labour. This chapter considers the work of women in reproduction:
child-care and lactation, cooking, water provision and the
problems of increasing shortages of fuel in many parts of the Third
World.

As in our other rural chapters Africa seems to pose most problems
in terms of definition. Jane Guyer (1981b) and Guyer and Pauline
Peters (1987) suggest that this is because of the permeability of the
boundaries of African households, whether defined in terms of
residential units or production/consumption groups. What they
mean by this is both the fact that the actual composition of groups
can fluctuate almost overnight, as people leave or arrive for short or
extended visits, and that groups are embedded in wider structures:
they are not discrete, but individual members have differential
rights and obligations in other groups, rights of land in different kin groups, rights in clientship or patronage networks, rights
of inheritance of status and moveable goods and obligations to
perform duties and to contribute to the maintenance of these other
groups.

Bearing these problems in mind, we consider first the characteristics and determinants of the composition of rural households with

particular reference to the principles and significance of kinship systems as they affect both household structure and wider forms of social organization. Second, we move on to consider the importance and roles of a household head. This is followed by a brief discussion of marriage as the process by which most households are formed. In the latter part of the chapter we turn to the issue of women's domestic (reproductive) roles in rural areas and in the final section we consider problems in analyzing women's status. It will be obvious that some of the material covered here has relevance to women both in rural and urban areas and it is therefore useful to read this chapter in conjunction with Chapters 6 and 8.

WOMEN AND RURAL HOUSEHOLDS

A household is focused around the management of the resources of its head (see below), together with those of a spouse where one exists, and the care and maintenance of any children. There are other things that households are responsible for, but the above very general set of principles serves as a starting point. Within households there is usually a division of labour among adult men, adult women and children: usually is added here since many rural households (and also those in urban areas: Chapter 6) have only one adult present.

Further, we should not expect that because a village group, tribal society, ethnic group or whatever has a stated 'norm' for residence or household form there should be residential homogeneity within a particular area. Two factors intervene to prevent this: first, the process of time, during which a household is created, develops and changes as those responsible for its formation have children and grow old. This is known as the 'developmental cycle' and is well studied within the anthropological literature (Goody, 1958; Fortes, 1958, 1970; Murray, 1987). The second set of factors is socio-economic and includes the integration of rural areas and their populations into nation states, and the consequences of labour migration and of increasing differentiation in wealth (Guyer, 1981b).

The norms which orient household composition are often those of kinship ideology, and in many Third World societies kinship is a fundamental principle of social organization. When we talk of kinship in these terms, however, we are talking not just of the fact of having parents, siblings and 'relatives', as we might in Britain, and having a vague notion of 'blood being thicker than water', that is, a notion, however attenuated, of kin obligation; rather we are talking of place in the local community and household organization being determined very largely by kinship ideology. Residence, access to resources such as land, herd animals or craft skills, choice of marriage partner, choice of friends, may all depend on kinship.[1] The centrality of a kinship system is given for both sexes, but what particular entitlements follow from place in the kinship system depend to a large extent on gender.

In most societies in the world, kinship status is dependent on who a person's father is, that is property is inherited and descent is traced in the patrilineal line. However, there is a significant minority of societies in which descent and property pass in the matrilineal line, that is, through women. This does not mean, however, that in these societies power is held by women. In patrilineal societies those in control of property and resources (land and so on) are men as fathers, paternal uncles, and sometimes sons of women. These societies are said to be patrilineal and patriarchal; power is in the hands of men. Contemporary matrilineal societies are not correspondingly matriarchal (although there has been some debate as to the existence of matriarchy in the past: see Coontz and Henderson, 1986). In matrilineal societies public power in the community is also vested in men, but in such situations the men are the maternal uncles, brothers and, again, sometimes sons, of women. Figures 2.1, a and b illustrate these differences.

In yet other societies, some aspects of status are inherited in the patrilineal line and others in the matrilineal line, but here again, power, in the sense of much of the decision-making and control of access to resources, is seen to be vested in men. These societies are said to be bilateral where the lines of descent are kept rigidly separate, or cognatic where the division is less rigid. A much more detailed discussion of descent and inheritance patterns can be found in Roger Keesing's *Kin Groups and Social Structure* (1975). In the empirical examples in Chapter 3 we include discussion of societies with each of these kinship systems, for example, patrilineal: Masai (Kenya), Luo (Kenya), Hindu (India), Pirá-Paraná (Colombia); matrilineal: Asante (Ghana), Rembau (Malaysia); cognatic: the people of Mafia Island, Tanzania. Just by stating that a society is patrilineal, matrilineal or cognatic, however, we cannot know anything specific about women's status or roles in it: although these are constrained by the kinship system, they are highly variable within it.

There have been attempts to associate the form of residential unit with 'types' of kinship structure, notably from those working with the Human Relations Area Files (see Chapter 3), who argue that in patrilineal societies the 'typical' form of residential unit is a patrilocal extended family group. In such groups, on marriage, sons bring their brides to live in their fathers' residence and their children are reared there with cousins on their fathers' side (patrilateral cousins) and several members of a grandparental generation. This kind of residential unit is found in some, but not all, patrilineal societies (Brydon, 1976; Verdon, 1983). Even in these reductionist studies, however, it is accepted that residential patterns in matrilineal societies are much more varied. For example, among the matrilineal societies of Zambia, the pattern tends to be for nuclear or polygynous (see below) male-headed residential units (Mitchell, 1956b; Richards, 1950; Turner, 1957). Among the Asante, although women may be married and formally 'living' with their husband they spend the bulk of their time in the houses and on the farms of their natal families, cooking (cooked food is sent to the husbands), bathing and dressing there, and only going to their husbands' houses to sleep when asked (Fortes, 1970). These examples not only illustrate the problems in making monolithic associations, they also show some of the problems in defining what a household is.

We must also bear in mind here the distinction between 'household as residential unit' and 'household as domestic (consumption/production) unit'. For example, the Yanomamo on the border between Brazil and Venezuela live in villages enclosed by a stockade. Inside the stockade there are separate cooking and sleeping areas, but nothing approaching separate 'houses'; thus here, the 'residential' unit is the whole village (Chagnon, 1968). Similarly for the Pirá-Paraná of Colombia (Hugh-Jones, 1978, 1979), the residential unit encompasses the whole village, but in this case its form is a longhouse inside which each wife cooks separately for a husband and children from food collected, hunted or grown by herself and her husband. Although we only have one 'residential unit' here, we have several 'domestic' units. Among the cattle-keeping peoples of eastern and southern Africa the residential unit may be large and patrilocal, but these larger units are composed of smaller domestic groups in which wives cook for their husbands and children from

PATRILINEAL SYSTEMS

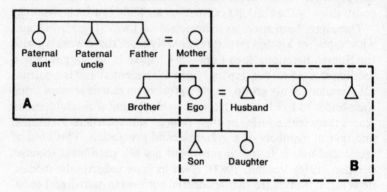

Figure 2.1a   Kinship and the Transmission of Rights: Patrilineal System

Group A is the woman's natal kinship group. She may retain rights to land and status in this group after marriage as in Avatime (Brydon, 1985b, for example) or not. Transmission and control over rights and resources are in the hands of a woman's father, paternal uncles and brothers. Group B is the woman's husband's kin group. A woman may have rights through her husband in this group, but unless she produces children, and in most cases, sons, then she loses rights in this group on the death of her husband (as among the Masai; Llewelyn-Davies, 1978, 1981). Where a woman's identification with her husband's kin group on marriage is very strong, on the death of her husband, whether or not she has produced children she will be married to a close relative of her former husband, having lost all formal ties to her natal group.

resources husbanded, if not owned, by themselves.[2]

Even in patrilineal societies the range of household form and residential structure varies enormously. Thus while residential units in 'traditional' societies in southern, central and eastern Africa, in high caste Hindu India and in societies where Islam is dominant might well be composed of patrilocal extended families, there are patrilineal societies where this is not the case. In most of Latin America, for example, where, although kinship is not so important a principle of social organization as in Africa or Asia, societies are effectively patrilineal, nuclear family residential units tend to be the norm, or increasingly, female-headed units (see below). It is only when we talk of nuclear family-based groups or female-headed residential units that we see any equivalence between 'household as residential unit' and 'household as domestic unit'. Perhaps in order

MATRILINEAL SYSTEMS

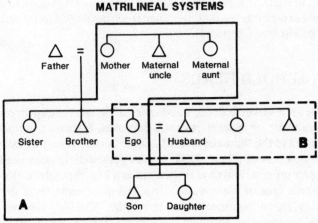

KEY
△ – Male   – – Sibling Tie
○ – Female | – Filial Tie
= – Marriage Tie

*Figure 2.1b   Kinship and the Transmission of Rights: Matrilineal
             System*

Group A is the woman's natal kinship group in which she never loses rights
and is the only transmitter of rights. However, control over productive
resources in Group A tends to be in the hands of a woman's maternal uncles,
her brothers, and, if they are old enough, her sons. A woman's involvement
with her husband's kin group, Group B, is minimal and confined to playing
wifely support roles at life-crisis rituals and working on her husband's
farms. She has no 'rights' to resources in group B.

to maintain consistency in distinguishing the two we should adopt
the term 'hearth-hold' for 'household as domestic unit' (Ekejiuba,
1984).

With the long-term influence of colonial rule and involvement
with the world capitalist system, many traditional forms of residential unit are much rarer than they were. Thus wherever there is a
significant migrant population whether in rural or urban areas,
residence forms may be changed: marriages might be 'neolocal', a
couple setting up residence in a new area as the nub of a nuclear
family unit, or single people hire rooms, live in company-provided
barrack-type accommodation or move in with kin or people from the
same home village. Where, traditionally, urban residence was the

norm, in parts of West Africa (among the Ga and Yoruba), in some Islamic areas or in Hindu India, then traditional residential patterns may persist (see Chapter 6).

HOUSEHOLD HEADS

Whenever a survey is done, whether for national census purposes or for academic or market research purposes, questions are always addressed to the 'household head'. Some questions may be asked of other members of a household, but the person designated head, on whatever criteria, is always singled out as a key respondent. Because the whole idea of surveys, censuses and questionnaires is derived from 'Western' approaches to knowledge (the idea that we can 'know' something through adding up replies to a series of questions), and because in the patriarchal societies of the West it is assumed that men have particular roles and functions as 'household heads', then in the Third World, too, both the notion of a household head is assumed to have similar relevance and men are presumed to be heads of households. Such glib transfers of Western academic technology obviously have their drawbacks when we come to consider problems we have with defining households in the Third World in the first place, and these are exacerbated if we further assume that a man has approximately the same role or significance as household head as his Western counterpart.

Even in the First World, in Britain and the US for example, recent work has shown that there is a considerable variety and range of household forms and that the nuclear family is by no means as preponderant as was formerly assumed (Wilson, 1985). One factor common to both First and Third Worlds in recent years has been an increasing frequency of female-headed households (both residential units and hearth-holds). Evidence from the Caribbean (for example, Smith, R.T. 1956; Clarke, 1957; Smith, M.G. 1962) shows that such groups have a long history. In addition, studies of Africa (especially in the 1950s and 1960s) found that where men move to work in cities, mines or plantations, they tend to leave their wives behind in rural areas, at least in the early stages of migration, thus creating *de facto* if not *de jure* female-headed households in rural areas (see Chapter 5). This distinction between *de facto* and *de jure* headship is common in the literature and refers to the differences between headship for everyday management (*de facto*) and in terms of the legal and jural norms of the society (*de jure*) (Chapman and Prothero, 1985; Brydon 1985a; Murray, 1981; Youssef and Hetler, 1983).

However, women are now assuming greater responsibility for household organization, and female-headed households are not simply those in which the male head is 'away' or has died. Women are heads of households in both rural and urban areas because they choose to set up house on their own, or are constrained to, because they have children and are not married (are divorced or separated from the fathers of their children). We might, in this category, regard widows as 'residual' household heads. Female-headed households occur even where we might least expect it, for example, some Islamic areas have a significant proportion of female-headed households: Celia Mather (1985) writes of 12 per cent in western Java, and the existence of female-headed households is also documented for rural India (Agarwal, 1987). In Sri Lanka, Rex Casinader et al. (1987) have shown how women have increasingly taken responsibility for their own and their children's welfare either with or without the support of a husband.

The Asian and Islamic instances of female-headed households are especially interesting since it is in these societies that men are often thought to exercise most control over women. In many, particularly East African, patrilineal, societies women have few rights as adults in the disposal of their labour or domestic services or of their sexuality, and yet here too we find an increasing number of female-headed households, not just in peri-urban squatter settlements (Nelson, 1978, for example), but also in rural areas (Feldman, 1984).

The early work on female-headed households in the Caribbean suggested not only that they were often the result of men working away in cities on other islands and in the US, but also, that they were a response to constraints imposed on women by the care of small children. Grandmothers were sometimes given the care of small children while their mothers worked. Such 'granny fostering' is now occurring in West Africa (Brydon, 1979; Asuni, 1988; Di Domenico, pers. comm.,) and in East Africa (Nelson, 1987).

Where women are on their own in rural areas with children to look after and without financial support from men or migrant offspring, they are often very poor. This position is reinforced by the fact that rural women may have little 'say' in local power structures, they may have limited access to land, or the division of labour and allocation of resources may militate against their production of key crops (Chambers, 1983; Mitchnik, 1978). Even in areas with rural development projects or where socialist governments have made radical changes in land-ownership, women may still be among the poorest, and the patriarchal orientation of 'development' ideology and of most governments works against any improvement in their lot (Crehan, 1984, for example; see also Chapters 4 and 6).

Whatever the reasons for the formation of female-headed households, they are now so prevalent that it is estimated that they make up around one-third of households world-wide (Bolles, 1986; Moser and Chant, 1985). Such estimates include both rural and urban areas. The relationships among 'development', urbanization and female-headed households are dealt with further in Chapter 6.

MARRIAGE

Just as studies of kinship, residence and household structure and organization have been largely the province of anthropologists in the past, anthropologists have also provided much of the empirical material and theoretical insights into 'marriage', the process by which most households are formed, whether it is a formal marriage recognized as legitimate by members of the community and/or state apparatus or whether it is an 'illegitimate' or transient union. Both 'marriage' and 'illegitimate' are singled out here as there has been much debate as to the applicability of the terms in cross-cultural contexts (Goody, J.R., 1971; Keesing, 1985).

While monogamy (the marriage of one man with one woman) is the norm in most of Central and Latin America and the Caribbean, polygamous marriages are found elsewhere in the world. Polygamy means simply plural marriage: polygyny is the marriage of one man to more than one woman simultaneously, and polyandry is the marriage of one woman to more than one man simultaneously. Polygynous households tend to be larger than others, consisting as they do of a man, two or more wives and their respective children. Here too, we must bear in mind the distinction made above between 'household' and 'hearth-hold': while a polygynous household may be comparatively large, each hearth-hold (each cluster within it) is similar in size to other mother–child units. The difference in a polygynous household is that the man/husband/father is shared among several hearth-holds. In all polygynous situations, hearth-

1olds are distinct. Although co-wives may cooperate in looking after :ach other's children and so on, they still maintain a separate dentity with their children from other units in the residential group, aving their own supply of food and/or money from which to feed and clothe their children.

Polyandrous marriages are much rarer than polygynous mar-iages and are found where there may be a demographic shortage of women (for example, through female infanticide) in areas such as Tibet. In these cases, the woman performs domestic services for her ausbands and sexual services are given on a rotational basis. Polyan-lrous marriages tend to be associated with scarce resources and their orudent management, rather than with wealth and displays of :onspicuous consumption.

Polygyny occurs in most African states and several parts of Asia and the Middle East. Islam permits a man to have four wives by law, out this depends on the wealth of the husband. Since all wives must oe equally provided for under the tenets of Islam, only very rich men :an afford the luxury of keeping more than one wife in *purdah*. In aon-Islamic societies, polygyny also tends to be associated with wealth: large individual (or family) resources are essential in order to afford the rituals, gifts and so on necessary to contract several narriages.[3] Of course, these marriages in turn may help to generate nore wealth: each wife brings into the marriage, not only her lomestic labour and potential as a mother, but also her capacity to work in whatever sphere there is scope, for example, agricultural oroduction (Goody and Buckley, 1973; Guyer, 1982, for example).

In Latin America polygyny is rare and found only among some indigenous groups. As we saw in Chapter 1, the great majority of Latin American people today is Christian (mainly Catholic). Thus aouseholds tend to be centred on a monogamous marriage, and here is not the same significance to distinguishing 'household as esidential unit' from 'household as domestic unit' (hearth-hold) as n other parts of the world. It is also for historical reasons that, unlike many of their African counterparts (see, for example, Peel, 968), even the indigenised Christian Churches in Latin America do ot promote polygyny as part of their ideology.

VOMEN'S ROLES IN RURAL AREAS

eventy-five per cent of the world's population lives in the Third

World, and 75 per cent of Third World population is in rural area
(UN, 1985). When we talk of 'rural women', therefore, we are in fac
referring to *the* major category of women in the world. What wome
do and are expected to do varies, of course, with economy, climate
political or religious ideology and culture, but there is throughou
the world a core of common tasks which women everywhere ar
required to perform. These include cooking on an everyday basi
(see Guyer, 1981a), 'housework' (sweeping, cleaning), care of sma
children and, very often, fetching water and fuel. Such chores ar
also performed by urban women (see also Chapter 6).

In addition to these service and management tasks, however, rura
women are also for the most part responsible for the production of
significant proportion of the household economic resources
whether this is production of crops for food, care of herds or work i
the storage and processing of crops, both for food and seed (produc
tion for use), or whether it is production of cash crops and/or craf
products for sale (production for exchange). Production in its wides
sense is the subject of Chapter 3 but here it is important to note tha
in spite of women's obvious contribution to the maintenance of th
household, there may be no necessary correlation with women'
status, either in the household or the wider community (se
Chapter 3).

Women's work in rural communities thus combines domesti
service and 'productive' work: it is often said that rural women mus
bear a 'double burden', working long hours in the farms or in craf
production and then equally long hours in child-care, food prep
aration, cooking, washing and cleaning. Jette Bukh (1979) gives a
account of the daily toil of a Ghanaian village woman: her typica
day involves rising before dawn (4–5 a.m.), preparing cooked foo
for sale and for her children to eat before going to school, selling th
food, getting the children ready for school, tidying up the house
going to farm, either preparing food for children at lunchtime o
giving them money to buy cooked food, procuring the ingredient
for the evening meal, preparing and cooking it, and then, perhaps
going again to the village market to sell once the children are asleep
In such a case, the woman's children help by fetching water fron
stand-pipes, but the community in which Bukh worked is unusual i
that it has piped water. Fetching water from streams, more usual i
rural communities, can involve a long trek and in the dry seaso
streams often shrink to a small trickle, thereby prolonging the work

Berny Horowitz and Madhu Kishwar (1984) give an example of a typical woman's day in an agrarian society in India, and Tahrunnessa Abdullah and Sondra Zeidenstein (1982) describe a day in the life of a woman in (Islamic) rural Bangladesh. Both are as long and arduous as that of Bukh's rural Ghanaian woman. Here too, as in other societies, separating productive, in the sense of remunerated work, from other work is rather a futile exercise (see Chapter 3; and Bennholdt-Thomsen, 1981). Even in the case of women who are producing for the market, for example a charcoal burner (Dankelman and Davidson, 1988, pp.80–3) or a 'kenkey' (steamed, fermented maize dough) maker in Ghana (Rocksloh-Papendieck, 1988, pp.163–4) the boundaries among remunerated work, subsistence production and reproduction are vague.

A slightly less stark picture of women's lives is given by Stella Odie-Ali (1986), who, while not denying that Guyanese women work hard, states explicitly that their lives compare favourably with those of women elsewhere in the Third World. Her description of the day in the life of one woman is typical of the 'fluidity and flexibility' of a woman's roles (1986, p.254). The day combines personal care (bathing, eating, and so on), care of livestock, both garden and field agricultural work, family care (cooking and caring for/overseeing children, housework), marketing activities (in this case, preparing and packing produce for sale next day) and recreation. Here the day begins at 5.30 a.m. and ends at 9.30 p.m. Odie-Ali's emphasis on time for personal care and recreation distinguishes her account from the others cited.

While men also sometimes share in the work undertaken by women, their tasks do not normally include quotidian domestic work. Men may play with small children, but it is not usual for small children to be left continually in the care of men. Once men return from their work, they tend to relax: to eat, bathe, gossip and/or drink. Men's domestic tasks, where they do any, tend to be communal: house-building or thatching, although in some societies construction and maintenance of houses is also the responsibility of the women (Llewelyn-Davies, 1978; Caplan, 1984).

In many parts of the world women's work has been made even more difficult by an increasing shortage of fuel wood. Thus, what was just one more rather onerous female chore has been made much more time consuming and laborious in that loads take longer to collect and have to be carried further because of increased felling of trees in both forest and savannah areas. Not only have women's burdens been exacerbated in this way, but also, degradation of woodland has consequences for quality of land and climate: desertification is the end result if the process is allowed to continue (Dankelman and Davidson, 1988; Cecelski, 1985).

The issues surrounding the fuel wood crisis serve as a succinct example of the problems women have in 'being heard' in many Third World communities. In areas of Uttar Pradesh, India, in 1974 women learned that a large acreage of woodland was to be felled to provide land for a business venture. Since their men were away working and since, in this area, women ordinarily need men to speak for them in the public arena (Jain, 1980; Kishwar and Vanita, 1984), the women could only take direct action: they physically surrounded the trees and prevented the bulldozers from moving in. The state government subsequently recognized their claim that the trees should not be felled and since that time a movement has grown, both for the protection of existing trees, and for the planting and nurturing of saplings (Dankelman and Davidson, 1988; Cecelski, 1985). This movement is known as *Chipko*, which means literally, 'to hug', after the Uttar Pradesh women's action in encircling 'their' trees.

Increasing shortages of fuel, either as wood or charcoal or in other forms has meant that costs have risen. This has meant that sometimes only one meal a day is prepared, instead of two. In other cases where formerly nutritious foods such as pulses were eaten (rich in protein and certain vitamins), these are now being replaced with less nutritious alternatives which do not take so long to cook. Although there have been some successful attempts to find ways of reducing fuel consumption or other alternatives (notably energy-saving stoves in India), these alternatives have either proved too expensive (for example, electricity) or impractical (solar-powered stoves).[5]

THE STATUS OF RURAL WOMEN

In spite of Barbara Rogers' (1980) derogatory comments on studies using the notion of the 'status of women', so many writers have focused on status that we must examine the concept more closely. Much of the work on women's status today derives from Engels' (1884, 1972) work in *The Origin of the Family, Private Property and the State.* He saw women's subordination particularly in capitalist societies as a result of their separation from 'production', by which he meant remunerated work. We discuss women, production and status in detail in Chapter 3, but it is important to look briefly at status as a concept, whether related to production or not.

Women, Nature and Biology

Those working from a 'symbolist' orientation see women's subordination as universal. Sherry Ortner (1974) is the modern feminist writer most associated with this approach. Her argument begins with the premise that, following Simone de Beauvoir (1953), women's bodies (which are everywhere similar) condemn them to being 'more enslaved to the species' than men: a much larger proportion of women's bodies is devoted to reproduction of an 'other' than that of men. The fact that it is women who are responsible for gestation and lactation reinforces women's association with the reproduction of the species. Thus, she argues, women are somehow 'closer to nature' than men.

Ortner combines a symbolist with a biological/behavioural approach (Rogers, 1978), and posits a universal opposition between culture and nature, following Claude Lévi-Strauss (1969). Culture, as opposed to nature, is the realm of men and Ortner's task at the outset is to show how women can be identified with nature thus forming a neat pair of oppositions, male: female :: culture: nature. Since she has proposed the ubiquitous existence of an opposition between nature and culture, and since the aim of men in culture is to control nature, women are everywhere subordinate to men. However, what she in fact demonstrates is that the 'problem' with women is not that they are *in* nature, but that they are partly in nature (as culturally defined) and partly in culture. As such they form a kind of intermediate category and are thus potentially dangerous and must be controlled (Ortner, 1974). Their subordinate (controlled) status is reinforced because they are confined to the domestic sphere by their child-care responsibilities. Men, on the other hand, control interaction and exchange in the wider society, and are thus dominant (Lévi-Strauss, 1969, 1972; Ortner, 1974).

Ortner's work is highly controversial and there have been many criticisms (see, for example, Rogers, 1978; MacCormack and Strathern, 1980). In particular, in 1981, Sherry Ortner herself, together with Harriet Whitehead, edited a collection of essays which strive to consider questions of gender and status in a more holistic way, and particularly the association between gender constructions and hierarchy. But still their explanation ultimately rests on the idea that it is the fact of women's biology, their sexuality and reproductive capacity, which condemns them to universal subordination although this may vary in degree. As Susan Rogers (1978) points out, however, general theories of sexual differentiation/women's subordination/status based on a denigration of women's physiology and childbearing and rearing responsibilities, together with an attitude that these are somehow 'constraining', is derived from our own culture and is thus grossly ethnocentric.

Ethnocentrism and Status

In addition to the charge of ethnocentrism in *analysis*, researchers working on women's status are also open to the charge of ethnocentrism in their *data collection*. The literature on this is already quite wide (Ardener, 1975a, 1975b; Sacks, 1976; Milton, 1979). For example, Annette Weiner's (1976) work in the Trobriand Islands off the coast of New Guinea has led to a realization that women are social actors in their own right and vital partners in their husbands' social manoeuvring, a fact previously overlooked or ignored in the ethnographic material from this area. Assumptions and 'data' that have formed the bases for our views and understanding of other cultures for many years are now being questioned from feminist perspectives, without the initial premise that only men are social actors and as such, 'superior'.[6]

Recently the emphasis has shifted away from trying to provide universal explanations of women's status, to more specific examinations of particular issues, both theoretical (for example, capitalist patriarchy (Coward, 1983, for example), and empirical (for example, Ifeka, 1975, 1982; Rogers, 1975)), which point us in the direction of re-examining our own evaluations and concepts. Susan Rogers' (1978) review of 'women's place' was a timely intervention here. While noting attempts by writers to 'measure' women's status through sets of externally imposed criteria, she suggests that the way forward is to try to see behind our own assumptions about status and power. Just because men may be prominent in public arenas, and Western cultures 'measure' power and status in terms of public position, this does not mean that in other cultures women are 'devalued', or subordinate. Thus, when we try to measure women's status in the Third World in terms of what are considered 'appropriate' indicators in the West, their participation in agriculture or their access to ownership of land (Chapter 3) or their visibility in public decision-making (Sanday, 1981; Ross, 1986), we are probably distorting whatever the empirical reality is. We must decipher status and power considerations in their own terms, and find out what lies behind public practices.

Of course, this poses problems when we come to deal with societies that have changed. Factors such as the introduction of a world religion, whether Christian or not, the experiences of colonial rule and incorporation into the world capitalist system have affected most societies at least within the last 150 years, and First World feminists argue that since these all entail patriarchal ideologies, women's status is therefore generally subordinate. But if we assume that these externally imposed influences have not entirely eradicated indigenous cultural logics and practices, an assumption which would guard against ethnocentrism on our part, the task of deciphering women's status is rendered more difficult. Thus, whatever women's status was in pre-colonial societies, it has changed and women in these societies have been incorporated into the new Third World nation-states in travestied ways.

Caroline Ifeka's (1975) analysis of the change in women's status among the Igbo brought about by colonial rule and colonial British assumptions about the universality of Christian, patriarchal and bourgeois/capitalist values provides an excellent example here. The Igbo are a patrilineal people living in the forest areas of Southeastern Nigeria surrounding the Niger delta. Their economy was based on agricultural production for subsistence and exchange (the area had long been incorporated into the world capitalist system through the slave trade, initially). Settlement was in villages connected not only by kinship ties, but also by a network of markets which were primarily the domain of the women. Yams were the most significant subsistence crop (grown by men), but women's processing of palm fruits and kernels into oils meant that they had direct access to the exchange economy. Igbo villages do not have chiefs, they are ruled by village councils and there is some evidence to suggest that parallel hierarchies of male and female elders were responsible for the political affairs of the village (Okonjo, 1976; Van Allen, 1976; Martin, 1988).

In the 1920s the British introduced 'Indirect Rule' to the Igbo.[7] Since there were no indigenous chiefs, the British chose men for the chiefship (usually those who had cooperated with them and often, those who were literate). The basis for their authority was their 'warrant' from the British: hence they became known as Warrant Chiefs. The chiefs were corrupt and unpopular, since they had to impose a poll tax on men, and further, they had been given authority over the markets, previously the province of women. However, while the *political* power of men might have increased, women gained in *economic* terms: the 1920s saw a great boom in the price of vegetable oils in West Africa, and as women were largely responsible for their production and sale, they became rich relative to men. By 1929 women resented the power of the Warrant Chiefs, especially in the area of the markets and they had become disproportionately wealthy with respect to their husbands so that the economic 'balance' in their marriages had altered. Finally, because of the actions of one chief, women felt that they, too, were to be taxed, and the word spread through market networks for the beginning of collective action against the chiefs and the British.

The form this action took was a particular traditional sanction open to women when they felt threatened *as* women. Such action is called 'sitting on a man': the women dress only in creepers, paint their bodies white and behave aggressively. Although there is no physical danger to the offender, the women taunt him with bawdy songs and surround his house, shouting and waving sticks in the air and banging on the roof. However, when the Igbo women decided to protest this way in late 1929, both against the chief and against the British, the British interpreted their behaviour as a riot and took 'defensive action': several women were shot and many were injured.[8]

According to Ifeka (1975) Igbo women 'rioted' in the eyes of the colonial administrators, but in their own cultural terms staged a perfectly legitimate protest, which had specific limits to its form and was thus in no sense a riot. The rumour of taxation was the last straw: women had lost control of the markets, which had given them status, they were becoming rich, as men had become rich, and they felt their remaining status as women, their power over fertility and reproduction, was also vulnerable. The specific form of the Igbo women's action reflects this perceived threat to their womanhood. Ifeka ascribes the differences in perception by the British to intellectual arrogance, but later goes on to expand the significance of her analysis.

Ifeka (1982) stresses the importance of appreciating the cultural relativity of perceptions of 'self' and 'gender'. Her analysis of Igbo social thought shows how it is possible to have such concepts which, unlike our own, are fluid and interactive. Thus, she states that to talk of 'dominance' and 'subordination' in Igbo society is not, strictly speaking, accurate. The roles and status of men and women are complementary in specific ways on different occasions, and so, even to speak of 'equality' is problematic, since this implies that we must be able to measure women's and men's status objectively.

This kind of work does much to show that it is both possible and valid to move away from Western-derived ideas of women's status, and in Ifeka's description Igbo society emerges not as 'strongly patrilineal' or 'male-dominated', terms which could have been applied to it on the basis of past analyses, but as a society in which women and men have particular roles to play and from which their statuses are derived situationally. Kamene Okonjo's work (1976), although more mechanistic, supports Ifeka's ideas and support also comes from a careful reading of Chinua Achebe's novel *Things Fall Apart* (1958), written from a male perspective.

The idea of gender complementarity is prominent in the work on the Igbo just discussed and is a key issue in studies of gender and status elsewhere in the world. Women in *mestizo* communities in Latin America are, on the whole, thought to be subordinate in status to men, largely because of the predominance and long influence of Hispanic colonial values and the Catholic Church. However writers on indigenous Andean communities (Harris, 1978, 1980; Isbell, 1976, 1977; but see also Harvey, 1988) stress the complementarity of gender roles rather than any across the board 'subordination' of women. Throughout the 1970s, too, there were several attempts to analyse the status of women in 'egalitarian' societies (Leacock, 1978, for example). Patricia Draper's (1975) account of the development of an evaluative hierarchy which systematically denigrated women and women's work among settled !Kung Bushmen of the Kalahari Desert, Botswana, is also valuable here, since it demonstrates the pervasive, and we might add, pernicious, influence of patriarchal values.

General Considerations of Women's Status

Women's status within rural households and communities depends
on a variety of factors: relative status within the kin group or
household, for example, whether a woman is wife, mother, daughter
or sister; on the type of kinship system, where this is important and
on ideology, (whether religious or political), the cultural norms of a
particular ethnic group or a combination of the above. We leave
consideration of the relative statuses of 'sister' and 'wife' to the next
chapter, but motherhood is also an important facet of most Third
World Women's lives (see Chapter 1). Fertility has a crucial place in
the world views of most Third World societies, both those of men
and women. While it is important for men in patrilineal societies to
reproduce, especially to reproduce sons to continue the lineage, it is
also important for men to have children for status reasons: it
conforms to the norm for virile men (see also Chapter 8). So
important has this been that in some societies impotent men have
persuaded brothers or friends to impregnate their wives on their
behalf. A further bonus from having children is the benefits of their
labour, and increasingly, the chance that one or more will become
educated and gain access to the wealth and prestige that accompany
bureaucratic jobs in many Third World states.

While most women marry, wifehood is only a stage, and not
mandatory in many cases today, towards the achievement of the
more prestigious status of mother. A woman gains status through
bearing children (especially sons in patrilineal societies), but in
addition, her position in an extended residential or kinship group is
consolidated through the bearing and rearing of children. In societies such as Masai (Llewelyn-Davies, 1978, 1981) or Islamic societies
(Jeffery, 1979; Mernissi, 1985) where residence is in patrilineally
extended units, women achieve their ultimate status in many ways by
becoming a mother-in-law. In so doing they have not only confirmed
their status as women by bearing sons, but also have the power to
command the labour of others (their daughters-in-law: see also
Chapter 1).

Women's status also varies with the prevalence of different
religious or political ideologies. In all of the major world religions,
Christianity, Islam, Hinduism, Buddhism, Confucianism, for
example, men are formally the power-holders in terms of being
decision-makers and controllers of productive resources. But every-

where, there is local adaptation of religious doctrines, dependent on tradition or on political design. Thus although we might feel that Khomeini's Iran exemplifies the working of Islam in its strictest form, Haleh Afshar's (1987) analysis shows how a particular form of Islam, in this case, Shi'ite, has been adapted to suit the political designs of a small cadre of rulers, and that in pre-revolutionary Iran, local custom played a much greater part in the day-to-day practice of Islam. She also shows how Iranian interpretations of Islamic law deviate from or ignore some of the basic teachings of Islam, especially in the sphere of women's rights (Chapter 1). Even Hinduism, which still primarily serves the cultures in which it developed, has had to adapt to encompass new status mobility and economic class divisions in modern Indian society.

Although socialist societies tend to play down the role of religion and culture, even these are increasingly having to take into account the significance of such factors in their everyday practices and policies (see for example, Deighton et al., 1983). In a way, the advent of socialism can be seen as an attempt to incorporate a new form of ideology in societies. However, just as there is no example of a 'pure' form of religious ideology operating anywhere, so too, socialism has its variations, in Vietnam, in Cuba, in Tanzania and so on. J.D.Y. Peel's (1973) discussion of the significance of cultural factors in development, although not specifically concerned with gender, deals in detail with the importance of tradition, religion and political ideologies.

CONCLUSION

In this chapter we have looked at the contexts of Third World rural women's lives in the household and the community and discussed aspects of household structure, kinship ideology and religious and other cultural factors. We have noted problems in separating rural women's 'reproductive' and 'productive' activities and have documented a range of their household tasks. The issue of status has also been introduced and is taken up again in the following chapter in the framework of a broad discussion of women's roles in rural production.

NOTES

1. In some societies, the state of slavery has even been likened to that of

having no kin. A slave was completely under the control of a master (and solely a member of his household) and had no rights in or duties towards any other group. Further, a slave could not rely on any support from outside the household: s/he had no kin to give it (MacCormack, 1977).

2. The idea of ownership in kin-based societies is highly complex. The simplest way of understanding some of the major problems is to separate rights in property into two: use rights and rights to alienate. While in the West ownership is regarded as consisting of both classes of rights, in many Third World societies ownership tends to mean use rights for the individual. Rights to alienate property: land, cattle or whatever rest with the kin group as a juridical body, that is, to alienate (sell) such property is a matter for group rather than individual decision.

3. Marriage in kin-based societies is often regarded as a union between two families rather than a union of individuals.

4. Dankelman and Davidson (1988; Chapter 3) provide a detailed discussion of water requirements and women's role in their provision and management in rural areas.

5. Solar stoves work well, in theory, but their designers failed to take into account the fact that meals are cooked in the early morning and/or the evening when there is little sun.

6. Rohrlich-Leavitt et al. (1975) and Goodale (1971) discuss these kinds of problems of collection and interpretation of data about Australian aboriginal women.

7. 'Indirect Rule', in theory, is rule through indigenous institutions, and was favoured by the British in their colonies. However, 'indigenous institutions' effectively meant 'chiefs', and so where there were no chiefs there were administrative problems, and the result was often the arbitrary creation of chiefs.

8. The British commissioned a report after the Women's War: some remained convinced, however, that the women could not possibly be responsible for what had happened and looked for male ringleaders for what they regarded as 'riots'.

3 Gender and Rural Production

In this chapter we examine women's roles in rural production. The first part looks at large-scale studies which have attempted to summarise and quantify rural women's work and the relationship between women, work and status. The second part is more substantive and focuses on the range and diversity of women's productive activities in rural areas, taking a regional and cultural perspective. First, however, we must look at how production is to be defined in rural contexts: as we noted earlier, the boundaries between 'reproduction' and 'production' in rural areas are often blurred. Although women in Cajamarca, Peru, for example, may not see their contribution to agriculture as 'production' (rather as 'helping out', Deere and Leon de Leal, 1981, 1982, for example), it must be regarded in any analysis as contributing to subsistence, and therefore as productive work. Similarly, Bangladeshi women who do not work in the fields, nevertheless play a vital part in the cultivation of rice (the staple crop) since they are responsible for preparation, storage and germination of the seeds (Abdullah and Zeidenstein, 1982). Is this 'work' (a contribution to production) or not?

Perhaps one way of defining 'production' is to say that if work is remunerated it qualifies as productive labour. But this is hardly satisfactory, since in many cases rural productive activities (the production of food, for example) are primarily subsistence activities and as such are not remunerated. Maybe we can tighten up our definition and say that it is only if there is production for exchange that 'work' is done. But things are becoming absurd here. Women constitute on average 47 per cent of the agricultural labour force in sub-Saharan Africa, 30 per cent in North Africa and the Middle East, 40 per cent in south Asia, 54 per cent in Southeast Asia, 40 per cent in the Caribbean and 18 per cent in Latin America (Dixon, 1983).[1] How can we know how much, if any, of this 'productive' labour is for exchange, and how much for use? The short answer is that in the gross sense, we cannot. For the sake of simplicity we include subsistence production as 'work', and recognise too, that in many cases, what is usually regarded as 'reproductive' labour, cooking, cleaning, child-care, water and fuel collection, can have a value in the productive sense (Chapter 2; Bennholdt-Thomsen, 1981).

LARGE-SCALE STUDIES OF WOMEN AND RURAL PRODUCTION: THE PROBLEM OF STATISTICS

Ester Boserup's (1970) *Women's Role in Economic Development* was the first attempt to provide a serious and comprehensive analysis of the issue of women's productive roles. Boserup argues that women's status varies with the nature of productive activity and their involvement in it, and further, that with economic development, women's status declines. Her work was germinal in exposing women's vital contributions to agricultural production. Despite the fact that anthropologists *had* written of women's labour in farming, the most common assumption had been that because male labour was central to agricultural systems in Europe, it was *ipso facto* central to farming in all parts of the world, another example of a totally misappropriate transfer of academic technology! As we shall see in Chapter 4, this kind of assumption has often been incorporated wholesale into rural development policies and in turn, has led to a decline in women's status, and in some cases, to a drop in the overall levels of production.

Very generally, Boserup's thesis is that where shifting cultivation is the norm, women do most of the agricultural work; where the plough is used, men do more work than women; and where land is irrigated, and farming is intensive, such as in parts of Southeast Asia, then both men and women are highly involved in agricultural production. Boserup concludes that women's status is high where their involvement in production is high, that is, in shifting cultivation systems or systems of irrigated agriculture. However, she notes that with economic development, broadly understood as the mechanization of agriculture, and increasing specialization and differentiation of non-agricultural tasks, women tend to become separate from production and their status correspondingly declines. Boserup's prescriptions for improving the fate of women focus on increasing their access to education, thereby improving their chances of competing on an equal basis with men in the labour market.

While the statistical empirical associations (drawn from official country census and survey data) between types of farming system and women's status remain broadly true,[2] Boserup's theoretical overview, or perhaps, lack of it, has been criticized. Lourdes Benería and Gita Sen (1981), for example, while praising the empirical range of Boserup's work, point out the drawbacks of relying to such an extent on empirical material in what is, or, according to them, should be, a predominantly theoretical work; they see Boserup as falling into the empiricist trap of bringing in ideas/ideology in idiosyncratic ways as 'filler' to block in areas of her thesis. Benería and Sen's criticisms can be divided into two: those directed at Boserup's reliance on models drawn from neo-classical economics and on assumptions of modernization, and, secondly, her failure to provide an adequate theoretical analysis of women's subordination, in spite of her overt concern with women.

These two lines of criticism are not mutually exclusive: Boserup's over-concentration on productive work outside the home (remunerated work) at the expense of domestic (reproductive) work, together with her failure to show the systematic nature of women's subordination with the imposition of capitalist relations of production (the hegemony of capitalist patriarchy), mean that her prescription for the future improvement of women's condition, 'education', is totally inadequate. Until we have a satisfactory theoretical analysis of the significance of reproductive work in different modes of production and with different cultural patterns of gender relations then such prescriptions must remain deficient; that is, any analysis of women's status must draw upon both economic and cultural/ ideological factors (see Chapter 1).

Whyte and Whyte (1978), in discussing the applicability of Boserup's categories to women in rural Asia, come to similar conclusions, but add the proviso that in Southeast Asia where intensive irrigated agriculture predominates, other 'cultural' factors mitigate the association between 'type of agriculture' and women's status, including religion, forms of marriage payments and residence. However, women's involvement in agricultural work remains the key factor in the ascription of their status and other factors are only brought into play to explain deviations from the expected pattern.

In northern India, for example, where plough agriculture is dominant, women's status is lower than in other parts of Asia because of their exclusion from critical aspects of production, what we should expect on Boserup's predictions, and Whyte and Whyte (1978) show for these areas that major religions (Islam and Hinduism), types of marriage payment and so on have acted to reinforce women's low status. In parts of Southeast Asia where irrigated rice is grown, Thailand, the Philippines and Java, for example, women have relatively equal status to men, whereas in other irrigated rice areas such as Bengal or Bangladesh, women's participation in production is frowned upon and their status is lower. Whyte and Whyte (1978) explain these differences by pointing to the fact that Islam is dominant in the latter countries, and this imposes far greater restrictions on women than in the former states where Buddhism is prevalent (see Chapter 1).

Carmen Diana Deere and Magdalena Leon de Leal (1981, 1982) critically analyse material from Andean regions of South America with respect to women and their productive activities. In Boserup's classification, the Latin American region is classed as a 'male' farming system, that is, one with settled farming, use of the plough, and so on. However, their conclusions indicate that the term 'male' farming system is perhaps a misnomer: 'family' farming system would be more appropriate. Andean women do, in fact, participate in agricultural activities, even if men do the majority of fieldwork. But their study also shows the differential influence of ideological/cultural factors on women's relations to production and women's status. Boserup's thesis, they argue, is only directly applicable to rural producers who have access to land, grow cash crops and are relatively wealthy, that is, the middle and elite peasant groups.

Among the vast majority of peasants however, land is not sufficient to support a family group and some members have to become involved in wage labour in one form or another. Although in theory land can be owned by both men and women in all groups, in practice, it is only among the poorer peasants where women have to work in the fields and for other people, that they have a significant 'say' in major agricultural and other decisions which affect the family. Here the interrelationship between class and production is singled out as a significant factor influencing women's status in ways not predicted in Boserup's work.

Both Whyte and Whyte and Deere and Leon de Leal provide specific tests of Boserup's ideas, as well as stressing other factors in their analyses of women's status and their involvement in production. In particular, Deere and Leon de Leal (1981, 1982) point out defects in the statistics used by Boserup: the usual design of surveys and censuses does not allow for accurate categorization and enumeration/evaluation of women's activities (see also, Rechini de Lattes and Wainermann, 1986). Ruth Dixon-Mueller's (1985) review of women in agriculture is positively directed at the problems of finding out about women's work in rural areas of the Third World. Her book is part of one of several series of monographs (in this case, *Women, Work and Development*) published by the International Labour Office (ILO) with the sponsorship of other aid agencies. The ILO has been extremely active, especially since the inauguration of the UN Decade for Women in 1975 (see Chapter 10), in promoting women's visibility in Third World states, both in rural and in urban areas. Dixon-Mueller's work in this case is a methodological text but it complements and highlights some of the problems singled out by other writers on the quality of official data on rural women (Deere and Leon de Leal, 1981, 1982, for example).

Different sets of official statistics can also be interpreted in varying ways. For example, according to Seager and Olson (1986), less than 10 per cent of the total agricultural labour force in Angola is composed of women. According to the Organization of Angolan Women (1984), however, women's participation in agriculture is 25 per cent (based on 1978 figures), but they do stress that their figures do not include ' ... the vast majority of working women' (ibid., 41). The discrepancy noted by Ruth Dixon (1983) between the ILO revised estimate (27 per cent) and her 'predicted' estimate (42 per cent) of women's participation in the agricultural labour force in Angola is one of the largest in sub-Saharan Africa, which probably indicates shortcomings in the basic statistics rather than a fault in the ILO's methodology (see also, OAW, 1984).

In Guyana, according to Seager and Olson (1986), under 10 per cent of the agricultural labour force is female. However, Stella Odie-Ali (1986), working under the auspices of the Women in the Caribbean Project, suggests, on the basis of her survey of four government-designated development areas, that women are involved in agricultural work to much the same extent as men and that their ownership of productive resources, particularly land and housing, is increasing. Ruth Dixon (1983) using ILO revised figures, suggests that women's participation in the agricultural labour force in Guyana is 32 per cent (the predicted figure in this case is 37 per cent).

These two examples illustrate the care which must be exercised in using official statistics uncritically. Even within her samples, Odie-Ali shows the extent to which factors of race and culture (East Indian, Negro, Mixed or Amerindian) influence women's participation in agriculture. Rather than relying on 'official' statistics to any great extent, Dixon-Mueller (1985) suggests ways in which information on women has been and can be obtained, depending on budgetary and time constraints. Problems with the use of official statistics and the lack of information about what women do are dealt with further in Chapter 4.

Bearing in mind the fact that we must be cautious in using figures, it is generally accepted that there is huge global variation both in the proportions of women living in rural areas and in rural women's involvement in production. Overall, in sub-Saharan Africa women's agricultural employment rates are high and their urban employment rates, low. In Latin America and the Caribbean, the reverse is the case: rural employment rates are low for women and those in urban areas, high. In the Middle East, North Africa and South Asia, women's employment rates are low both in the cities and the countryside, and in Southeast Asia, women's participation rates are high irrespective of location (Townsend and Momsen, 1987). In sub-Saharan Africa, where overall, a relatively small percentage of the population is urbanized, women are at least 30 per cent of the non-subsistence agricultural labour force (Seager and Olson, 1986). According to Dixon (1983) in most of the sub-Saharan African states women in fact form well over 30 per cent of the agricultural labour force, and in many areas, over 40 per cent. It could be the case that women constitute a high proportion of the agricultural labour force simply because they form the bulk of the rural population: in Zimbabwe, for example, women are 75 per cent of rural inhabitants (Chimedza, 1987). Nevertheless, proportional activity rates for women living in rural areas in Africa are far higher than those of women in towns: in Malawi, 23 per cent of women between 15 and 69 are employed in urban areas, while the corresponding figure for rural areas is 58 per cent (UNCHS, 1985).

Latin America has a higher proportion of its people living in cities than in any of our other regions: 62 per cent of the population lives in settlements of 20,000 or more inhabitants (Gilbert and Gugler, 1982). Since women predominate in urban migration (Chapters 5 and 6), they are often outnumbered by men in rural areas, which could, in part, account for low rates of female labour force participation here compared with cities (Butterworth and Chance, 1981; see also Chapter 7). However, women's proportional activity rates, allowing for the fact of their reduced numbers, are low in rural areas. In Brazil, for example, 31 per cent of all urban women between 15 and 69 were classified as employed, compared with only 17 per cent in the countryside (UNCHS, 1985). This, combined with a relatively small rural female population plus systematic under-recording of women's work (discussed above) means that there appears to be a very low rate of female agricultural labour force participation in Latin America.

In Southeast Asia, as we noted earlier, women's labour force participation is high in both rural and urban areas. In the Republic of Korea, for example, in 1975, 31 per cent of all urban women and 61 per cent of rural women aged between 15 and 69 were employed (UNCHS, 1985). In Islamic areas (the Middle East and North Africa and also Pakistan and Bangladesh) female participation rates tend to be low: for Morocco, the figures are 15 per cent of urban women employed compared with 9 per cent of rural women, while in Pakistan, the figures are 9 per cent in both rural and urban areas (UNCHS, 1985).[3] In India the ILO revised estimate for women's participation in the agricultural labour force is 47 per cent. Obviously there are huge regional disparities and severe problems in synthesizing from widely divergent data sources, and in all of these areas, labour force participation is strongly influenced by both cultural and economic factors, which sometimes reinforce and at other times, work against each other: these variations are discussed in detail in the second half of the chapter.

The Human Relations Area Files

Without doubt, the most 'scientific' (in the sense of positivistic hypothesis-testing) work on women's roles and status in production and related activites, and that which is on the largest scale comes from those working with the Human Relations Area Files (HRAF). Since the 1930s, G.P. Murdock and successive associates have been working to try to understand the nature of various phenomena cross-culturally. To this end, Murdock was the prime mover in organising the Human Relations Area Files which provide information in coded and code-able form, on societies throughout the world. The Ethnographic Atlas and the journal *Ethnology* are the best-known indicators of their work. In 1969, in order to make comparison in cross-cultural work easier, Murdock and White compiled the 'Standard Cross-Cultural Sample' (SCCS) from the Ethnographic Atlas and HRAF data, and Murdock and Provost (1973) coded information on the sexual division of labour for 50 tasks.

The use of the HRAF and SCCS as a valid sample for sophisticated statistical testing has been criticized severely (see, for example, Leach, 1982; Dixon-Mueller, 1985), and in particular its use of data not collected specifically for the HRAF tests, but drawn from a variety of historical and ethnographic sources. But this has not deterred many writers from using it, often in attempts to try to systematize Boserup's thesis, to refine ideas about the division of labour by sex and its relation to 'type' of agriculture and to correlate both with the status of women. Most of these studies rely on data from Africa since it is here that women's contribution to farming is highest (White, Burton and Dow, 1981; Burton and Reitz, 1981; Burton and White, 1984; Ember, 1983, for example). For what they are worth, their findings are that although specific tasks do not appear to be correlated in any significant way, there are 'implicational sequences'. By this they mean that if women perform one set of tasks, then they are likely to perform a range of specified and related tasks, and that these can be predicted to be 'women's tasks' because they are compatible with the constraints of pregnancy, lactation and child-care (Brown, 1970). However, caution is advised by Martin King Whyte (1978). Although he set out specifically to test various hypotheses about women's status, using HRAF data, Whyte's conclusions are essentially negative: there are 'no grounds for assuming that the relative subsistence contribution of women has status implications' (ibid., p. 169). He further argues that there is no such thing as *the* status of women cross-culturally and that when researchers think they are looking at aspects of women's status, they are 'dealing with essentially unrelated things' (ibid., p. 170).

Carol Ember (1983) suggests that with agricultural intensification ('development' or advance in agriculture) women's work in the fields will decline: with the concomitant improvement in harvests women do more in crop storage, processing and preparation. Their work in food preparation increases since, Ember argues, with intensification there is a shift from root to cereal crops and cereals involve more work in their preparation as food (threshing and grinding usually as a minimum). She further suggests that with intensification the physical maintenance of the house increases (clothing and pottery become more elaborate) and fertility will increase, hence more time will be spent on child care.[4] As women are more and more occupied in the domestic sphere, according to Ember, so men consolidate their relationships with others in the society and with those outside the society, and women's overall status declines.[5]

Ember's article emphasises that there is no necessary increase in 'male dominance' with the intensification of agriculture, and thus takes a stance against the socio-biological assumptions of some writers (for example, Divale and Harris, 1976).[6] Because of the suggestive rather than prescriptive nature of her conclusions, Ember's work can be compared with that of those like Sacks (1974, 1979, see below) who see women's separation from 'social' production as the key to their declining status. As such, work such as Ember's supports the more overtly theoretical approaches which rely less on dubious macro-level statistics for their validity.

WOMEN'S WORK AND STATUS IN RURAL COMMUNITIES: EVIDENCE FROM CASE STUDIES

Karen Sacks' work (1974, 1979) is explicitly an attempt to 'revalue' Engels' thesis. She uses ethnographic material from the database of the HRAF to compare women's status in four African societies, although the theoretical implications of her argument are much wider. Sacks suggests a threefold classification of societies, based loosely on mode of production: 'communal societies', in which the mode of production is hunting and gathering; 'kin corporate societies' based on agriculture, pastoralism or a combination of the two; and 'pre-industrial class societies', where, although subsistence production may be similar to that in kin corporate society, differentiation in wealth and status means that different groups in the society, other than gender groups, have different relationships to the means of production.

In communal societies access to the means of production is effectively open to all, irrespective of gender. Women in these societies suffer little, if any, subordination or exploitation. Kin corporate societies can be divided into two: in the first, women have significance in adulthood in the wider community as 'sisters' (in kin groups). Here they have community-wide roles to play, access to resources in their own right and may play an important part in decision-making processes within the kin group. In the second, women's adult roles are primarily as 'wives', and although they may be responsible for labour, both reproductive and productive, their status in the community is relatively low: they play little part in decision-making processes, and have little or no direct access to the means of production. They are dependent upon their husbands for their livelihood and have effectively no say in the affairs of their own kin groups.

In pre-industrial class societies there is the added dimension of social stratification. Elite women's status may be higher than that of lower-class men, but in a different way. However, the relative significance of 'sisters' and 'wives' is still important. Sacks argues (1974, p.220) that 'class societies tend to socialize the work of men and to domesticate that of women'. This has resulted in a devaluation of women's worth and labour: it suits the ruling groups in a class society to use the labour of men (men are infinitely more exploitable than women since they are not responsible for reproduction), and in return for their loss of economic autonomy, men are given social adulthood and the guardianship of women. Sacks concludes (1974, p. 222): 'The key aspect, then, of women's position, . . . is social adulthood, and this comes from participation in *social* production' (emphasis added). While Engels' thesis that women's incorporation into production would lead to emancipation has been largely discredited, Sacks' reformulation in terms of 'social' production, as with other more recent feminist work, allows us both to escape the unilinear evolutionary straitjacket of vulgar Marxism and to incorporate cross-cultural analyses into an understanding of 'women's status'. By adding 'social' to production we thus include local socioeconomic and ideological factors in an analysis of women's positions.

As an alternative, however, Jane Guyer (1980, 1988) suggests that a 'bottom-up' approach to women's work and the evaluation of what they do might be more fruitful and she is also concerned to show the significance of historical change. Drawing on her own fieldwork in Cameroon (among the Beti) and in south-western

Nigeria (Yoruba) she has tried to develop more general and sensitive models of women's involvement in production which take cultural factors into account and are based on a detailed knowledge of what crops are grown, the agricultural year and the complex system of forest clearance and subsequent land use. Guyer's analyses (1980, 1984a, 1984b, 1988) raise questions as to the 'naturalness' of the division of labour by sex and, more fundamentally, the value of such a term. At the same time she shows that variation in agricultural patterns is possible even where two societies appear to be generally similar (see below). This kind of 'bottom-up' approach in theories of women's work, their roles and statuses, has as much to commend it as similar approaches in development policy (Chapters 4 and 9).

In the remainder of this chapter we look at what rural women do. Although space is limited, we include description of women's activities in all of our regions and focus attention on the sexual division of labour, status, access to land or other productive resources such as livestock and tools, which crops women grow and how they are grown (technology and access to labour), and women's control of what is produced (marketing and distribution). This section is rather heavily weighted towards sub-Saharan Africa since it is here that most rural women are involved in farming.

WOMEN AS RURAL PRODUCERS: A REGIONAL ANALYSIS

Latin America

Among indigenous Indian groups such as the Pirá-Paraná (Hugh Jones, 1978; 1979) of the Vaupes Region in Colombia and among the Laymi of the Bolivian Andes (Harris, 1978,1980) there is a complex interweaving of men's and women's lives, in which female and male principles, identifiable in particular crops and activities, are seen as vital for the reproduction of the society. Pirá-Paraná women's work centres on the cultivation and processing of bitter manioc, but Christine Hugh Jones' analyses show that trying to separate production from reproduction, 'economic' from 'domestic' labour, is not valid in cultural terms. There is a strong gender complementarity in productive tasks and questions of relative gender status do not enter into her work. We have already discussed the ethos of *machismo* in

Latin America (Chapter 1), and although we can generalize to say that it is a relevant concept in gender relations among peasant groups and urban populations, long-influenced by colonial rule and the Catholic Church, it is not a valid concept when discussing indigenous peoples. Lifestyles may be separate but not particularly inegalitarian, as among the Pirá-Paraná (Hugh Jones, 1978, 1979), or gender subordination may be very obvious, as among the Yanomamo of Venezuela (Chagnon, 1968). A critical 'interstitial' case is given by Elisa Buenaventura-Posso and Susan Brown (1980, 1987) who discuss the shift from gender egalitarianism to male dominance among the Bari of Colombia because of outside influences on both ideology and mode of production (Christianity and oil exploration).

In Kallarayan in the Peruvian Andes, Sarah Radcliffe (1986) describes how women contribute to agricultural production and also the strategies used by women to ensure household survival. Her data support those of Deere and Leon de Leal (1981, 1982) who worked in another Peruvian community, Cajamarca. In poorer families in Kallarayan, women may work in the fields, especially at busy times of the year such as harvesting, but the preference is for men to be hired or male labour exchanged in reciprocal agreements if the men of a household cannot meet all labour demands at any one time.[7] In many Andean communities the plough is associated with men and virility; women do not plough and it is an ill omen for them to touch one. Women are, however, symbolically linked with fertility and their role in planting is crucial. At other times of the year women's contribution to agriculture is regarded by both men and women as 'helping out', rather than substantially important (Radcliffe, 1986, p. 36). Women can inherit land, but their husbands gain control of it on marriage. Crops grown include potatoes and other tubers, grain (barley and maize) and vegetables.

The bulk of women's work in the Peruvian Andes is in food storage and processing, care of livestock and also in transport and marketing of crops as well as cooking, cleaning and childcare. Radcliffe's description of the emergence of a division of labour in crop retail where women are responsible for marketing any surplus subsistence crops in local markets, while men sell barley, grown for the local brewery, is typical of many Third World patterns. Thus while women do have money, men earn more.

In most rural areas outside of the rain forest there has been a long process of gradual commoditization of land and crops, and a widespread 'peasantization' of production. To some extent, there-fore, it is easier to generalize about these communities. According to Carmen Diana Deere and Magdalena Leon de Leal (1981, 1982) women's role in agricultural production varies inversely with the wealth of the household (see above). They suggest that women's status in richer households is lower than that in poorer groups where women are more closely involved in production and in productive decision-making. Evidence from Oaxaca, Mexico, supports this finding, and also shows that in wealthier households women may well be involved in non-agricultural productive work on their own account (sewing or catering), or in a family enterprise (Young, 1978). Thus women's status in richer Latin American peasant households is somewhat higher than expected and it is women in the middle-income groups (*medios*) who are worst off, having little or no voice in productive decisions and little chance of any well-remunerated work.

Where there is agricultural mechanisation, then women do not work in agriculture (the association between men and the plough seems to be extended to men and agricultural machinery). Thus it is frequently suggested that women leave rural areas in Latin America because there is nothing for them to do (Clarke, 1986; Rochin, 1983). Radcliffe (1986), however, sees female migration as a positive strategy in rural household survival (see Chapter 5).

The Caribbean

In the Caribbean, rural land tends to be individually owned and inherited through a formal legal system imposed by the colonizers. Women do similar kinds of agricultural work to men, although in practice they do so less frequently. Stella Odie-Ali (1986) in her study of Guyana shows that agriculture accounts for a growing proportion of GNP and that, more and more, women are taking an active part in agricultural work rather than being content to be merely the 'partners' of their spouses. However, Janet Momsen (1987) writing of the Caribbean islands, suggests that in the 1960s and 1970s high proportions of women either owned farms or were the decision-makers on them (around 50 per cent). This has led to a marginaliza-tion of agriculture: women's farms tend to be given over to subsis-tence production and women are often excluded from access to government extension services. But now with decline in opportunities for male migration and in the real value of remittances from migrants, she argues that the proportion of female farmers is decreasing. What consequences this may have for the status and roles of women and for agricultural output in the Caribbean remains to be seen.

Sub-Saharan Africa

It was not until the late nineteenth century that the vast majority of Africa was brought under direct European control. European influences in Africa, unlike Latin America and the Caribbean, have thus had less time to penetrate and transform the (largely rural) indigenous societies. It is at least partly on this basis and particularly given the survival of indigenous kinship-based and other forms of social organization, that Goran Hyden (1986a) has written of the difficulties of categorizing 'African social systems' and the problems of African development. When we look at agricultural systems in Africa and women's roles within them, therefore, we are faced with an overwhelming multiplicity. We cannot realistically generalize about women's roles in farming. What we can do, however, is to give some examples of the range and variety of women's work in agriculture. It is also in sub-Saharan Africa that other than agricultural subsistence types occur with most frequency, and thus we must also consider hunting and gathering and pastoral societies.

In hunting and gathering societies such as the !Kung of Botswana, where women do most of the gathering and may be involved in communal hunting, patriarchal power and exploitation of women are not apparent (Marshall, 1960, 1961; Sacks, 1974, 1979,). Gathering is compatible with reproductive work, such as care of young children, and gender stratification, if it exists at all, is minimal. However, the apparent gender egalitarianism disappears if people are settled, and women's status declines (Draper, 1975).

In predominantly pastoral societies, however, such as the Masai of Kenya, although women 'control' the herds in the sense that they make everyday decisions as to which cows to milk and how muc'ı milk to take, they have no rights in the disposal of cattle, the most valued productive resource (Llewelyn-Davies, 1978, 1981). A married Masai woman is allocated the care of a section of her husband's herds, and is responsible for its maintenance and reproduction, but she never owns it. Masai women are responsible for maintenance of both the herds and the settlements: they collect the cattle dung for house-building and repair, and fuel. Nevertheless, if a woman has male children, even if her husband dies, she may retain control over 'her' herd by virtue of being the heirs' mother. If she has no children, however, she is dependent on widowhood, on the goodwill of her husband's or her own kin. When a woman bears only daughters she tries to persuade her husband to allow one of them to stay with her to reproduce for her in the hope of producing male heirs in this way (Llewelyn-Davies, 1978, 1981). Thus, only by having male children can a Masai woman hope to improve and consolidate her status, ensuring her access to productive resources (cattle) and, in addition, when her sons marry, giving her some control over the labour of daughters-in-law. In these respects Masai society is not atypical of other African pastoral groups.

It is when we consider agricultural societies that we are faced with a daunting variety in women's roles and status. A major difference between sub-Saharan Africa and most other world regions is the absence of the plough. Agricultural tools are hand tools: cutlasses of various types for cutting and clearing, sticks (dibbers) and hoes. Although hoe blades vary in shape and size from area to area they are invariably short-handled and are essentially women's tools. The absence of the plough in sub-Saharan Africa has often been singled out as the independent variable in trying to explain other factors in African social organization, such as women's involvement in production, forms of residence and patterns of inheritance (Goody, 1976; Goody and Buckley, 1973): it is here that 'female farming systems' are most likely to be found (Boserup, 1970). In some areas of sub-Saharan Africa, root crops predominate, in others, cereals, while in yet others, both root *and* cereal crops are regarded as staples. In addition, the range of patterns of land-holding is as varied here as the range of kinship and inheritance patterns, with or without an overlay of Islam, Christianity or modern 'bureaucracy' (state control).

Generally, it is men who are responsible for the annual tasks associated with landclearing where agriculture is based on shifting or rotational patterns. Possibly, an important variable in explaining sexual divisions in African agricultural work is crop antiquity. Older or indigenous crops may be subject to a culturally specific division of labour (yams, upland rice, millet or bananas, for example) while more recently introduced crops such as maize or cassava[8] may be cultivated by both sexes, where both men and women farm. Thus among the Kpelle of Liberia (Bledsoe, 1980) it is women who are almost entirely responsible for the production of upland rice, while in Avatime, Ghana (Brydon, 1981), women are ritually prohibited from cultivating rice. Techniques of planting, care and harvesting in both areas, however, are very similar. The popularity of cassava, the most recently introduced African staple and grown by both men and women (where both farm), is largely due to the fact that it is relatively easy to cultivate and grows even on poor soil, but its nutritional value is much less than most other staples. In recent years, an urban market has begun to develop for cassava and more men are beginning to go into its production for exchange (Guyer, 1987).

In Africa, as elsewhere, cash crops (coffee, cocoa, tea, for example) tend to be grown and marketed by men (cf. Radcliffe, 1986). In the Volta Region of Ghana, Jette Bukh (1979) has shown that cash crop production (in this case, cocoa) is concentrated in the hands of men and they tend to take over the best land for this purpose. This has meant that women have been denied access to income from cash crops and that men have been seen as the 'breadwinners' in the community, in spite of the fact that it is women who remain responsible for the bulk of subsistence production. In the matrilineal cocoa-producing areas of Ghana, where we might expect women to be prominent in cash crop production on their own account because of their access to land by inheritance, studies have shown that they face many more problems than their male counterparts and are being squeezed out of production (Mikell, 1984, for example). Gwendolyn Mikell also argues that matrilineal principles operate against the inheritance of cocoa land by daughters, even if a farm was bought and worked by their mothers: sons inherit the cash crop-producing land and daughters are 'relegated' to the subsistence sphere (see also Okali and Kotey, 1971; Okali, 1983).

Bukh, Mikell and Okali all point to the impact of colonial rule and ideologies of capitalist patriarchy and Christianity in denying women economic opportunities. Tensions between different ideological systems in respect of production and property and their effects on women are also discussed by Patricia Caplan (1984) in her study of the people of Mafia Island on the Tanzanian coast. Caplan regards the customary division of labour and access to property for both men and women as egalitarian: both men and women histori-

cally had access to land and women were not subordinate to men
(cognatic descent is the norm in this area). However, the indigenous
ideological set has been complemented by Islam, and under Islamic
law women are entitled to inherit only half the amount of their
brothers. While women thus have access to subsistence productive
resources, it is much more difficult for them to gain access to
coconut trees, which produce copra, a cash crop (used in making
rope). Caplan regards the influence of Islamic ideology, however lax
in its application, as detrimental to women's status and suggests that
in addition, the women are losing out under the influence of
Tanzania's socialist ideologies. The idea that change and 'development' has had negative consequences for women is obvious from
these African cases and will be taken up again in Chapter 4.

Jane Guyer (1980), however, brings out the complexities of the
incorporation of cash crops and their effects on gender relations in
her comparison of two West African societies, the Beti of Cameroun
and the Yoruba of south-western Nigeria. In the Beti traditional
division of labour, men cleared the forest land and planted crops for
the first season. In subsequent seasons, before the land was fal-
lowed, women planted groundnuts, vegetables and, in this century,
cassava. Beti women are symbolically associated with production
from the earth. Yoruba farming is unusual in Africa in that traditionally it was a male farming system, yams being the most important
staple. In both systems the 'other' sex was expected to contribute
labour if necessary, but the Yoruba, and Beti, men could mobilize
women's (their wives, primarily) labour, while Beti women could not
mobilize male labour on their own account. The introduction of
cocoa as a cash crop affected labour and resources differently: in
both areas men and women planted and tended young cocoa plants
but for subsequent care and harvesting, Yoruba tend(ed) to hire
labour, while the Beti men used their own and their wives' labour.
The fact that cocoa became a 'male' crop in both areas Guyer
attributes to factors within the respective socio-economic forma-
tions rather than to effects of colonial rule (ibid., p. 364).

In the 1960s, although both groups still produced cocoa, the Beti
produced 80 per cent of their food, whereas by 1951 Yoruba
subsistence production had declined to 32 per cent. Guyer estimates
that 83 per cent of labour in food farming among the Yoruba is male,
while 84 per cent of food farming labour among the Beti is female.[9]
The fact that Yoruba women have long been associated with com-

mercial activities, trading, cloth and pottery production in Yoruba areas meant that there was potential for the development of trade in foodstuffs and cooked food in these areas. Women did not therefore have to concentrate on food *production* to live. Among the Beti, however, with no traditional markets, women's workloads, especially in food farming, increased. There was no scope for them to broaden their horizons in terms of commercialization of food. Thus, we cannot simply say that the impact of colonial rule advantages men in terms of cash crop production: we must always be aware of specific pre-existing socio-cultural configurations if we are to make sense of any changes. In addition, Guyer's work has much to say to debates about the relative values of male and female labour: does food farming become devalued when practised almost exclusively by women? (Hence the 'relegation' of Akan women to the subsistence sphere, see above.) In the Beti case, this does seem to have happened, but Guyer urges caution in generalizing from a specific instance. Relative values of women's and men's labour are discussed further in the urban context in Chapter 7.

In some East African rural communities Islam is an important factor in influencing women's involvement in rural production. Caplan (1984), for example finds in the Islamic communities of Mafia Island in Tanzania although women are not in *purdah*, there is some restriction on their mobility. In the Islamic Hausa areas of Northern Nigeria, however, even rural women stay in *purdah* if their husbands can afford it. Mary Smith's (1954) account of the life of Baba of Karo gives us a picture of Hausa women's traditional work roles in the early and middle years of this century, mainly in food processing and craft production, and Polly Hill (1969), for example, has described secluded women's control of the grain trade in relatively small communities in Katsina. While these women do have access to a cash income their 'status' and ability to command other resources is severely limited by the constraints on their public appearances, as is also the case with many women in the Middle East, North Africa and South Asia.

North Africa, the Middle East and South Asia

It is convenient to deal with North Africa, the Middle East and South

Asia in one section because religious and cultural patterns in the area (primarily Islam and Hinduism) confine women largely to the home or to 'invisible' activities. Male farming systems and the use of the plough are widespread throughout the area. While rice is ubiquitous as the staple in South Asia, it is also grown, along with other grains (maize, wheat, for example) in North Africa and the Middle East.

When we examine rural women's productive roles in these areas not only do we have to consider variations in division of labour, but also the question of status. Only poorer women, who *de facto* have lost status, work in the fields in many areas. Where women's work is effectively confined to the household as in the case of many Muslim women, the division between 'productive' and 'reproductive' work is even more entangled than for other rural women.

Among rural women in Bangladesh or among the women of the Delhi shrine (Abdullah and Zeidenstein, 1982; Jeffery 1979), being in *purdah* does not mean that women are confined to the women's quarters (*zenana*) of large houses. They occupy their own rooms within the house, but their work is carried out in the courtyard spaces on to which the rooms face. Abdullah and Zeidenstein (1982) also suggest that women may leave their compounds if they remain within the neighbourhood, such is the construction of their social and physical environment: houses are separated by secluded paths and people in the same locality tend to be kin because of prevailing marriage patterns.

Even where women are not involved in field work their role in subsistence may nevertheless be crucial. In Bangladesh, rural women are responsible for overseeing the initial germination of seed rice, as well as for the processing and storage of rice for consumption and seed (Abdullah and Zeidenstein, 1982). In addition, it is women who have responsibility for the care of the cattle, which are not only draft animals, but also give milk and are a source of prestige in the community: this involves feeding and watering them, cleaning out their sheds (and storing the dung for fertilizer), taking them to bathe and making sure that if any do fall ill, they are able to cure the illness from a range of traditional and modern remedies. Women are further indirectly involved in rice production in that it is they who cook food for communal (male) work parties. As in other areas where women are members of an extended family group then a woman's 'position' and roles in the household depend to some extent on her age and status: as a newly-married wife she must work hard and do as her elders tell her, as she gets older and, particularly, if she produces sons for the family, then she may be able to delegate some of her duties to daughters and eventually to daughters-in-law of her own (ibid.; see also Chapter 1).

Vanessa Maher's (1974, 1978) and Susan Davis's (1978) descriptions of rural women's work and options in Morocco is very similar. In the Moroccan case, the restrictions on women are not so severe: for example, women may market agricultural produce in the absence of their husbands or sons, something which is not possible in Bangladesh.

Berny Horowitz and Madhu Kishwar (1984) describe women's lives in the Punjab in a village mainly occupied by a middle-ranking peasant caste of Sikhs, the Jats; the remaining inhabitants are mostly from the 'scheduled' castes (low-status groups). In spite of differences in economic status between the Jat and other women (Jat women tend to be married to men who own land), there are similarities in their lives. Both groups of women work anything up to a 15- or 16-hour day, in the fields and at home. Women's work here, as elsewhere, includes care of cattle. The opportunities for landless women to work for money are fewer than those of men. Women are not involved at all in weeding, for example, and the only reliable work that women have is during the cotton harvest and, occasionally, during the wheat harvest. Some work in gleaning is also available. Women are never taken on by landlords as permanent labourers, but are always hired and fired as the need is perceived. Again we see similarities between rural and urban women's employment conditions (see Chapter 7). Maria Mies et al's (1986) study of rural Hindu women's work in Andhra Pradesh supports these findings, and focuses particularly on changes in women's lives, work and status in recent years. Many Indian landowners are not mechanizing their farms since the labour of women is cheaper. The relatively low cost of women's labour is likely to continue, she argues, as more and more women compete for what agricultural work there is as village craft specialization is swamped by urban mass-produced goods and mechanized services. Whatever their actual tasks, these women perceive their lives as hard: although they put in so many hours' work, they receive less food than the men, less general health care and are denied access to medical care (Horowitz and Kishwar, 1984). Mies' (1986) analysis and that of Horowitz and Kishwar together with the other articles in the same collection (Kishwar and Vanita, 1984) have the more general underlying theme of emphasizing women's continuing disadvantages and oppression in rural Indian society.

However we cannot assume that such exploitation of women is universal in India: Manipur in north-east India is a small state whose population is divided between the Hindu Meiteis of the valley areas and the tribal peoples of the hills. Women are very visible in production in this area (Jain, 1980), both in the markets of villages and small towns and the state capital, Imphal. While men are largely responsible for rice cultivation women have charge over the production of vegetables and mustard seeds intercropped with the rice. Women in Manipur have economic security by virtue of their access to productive work, and they have a public political presence, mainly through market networks which act as a focus for spreading of news and the planning of possible collective action.

However, here, as in other areas, in spite of economic and political autonomy, social security and status are conferred on women only through marriage, that is, through their relationship to men. This point is also emphasized by Abdullah and Zeidenstein (1982) in their study of rural Bangladesh. They stress that the quality of the male support is irrelevant and the male may be husband, father or son (depending on stage in the life cycle). Male support is more than economic: 'it is a matter of acting for women in "male space", the public world they are not supposed to enter' (ibid; p. 89; see also Sharma, 1978).

The ultimate reliance on men to mediate with the public world is also a key issue where rural women are involved in non-agricultural productive work, and is dealt with both by Maria Mies (1980, 1982) in her discussion of lace-makers of Narsapur and by Haleh Afshar (1985) in her discussion of carpet-weavers in rural Iran. In both of these cases women produce for the world market, but in both cases also, it is men who mediate the sale of their produce, and hence, any relation they have to the public domain. Money made from lace-making or carpet-weaving does not become the property of the women responsible, but goes to enrich family coffers. In the Indian case, it is the coffers of a woman's husband's family, and while this is true to some extent in the Iranian example, wily fathers are now delaying their daughters' marriages in order to prolong their control of such valuable assets.

Southeast Asia

As we saw earlier the subordinate status of women in Islam and

Buddhism is mitigated by other cultural factors in Southeast Asia (Whyte and Whyte, 1978). In Indonesia, for example, some women do have access to the public domain and *purdah* is not as common. Kinship is also an important principle in social organization and although both patrilineal and matrilineal descent are found, the frequent occurrence of cognatic kinship systems means that women in these areas inherit property on the same basis as men (see Chapter 2). In Muslim areas, however, Islamic rules of inheritance have come to be the norm (daughters inherit half the amount of sons). Although women have a degree of economic autonomy, both in agricultural and craft production, there is strong pressure on them to marry: for a woman to remain unmarried implies a lack of status and in marriage, men are regarded as 'controlling' their wives (Mather, 1985). Thus, as in South Asia and the Middle East, in rural areas of Southeast Asia women's positions in society are ultimately dependent on men.

Maila Stivens (1985) has discussed the fate of women's land rights with the influence of capitalism from 'outside' in Malaysia. The people of Rembau, Negeri Sembilan are matrilineal (see Chapter 2) and because of the combined effects of the traditional inheritance system and the growth of petty commodity production in rubber, together with a decline in the position of the peasantry nationally, during this century more and more land has come under the control of women. In pre-colonial times, Stivens suggests that there was much greater leeway in inheritance patterns and that only with colonial codification of the law has the feminization of land-ownership taken place. She does not, however, suggest that in the pre-colonial period Rembau women's access to land was restricted: her analysis indicates that the situation is much more complex.

Rembau women are responsible for the subsistence production of rice, although men do play a part in land clearing and 'help out' women with other stages of cultivation. However, in contrast to the cases we discussed in Africa, especially the matrilineal Akan systems, cash crop land (in this case, rubber) is also increasingly owned by women. Stivens relates this to an overall decline in rural production; the takeover of the best land by capital-intensive rubber estates, and in addition, a decreasing population in the rural areas as people are tempted away to work as wage labourers. Her analysis shows very clearly how pressure to change ideological and cultural systems (in this case, the values engendered by matrilineal descent and the status of women) have so far been resisted, but that with the immiseration of the rural areas, where now people must buy rice to eat, she is pessimistic about the prospects for the future.

Although plantation agriculture is not confined to Southeast Asia (tea plantations in Kenya and India, sugar in the Caribbean, coffee in Central America, for example) its relative prevalence in this region justifies its discussion here. According to Noeleen Heyzer (1986), women form over 50 per cent of the labour force on Malaysian rubber estates today, although originally only male labour was recruited. In the 1920s, however, an ethic of 'family formation' on the estates was encouraged. Male labourers were granted company housing and encouraged to bring their wives to live with them and in many cases, to work with them. This tied families to the estates and allowed the exploitative and discriminatory wage system to continue. Throughout the colonial period, women workers were paid less than men: the men were mostly tappers, the women, field workers, and a 'reserve army' of tappers for busy times (ibid; p. 72). The women of these largely Hindu communities, already isolated geographically on the estates, were totally dependent on their husbands and isolated from each other.

Although the absolute numbers of women working on rubber estates has declined since the 1960s (because of competition from synthetic products), in relative terms, their numbers have grown (from 47 to 57 per cent), and women now have equal pay for equal work agreements. However, it is still men who dominate the top positions in the plantation hierarchy. In addition, women are partly responsible for feeding the labour force (they grow vegetables and fruit on small plots), and they also reproduce it: these conditions of exploitation should now be familiar. The proportion of families living below the official Malaysian poverty line on the estates is only slightly larger than that nationally, but one of the most insidious features in the plantation system here is its cyclical nature: because under the new equal pay conditions women are allowed no time off for reproductive activities, (visiting or feeding children in the crêche, for example), this means that a substantial portion of reproductive work must be carried out by children. Since the schooling children receive is therefore minimal, families therefore remain trapped in the rubber plantation network from generation to generation, in spite of increased opportunities for more remunerative wage-earning in towns and on palm oil plantations.

CONCLUSION

Having given an indication of what rural women do and how their status varies we can see clearly how difficult it is to make generalizations about gender and rural production, let alone to select 'crucial' parameters of women's work and status. In many cases a productive/reproductive divide is meaningless and the separate examples of variation in women's access to productive resources in matrilineal systems in Ghana and Malaysia suggests that we cannot pinpoint 'kinship' as a significant factor, whether patri-, or matrilineal or cognatic. Several of our examples have referred to women's roles and status both in terms of a 'traditional' system and with the impact of colonial rule and incorporation into the world capitalist system. In the majority of these (for example Caplan, 1984; Guyer, 1980; Bukh, 1979), women have been adversely affected. Even in the case of Tanzania with its socialist development policies, women have lost out in land ownership and access to and control of productive resources (Caplan, 1984; Croll, 1979). Men are still recognized as 'household' heads by those in power, resources are channelled to them and products bought from them. This is a major issue in development policy, the subject of the next chapter, and we discuss the effects of development projects designed for rural areas and show that they have, at least until very recently, systematically 'neglected rural women' (Nelson, 1979a).

NOTES

1. These figures are calculated from Dixon's Table A (1983) simply by taking the mean from the means given for her sub-regions: they are meant to serve here as a rough indication of female agricultural labour force participation.
2. Ruth Dixon (1983) supports the general associations pointed out by Boserup between women's involvement in farming and status.
3. However, Dixon (1983) states that women constitute 31 per cent of the agricultural labour force in Pakistan.
4. But note here that Guyer (1980) warns of positing one way implicational sequences when we are uncertain as to direction. It is just as likely that the invention of pottery, weaving and so on meant that more intensive agricultural techniques had to be found so that women's labour could be released.
5. The assumption that status is lost with association with the domestic

sphere and exclusion from the public domain has its roots in Lévi-Strauss (1969). See also Ortner (1974).

6. There are published criticisms of Divale and Harris, on one hand pointing out their incorrect use of sophisticated statistical techniques and a skew in their sampling relating to Latin America (Hirschfeld et al., 1978), and on the other, pointing out deficiencies in their basic definitions and biases in their use of interpretive data (Lancaster and Lancaster, 1978). Both large-scale states and small groups are included in the sample, without any reservations, as comparable, a facet of this kind of work criticized by Leach (1982). These obvious biases and faulty assumptions, let alone invalid use of statistical procedures render Divale and Harris's conclusions null as far as we are concerned, but there are still writers who persist in trying to 'prove' statistically biologically-based assumptions about culture. We emphasize that while such large-scale work provides interesting and useful supports to theoretical and smaller-scale work, its results can never, based as they are upon such an inadequate database, be used without major reservations.

7. 'Household' and 'family' are usually equivalent in Latin America.

8. The manioc grown in Latin America is bitter manioc and contains a cyanide compound when unprocessed. The cassava (manioc) grown in Africa is a non-poisonous sub-species and can be simply peeled and boiled to eat. The leaves are also edible.

9. Recent evidence has indicated that Yoruba women are becoming more involved in farming (Adeyemo, 1984; Roberts, n.d.; Spiro, 1987).

4 Gender and Rural Development Policy

Two themes of particular relevance to women and rural development policy have figured prominently in our discussion so far: one is the problem-ridden conceptualization of women's work in rural environments and in particular, the failure (by census-takers, gender-blind researchers, and so on) to recognize the importance of their reproductive labour (however that is defined) as a vital component of agricultural production. When these underestimations and undervaluations of rural women's work slide, as they so often do, into the sphere of development planning, the consequences are even more serious. Failure to acknowledge the importance of women's multiple contributions to rural survival means that practical policy interventions are not only frequently detrimental to women themselves, but also to the rest of their communities.

The second theme is that of the generally negative consequences of 'external influences' (colonialism, incorporation into the world capitalist system, world religions) on the lives of Third World women (see, for example, Abu-Saud, 1984; Caplan, 1984; Ifeka-Moller, 1975). Given that development planning also represents an intrusion of outside influences and ideologies into rural communities, it is highly likely (unless those responsible for designing and implementing rural development projects are particularly concerned with improving women's situation), that the outcomes will also be unfavourable. As such, both the above issues are critical to our discussion here.

In this chapter, then, we are concerned on one hand with changes that have been introduced 'successfully' or otherwise, from outside, either by Third World governments, their agencies or by international development organizations including various offices of the United Nations, the European Economic Community (EEC), the International Labour Office (ILO), the World Bank (International Bank for Reconstruction and Development: IBRD) and non-governmental organizations such as Save the Children and Oxfam. This not only includes discussion of the design and consequences of specific rural 'development projects', but also the implications of governmental decrees on such issues as land reform, or resettlement. On the other hand, we also look at changes that have been initiated from within, often by women themselves ('bottom-up' approaches to development) and assess their merits and demerits in comparison with externally-introduced initiatives in rural areas.

The 'inclusion' of women in development ideology at the formal planning level is a relatively recent phenomenon and is one focus of Barbara Rogers' (1980) book. We take 1970 as a convenient watershed for change in orientation towards women, and, in addition, the UN Decade for Women (1975–85) had a major impact on the visibility of women and their viable incorporation into development planning. (This is discussed further in Chapter 10.)

The chapter is divided into four sections: the first considers the design and methodology of rural development; the second and third deal respectively with the failures and successes of rural development schemes in capitalist states. The final substantive section looks at rural development in socialist countries. As with our earlier chapters, the problems associated with 'status' are implicit throughout.

THE DESIGN AND METHODOLOGY OF RURAL DEVELOPMENT

Many of the assumptions underlying the design of development schemes and projects, certainly up to the early 1970s, were those we have already criticized as of the 'modernization' approach. If women were considered in rural development programmes at all it was, at best, as adjuncts to their husbands, or as daughters or mothers. It was assumed that women's 'position' would improve as did the economic prosperity of their husbands (see also Cubitt, 1988). However, this assumption 'denies the unequal power relationships which exist between people of different castes, races and classes and between men and women' (IBG, 1984, p. 107). Furthermore, it takes for granted the notions of male–head–breadwinner and female–housewife: an ILO report discussing the design of such programmes severely criticizes this model stating:

Among the rural poor in most countries it is quite ridiculous to presume a male head of household who provides for the family's needs and a dependent wife who looks after the house, the children, the elderly and the sick. Yet this (urban middle class) model underlies the approach that has generally been taken to assisting women in developing countries. (Ahmad and Loutfi, 1985, p. 5)

Zubeida Ahmad and Martha Loutfi (1985) also go on to criticize more generally projects designed by outsiders *for* rural women, without taking into account their views, attitudes and abilities, and the constraints upon them. They advocate a 'bottom-up' approach and stress the importance of initiating change through a more positive evaluation of the work that women already do. This, they argue, will lead 'naturally' to a more equitable distribution of resources within the household and community and have the effect of raising the status of women.

As part and parcel of a 'bottom-up' approach, Ahmad and Loutfi urge the active participation of women in the design and implementation of rural development projects and cite several examples in which women, through their own initiatives, have successfully organized to improve both their economic power and status in rural communities (see Chapter 9 for a fuller discussion of 'participation'). Although they recognize that women face several obstacles to participation, on account of various cultural prejudices, they feel that the active involvement of women in development programmes is the only way forward. Nevertheless, the section on 'Violence' in Madhu Kishwar and Ruth Vanita's (1984) collection of articles from *Manushi* (an Indian magazine), highlights the extremely formidable nature of the obstacles to the improvement of women's positions in society: landlords, police and bureaucrats often collude in denying women their rights under the law (see also the section on 'Violence against Women' in Davies, 1983). Thus, while we support the general idea of female participation as a means of improving the status of women, we stress how difficult it is to implement such schemes, quite apart from the fact that they in no way guarantee change for the better (see also Chapter 9).

Until the early 1970s, programmes devised to improve productivity, basic amenities and living conditions in rural areas tended to have two major design faults. In the first place they took little or no account of local knowledge of the environment and cultivation methods, and secondly, they tended to be addressed to household heads, using the type of model criticized above. Almost invariably, these schemes resulted in failure in the sense that although productivity may have been improved for a short time (usually only as long as the inputs from the aid agency lasted), once this initial phase had passed, then transfers to local control were fraught with problems of both supply and distribution. Bureaucratic inertia, national balance of payments problems and in some cases corruption meant that supply inputs such as 'hard' (foreign) currency to buy fertilizer, spare parts for machinery, fuel and lubricants, and seed for new crops, either HYVs (high yielding varieties) of crops already cultivated or new crops grown for export, became increasingly scarce. At the same time the distribution of inputs (if and when they came), and of profits and/or payments owed to the participants in the scheme were subject to delay and often did not materialize at all.

The second problem in the design of rural (and urban) development schemes up to the early 1970s, that of channelling initiatives to (male) household heads, resulted from a failure (and perhaps, unwillingness) to recognize the work done by women. It was generally assumed that women worked as part of their wifely duties, as something natural, as part of the marriage contract, which was therefore not open to discussion, negotiation or seen as having the potential for change in its own right. These assumptions owe much to sociological theories which see the family as a natural unit and one in which the relations of household production and reproduction are somehow separate from relations of production in the wider society. Both Functionalists and Marxists are guilty here (see Chapter 1).

Several writers have criticized both the problems identified in the design of rural development projects and the early attempts to 'integrate' rural women into development. Some take as their starting point Hanna Papanek's (1977) assertion that 'a curious ambiguity in the concept of *integrating* women in the development process hampers the achievement of the goal from the start. For women are full participants in all processes of social change' (Papanek, 1977, p. 15; quoted in Roberts, 1979, p. 60). Pepe Roberts (1979), from whose work this quote is drawn, criticizes both the design of 'gender-blind' schemes and the earliest attempts to 'integrate' women into the development process. Her work draws on field experience in Niger evaluating government-sponsored programmes designed to increase rural Hausa women's economic production outside the home. The assumptions underlying the scheme were that, since in existing conditions, women worked on family plots for some of the time as their husbands desired (the *gandu* system), but were also entitled to cultivate their own small plots when not working on the family farm, then the women's own plots could be 'developed'. The scheme aimed to increase women's productivity and personal income by giving them access to inputs of fertilizer and seed, and to advice from the *Animation Feminine* extension workers. The planners also assumed that women had time to cultivate these smaller plots more intensively. However, when the women's plots became highly productive as a result of increased inputs they were promptly taken over by the men for *gandu* production. There was no compensation for the women: they were not given new plots but the proportion of their time spent in *gandu* labour increased and they experienced more, rather than fewer, constraints on their productive activities. Further, since men in this rural Hausa society control access to resources, it was men who were most often given the fertilizer, leaving little or none for the women (Roberts, 1979).

The 'neglect' of rural woman along with the problems of incorporating them into the design and implementation of development schemes, are discussed in detail for Asia by Nici Nelson (1979a) and more generally by Ingrid Palmer (1979) and by Sue Ellen Charlton (1984). Nelson's review of the South Asian literature, brings out the points we are concerned with here: the general failure of planners to appreciate what women do, whether in the household or outside; their totally false assumptions about women's existing responsibilities and their capacity for extra work; and their blindness to existing gender inequalities in control over resources which hampers equitable development. Nelson (1979a, p. 45) also criticizes the design of schemes based on 'the myth of the ever-present male head', when many rural households are at least *de facto* female-headed, and besides, it is frequently the case that resources directed to families through male heads do not end up in the hands of their wives and children.

Palmer and Charlton trace change in the design of development schemes to the early 1970s, and both recognize that there are major pitfalls to be overcome if women's status is to be improved, notably in the area of cultural assumptions about women held both by rural populations and planners (see Barbara Rogers, 1980, on the integration of women in development as both participants and policy-makers). Charlton sets out three 'levels' of development into which women have to be incorporated: the micro-level, integrated regional projects and the macro-level, although it is difficult to differentiate the micro-level from the integrated regional projects (Charlton, 1984, pp. 176ff). Macro-level change, according to Charlton, involves major shifts in state ideologies, such as the change to a socialist government or the introduction of large-scale land reform.

Our discussion thus points to the fact that it is all very well to talk about the 'integration' of women into development schemes, but we have then to ask the question, on what basis? If women are to be reached and their incorporation made possible, we have to know what women do, the range of their activities, and what time they have at their disposal beyond that taken up by existing tasks. In a way, discussing how to improve women's chances in rural development schemes is jumping the gun: one of the most problematic areas in the design of projects is assessing both the nature and value of what work is done already. We have already hinted that 'Western' survey methodology is inadequate when it comes to trying to assess women's status, and it is equally ineffectual in shedding light on what rural women do, how much time they spend doing it or what value is placed on their 'work' (both productive *and* reproductive). In all areas, both in initial assessments and in roles for the future, women lose out.

Until the 1970s, the dominance of the positivist assumptions of the main body of social science meant that information on which development projects were based was derived either from existing national census figures or agricultural survey data for example, or from data collected for the purposes of specific projects, all of which were based on Western academic survey techniques. It is hardly surprising, therefore, that women were neglected in the information considered by planners fundamental to designing rural development projects. Households were the study units, and the premise was that the 'ever-present' male head identified by Nelson (1979a), was the person with whom the planners and their extension workers should communicate. The male head would act as the planners' agent within the community and distribute the ideas and profits from his participation in the development project among the various members of his household.

When the emphasis began to shift in the 1970s and planners increasingly recognized that women's contribution and participation were crucial if 'development' was to have permanent effects (see Charlton, 1984; Nelson, 1979a; Palmer, 1979; Rogers, 1980), they also realized how difficult it was to design projects to incorporate women when they effectively knew nothing about what women did. (Although there were numerous highly specific ethnographic descriptions by anthropologists, but these too tended to be gender-blind.) The task facing planners was twofold: first, to uncover the range of work that women did, in a qualitative sense, and second, to find a way in which this work could be 'operationalized', made usable for survey techniques so that women's contribution could be quantified. At this stage, the values placed on women's work in the cultures themselves were not apparently considered problematic: only later was this issue taken up.

Since the early 1970s there have been various suggestions of how to collect and organize information on women and their work for development planning. Carmen Diana Deere and Magdalena Leon de Leal (1982) in their study of women in Andean agriculture show that, although official census data suggest that Andean women are scarcely involved in agricultural production, and that what involvement there is seems to be declining, this apparent trend is probably an artefact of data collection techniques: in recent years, women's contribution to production, rather than declining, has been systematically ignored (see also, Deere and Leon de Leal, 1977, 1981; Rechini de Lattes and Wainermann, 1986). The methodological problems of incorporating women in data collection are also discussed in Sondra Zeidenstein's (1979) *Learning about Rural Women*.

The ILO has also looked for ways to incorporate women into both data collection and the design of development projects. We have already discussed the critical evaluative work of Deere and Leon de Leal (op. cit.) and a survey of what has been done to date is provided by Ruth Dixon-Mueller (1985). She assesses in turn the sexual division of labour, time-use surveys, problems with the measurement of productivity and of the use of employment statistics in the assessment of women's labour force participation rates. Her overall conclusions, in terms of suggestions for research and policy formulation, give an indication both of the amount of work to be done and the kinds of question that must be asked if valid evaluations of women's 'work' are to be made, and hence, effective and realistic policies designed (Dixon-Mueller, 1985). On another tack, in recent years, Christine Oppong has been working out a model for understanding what women do in terms of seven roles and statuses often allocated to them. Although her material is based on empirical data from Ghana, her model is designed to be universally relevant (Oppong, 1980; Oppong and Abu, 1985, 1987).

The critical importance of making women visible in the design stages of development projects is also recognized by Joycelin Massiah (1986a) in her overview of the Women in the Caribbean Project. This project was given direct impetus by the inauguration of the UN Decade for Women in 1975. The UN Decade for Women (discussed in more detail in Chapter 10) was also relevant more generally here in that with its inauguration came a call for more female-centred research (Massiah, 1986a, p. 3). The Women in the Caribbean Project is seen as relevant for the Caribbean region as a whole and has five major objectives:

1. To find out more about women's subjective conditions and what objective realities women face.
2. To devise a theoretical framework for the study of changing aspects of women's roles (also implied here is an analysis of what women do).
3. To use the information generated for coherent policy formulation (and implementation).
4. To use the information generated directly in the planning of development programmes.
5. To produce a group of women who have skills in data collection, analysis and communication and dissemination of results to ensure continuation of the project.
   (paraphrased from Massiah 1986a, pp. 1–2)

All the examples we have discussed above deal specifically with the task of enabling women's incorporation into development schemes and projects. In more general terms, the 1970s saw at least a recognition of the problems of large-scale farming schemes, export-oriented programmes and initiatives deemed scientifically appropriate by expatriate experts, and a move towards development focused on recognizing the needs and wants of indigenous cultivators. The two formally labelled approaches relevant here are the 'Basic Needs' approach and 'Farm Systems' research. The Basic Needs approach (see Webster, 1984; Palmer, 1979), crudely speaking is what it appears to be: its proponents set out to find out what rural people need and to help them fulfil those needs. However, there are several criticisms to be made here from the point of view of women (Palmer, 1979). First, there is no easy solution to the problem of how to go about identifying women's needs, and second, there is no provision in theoretical terms, for redistribution of resources and power between men and women. (See Palmer, 1979, for criticism of this in rural contexts, and Chapter 9 for a discussion of similar issues in urban areas.)

Farm systems research, which rose to prominence in the early 1980s, might also prove valuable to women (Charlton, 1984; Moock, 1986). In this approach rural households or other groups identified as production units by the scheme are regarded as systems within which there are sub-systems embracing different aspects of productive and reproductive work, but which are also integrated into wider community and regional systems. Such an approach allows for the recognition of women's contribution to all kinds of work and can incorporate cultural evaluative elements. Moreover, it seems to fit the requirements both of economically-minded social scientists and cultural/socialist feminists, who stress the necessity of looking at relationships within the household. 'Participation' (see Chapter 9) and a 'bottom-up' perspective are integral to both of these approaches to development (see also Nelson, 1981).

Although much valuable research on the neglect of rural women and ways in which their incorporation can be improved has come from those working at the ILO, at the same time gender-blind studies from within that organization continue to be produced. On one hand, the World Employment Programme of the ILO produced *Rural Development and Women in Africa* (1984) and *Rural Development and Women in Asia* (1982) which focus entirely on the problems of and for women and development, and on the other the same Programme produced *Poverty and Landlessness in Rural Asia* (1977) and *Agrarian Policies and Rural Poverty in Africa* (Ghai and Radwan, 1983). The wider body of the ILO also produced *Studies in Rural Participation* (Bhaduri and Rahman, 1982) and all of these effectively ignore women in their analyses. It is as if 'real' studies, about whole countries, need not be concerned with women at all, let alone especially focused on women, and only those concentrating on particular sectors, or written largely by women, may single out questions of gender as of specific importance (see also Robertson,

1987, for similar criticisms). The continuity of gender blindness in the literature is not confined to the ILO; Hirashima's (1977) *Hired Labour in Rural Asia* among many others is also guilty. Just as serious a distorting device as problems with enumeration and evaluation of women's work and status is 'a set of cultural assumptions about the secondary importance of anything women do' (Elise Boulding, quoted in Charlton, 1984, p.40).

The widespread undervaluation of women's work on the part of governments, planners, academics and others has been one of the major obstacles to change and even though some positive trends in gender-aware rural development policy may now be identified, there is still a very long way to go. In the words of the Women and Geography Study Group of the Institute of British Geographers, 'Discussions about the impact of development policies on women see them as *objects* rather than *agents* of change' (IBG, 1984, p.107; our emphasis).

GENDER AND RURAL DEVELOPMENT IN CAPITALIST STATES: INGREDIENTS FOR FAILURE

These two sections deal with 'failures' and 'successes' in rural development, broadly considered. Two interrelated analytical themes underlie the organization of these sections, first, the 'orientation' of the scheme, whether 'top-down' or 'bottom-up'; and secondly, whether project design and plans for implementation take into account cultural factors. Under the first head we include both those schemes imposed from the outside with no design input from the community supposed to benefit as well as those directed at 'household heads', with the assumption that all household heads are male. The second theme involves an analysis of situations where projects have unforeseen 'ripple' effects and where consideration of local cultural and religious factors would be well-advised.

There are obviously practical problems in separating out the two themes; if project design is 'top-down', there is a good chance that it will ignore local customs; conversely, if the orientation is 'bottom-up', it is much more likely that cultural constraints will inform both design and implementation. A further point is relevant here: although intended to help the poorest members of communities, project inputs tend to be monopolized by richer peasants at the expense of their poorer neighbours. Although a discussion of the differentiation and stratification of the peasantry is beyond the scope of this book, this is an important factor to bear in mind since many of the poorest members of rural communities are women, and until recently neither this nor the existence of women-headed households in rural areas was recognized (Chambers, 1983).

When considering failures in rural development schemes, it is probably best to start with projects which have had unintended side-effects on women through blindness to their needs as a specific group. One such project was the creation of Lake Volta in Ghana in the early 1960s. A new dam was inaugurated at Akosombo on the Volta River, both to provide hydro-electric power to fuel Ghana's development and to provide plentiful resources of fish: in the process of creating the lake, the water flooded many villages whose inhabitants had to be resettled (Graham, 1982). Resettlement was undertaken without adequate compensation for lands and crops lost through inundation and with no thought for local social organization and practices. Land in the areas to which people were moved was poorer than that which had been flooded and the new houses constructed by the government took no account of prevailing polygynous family structures. Thus there were no separate sleeping rooms for individual wives, nor were there separate kitchens or store areas. Although D. Paul Lumsden's (1975) account of the adverse effects of resettlement of one particular group (the Nchumuru) does not deal specifically with the problems of women, it is obvious from his work that they probably faced more problems (economic, social and psychological) than anyone else.

The projects discussed by Elliot Morss et al. (1976) are also characteristic of this frequently gender-blind, 'top-down' approach. No Asian countries are included in their survey but in Latin America projects in Bolivia, Colombia, Ecuador, Mexico, Paraguay and Peru are discussed, and in Africa, Gambia, Ghana, Kenya, Lesotho and Nigeria. Inputs are given to household heads (presumed to be men) in the vast majority of cases; female-headed households do not feature, and success or failure is judged largely in economic terms. In spite of the 'modernization' orientation of Morss et al.'s work, on the whole they are sceptical of the claims to success made by various project personnel. For example, although ignoring gender entirely, they criticize the over-protective attitude of planners from Cornell

University in the early phases of a rural development project in Vicos, Peru. When, after some years, potato blight devastated the villagers' crops, and outside influences, both corrupt and well-meaning, were allowed in by the Cornell staff, the peasants had no innovative resources to fall back on and reverted to their previous, apparently precarious, subsistence production techniques (Morss et al., 1976; Mickelwait et al., 1976). In a second case, they discuss, with some scepticism, the efforts at motivation (devised in advance and of the 'carrot and stick' variety), for community development in the 'Futures for Children' project in central Colombia.

Donald Mickelwait et al.'s sister volume (1976), however, does focus on women, although the list of countries covered is more restricted: Ghana, Kenya, Lesotho, Nigeria, Bolivia, Paraguay and Peru. Many of the projects discussed are the same as those in Morss et al., but it is difficult to realize that this is so. In Mickelwait et al.'s study women seem to have been 'slotted in', assumed to be members of households, in most cases, headed by males (although some recognition is given here to the existence of female-headed households). The projects evaluated here focus primarily on reproductive aspects of women's work: nutrition, health, sanitation and needle-work, they are 'family-centred', and no great changes in women's personal economic security or status is intended (see Chapter 9 for a more detailed discussion of these kinds of projects in urban areas.)

Top-down rural development schemes in Latin America all tend to see women as 'reproducers': women are considered only as 'wives' or 'mothers' and not as independent adults. The primary target group for agricultural inputs is men and projects for women are restricted to 'home betterment' (Mickelwait et al., 1976). There is not the same focus on income-generating activities for rural women in Latin America as there is for women from other regions. Perhaps this can be seen as a reflection of the general acceptance that most Latin American rural producers are 'peasants' on the European model, with a division of labour that, for the most part, limits women's contribution to production to 'helping out' in the general conception of things, if not in reality (Deere and Leon de Leal, 1982, for example).

This is not to say that projects which focus on improving women's income-generating opportunities can be considered successes: here, too, there are problems with top-down approaches which do not take cultural constraints into consideration. For example, Morss et al. (op. cit.) evaluate an agricultural development scheme in the Gambia, focusing mainly on rice (the staple food) and vegetables. Although they mention in passing that one of the consequences of the scheme was a change in the sexual division of labour in rice production, they do not elaborate on the consequences of this for women. However, this is taken up by Jennie Dey (1981) who found that in the areas affected by the projects, women had been largely responsible for the cultivation of rice before the implementation of the development scheme. With the introduction of outside 'help', directed at household heads and based on the assumption that these are men, women have been pushed out of rice production, one of their most basic sources of economic security and status within the communities. Thus far from providing a long-term improvement in the 'condition' of women (the assumption underlying these 'trickle-down' approaches), women's lot here has deteriorated. Similar criticisms, deriving from the 'male–household–head', and, in these cases 'primary-producer', models, can be made of the agricultural extension work discussed by Jette Bukh (1979) in Ghana, and the schemes discussed by Anna Conti (1979) in Burkina Faso (formerly Upper Volta).

Another major problem in top-down projects stems from lack of attention to other cultural factors. In areas where women are in *purdah*, for example, it is obviously difficult to talk to them unless their husbands give permission and/or researchers are women (see also Chapter 9). In other respects, attempts at development in rural areas in Asia tend to be subject to similar criticisms as those elsewhere. Vina Mazumdar (1979), for example, in her survey of rural women in India, includes a discussion of the problems of government-backed rural credit associations for women, *mahila mandals*. She cites lack of clear objectives, adequate training of those responsible for supervision, failure to involve the poor and a focus on women's household activities as reasons for disillusionment with the associations both on the part of the rural women themselves and the planners. Devaki Jain's (1980) assessment of women's involvement in another Indian government-backed project, this time a milk-producing cooperative in Kaira, reveals that even where women were recognized within the scheme as workers, their limited rights to customary ownership and control in the wider community severely restricted their chances of 'success'. Women rarely owned cows and were cooperative members in only a small minority of cases (see also Dixon, 1978, p.50–6). A study of women artists in Madhubani, also in India (Jain, 1980), reveals similar constraints: even though women's art was a major source of income in the communities involved, women were neither in charge of selling their paintings nor in control of the income derived from the sales. They remained subject to the control of their husbands and fathers (see also Mies, 1982). Again, although such schemes are formally 'gender-aware', the roots of failure lie in both a top-down orientation and failure to engage local cultural constraints. Jain (1980) also suggests that in order for development to 'succeed' we have to begin by looking at relations within the household (the reproductive sphere), although she does emphasize that these are related to class and gender relations in the wider community (see also Chapter 9).

GENDER AND RURAL DEVELOPMENT IN CAPITALIST STATES: RECIPES FOR SUCCESS

Since the mid-1970s there has been an increasing awareness on the part of planners of the integral role women must play in any development scheme and an emphasis on looking both at projects specifically designed for women and which build on existing skills, practices and knowledge. In short, there has been a discernible move towards schemes which are gender-aware, bottom-up in orientation and take at least some cognizance of cultural practices. These include both initiatives on the part of the women themselves and those initiated from outside the community. Schemes into which women have been 'fitted', and are not the primary focus for development plans are not considered here as 'successes', and hence many rural Latin American initiatives which consider women only in relation to reproduction ('home betterment', 'family-centred' projects; see Chapter 9), and not as the primary focus of 'development' both inside and outside the home, are not discussed.

In contrast to the numerous schemes in Latin America where women are not singled out as autonomous actors, several Caribbean development initiatives have focused on increasing women's income-earning opportunities. We have already mentioned the 'Women in the Caribbean Project' (Massiah, 1986a) which concentrates on improving both the economic participation and status of women in rural communities. Sonia Harris (1986) discusses women's participation in precisely these terms in her analysis of Church-initiated projects in Jamaica. These grew out of the already existing 'Women's Federation' and, as well as providing income for women (in the area of tourist handicrafts, tie-dyeing, sewing and baking), have also improved their self-image and made them more aware of the possibilities open to them, even though they have not expanded the range of skills women already had.

Women's Income-Generating Initiatives

Although many development projects *for* women are just that, they have been designed by planners in cooperation with local women, there are instances where rural women themselves have taken the initiative. For example, Achola Pala Okeyo (1979) describes the activities of Luo women in Kenya, whose livelihood depends on both trading and subsistence farming. These women have organized themselves into cooperative work groups for both market and farm work, and not only do these provide exchange labour and travelling companionship for itinerant traders, but also, permit the sharing of child-care.

Similarly, without any outside influence, women in the Lake Titicaca area of Bolivia have gained access to cash through developing market networks and gradually setting up enterprises on their own account (Benton, 1987). In 1971, when Jane Benton first worked in the area women were 'invisible', 'helping' their men in agricultural work, denied access to all but the most basic education and oppressed both by an unrelenting cycle of pregnancy and lactation and by the violence of their husbands. Ten years later in a re-survey, Benton found that women were at the forefront in marketing, they had developed small-scale workshops, including a bakery employing four men, and had taken full advantage of the regional tourist trade. Access to secondary education for girls had become a matter of course without which even the most die-hard of fathers knew that their daughters would not be able to realize their full potential. As a result of these changes, the women were more open and confident, especially in their technical skills, and had even made inroads into the hitherto male preserve of fishing in the lake. Attitudes to their own lives were also more positive. From being resigned to the fate of marriage as at least providing some security, now most young women postpone marriage until after they have established themselves economically, and aim to have at most only two or three children so that they can be better cared for and educated. Some women have even suggested that marriage is not necessary: they may have a child without being married (and most do want children) and without being subject to social disapprobation and stigma as they would formerly have been.

Susan Caughman (1981) analyses an initiative on the part of women in Markala, Mali, with the help of a prominent Malian middle-class woman. Using this woman's 'voice' and connections, the Markala women have obtained some agency and government support for their cooperative cloth-dyeing and soap-making schemes. In the discussion, which takes into account the 'traditional' and current patterns of the sexual division of labour, Caughman shows how women need the income from the cooperative to meet family obligations (food, fuel and clothing), which should be provided by men. The Markala women's success at meeting these family obligations means that women now control their own incomes, and their status in the community has improved (Caughman, 1981, pp.8–9).

In India a vast organization has grown up, originally on local women's initiative, of *pappad* rollers. *Pappads* are thin biscuits/crackers (as in pappadums) eaten as snacks and as part of meals. Again, although begun without outside help, the organization (*Lijjat*) has grown with external support and is now fairly widespread in India (Jain, 1980). *Lijjat* has developed in such a way that women can combine their own domestic work with rolling out the *pappads* in their homes (they are taken to a central bakery for cooking). This work both provides poor women with an income and does not offend prevailing moralities, notions of gender purity and seemliness, prominent in the south Asia region.[1]

Credit

All of the initiatives we have discussed so far involve a positive change on the part of local women, with or without additional funds from outside. In parts of West Africa informal kinds of support predate the 'development era'. For example, 'rotating credit associations' have a long history in the area and provide capital either for reinvestment or diversification of produce and/or a fund for buying foodstuffs so that produce grown does not have to be sold cheaply in times of glut, but can be stored and sold when prices are higher (Ardener, 1964; Bascom, 1952; Geertz, 1962; Little, 1965; Ottenberg, 1955).

Elliot Morss et al. (1976) and Donald Mickelwait et al. (1976) discuss government backing for these credit institutions among the Tiv (Nigeria), where they are known locally as *bams*.[2] Both men and women have access to membership of these state-sponsored *bams*, but although women may constitute the bulk of the members, leaders are usually men (see also Chapter 9). Each member agrees at the time of formation of the *bam* to contribute a small sum of money at fixed intervals for a year. At each meeting, funds already collected are made available to individual members for specific projects such as school fees, taxes, land purchase, funerals, and so on. Members pay a low rate of interest on the loans which are limited by the size of the contributions. At the end of the year the *bam* is disbanded and any remaining funds distributed. Mickelwait et al. (1976) suggest that membership in such associations helps to increase women's influence in decision-making within the family as well as providing them with a lump sum of cash when they need it. Kamene Okonjo (1979) discusses women-only rotating credit associations in the Igbo area of Southeastern Nigeria: in these schemes women contribute small sums on a regular basis and each is entitled to receive the total contributed at any one meeting on a rotational basis. Such associations provide women with capital (which their husbands should give them, but usually do not) for investment either in agriculture or off-farm work. In the areas discussed by Okonjo, the women invest both in retailing and in membership of a cloth-weaving cooperative.

Although government intervention in bottom-up initiatives can, as in the case of *bams*, be positive, in many cases it hinders their success. Patricia Ladipo (1981) discusses two women's cooperatives near Ife, Nigeria, initiated by the women themselves as a response to what they perceived as their worsening economic situation *vis-à-vis* men. Ladipo compares two schemes, one which adhered rigidly to government guidelines for cooperative formation and a second, which adapted the guidelines to its own purposes and perceived needs. The former scheme, although having access to credit, did not survive. The latter had difficulty in gaining credit because of its nonconformist constitution, but eventually did and was regarded as a 'success' by its participants. Availability of credit is therefore not a sufficient guarantee of 'success', cooperatives also need to be flexible to adapt to local circumstances.

The Sri Lankan women studied by Rex Casinader et al. (1987) have access to government credit for the purchase and processing of cashew nuts. In an area of high male unemployment, women have in some cases become the family breadwinner because of the income derived from sale of cashews. Since cashew-processing is traditionally 'women's work', men are loath to take it up for status reasons, and even where they do, they are less skilled than their wives. Because of the increased economic power of women, some women have opted to do without their husbands, considering them at best as an extra mouth to feed and at worst, a violent oppressor and an alcoholic drain on family resources. Although these women are 'successful' in economic terms, being able to feed, clothe and house their children, their status is questioned by the men (who are the power-holders) in the community: some have been accused of being prostitutes (as have some economically independent women in urban areas in Sri Lanka (ibid., p.319), a course which denies their validity as women since a prostitute is the antithesis of the cultural ideal of wife and mother. This abuse of women in the face of economic success is remarkably similar to the process noted by Siegfried Nadel (1952) in the 1930s in Nupe, Nigeria, where successful women traders were not only accused of being prostitutes, but also witches.

Integrated Rural Development

Integrated Rural Development (IRD) 'considers the interrelationships between all the factors that contribute to the well-being of rural peoples' (Charlton, 1984, p.180). As such, IRD in theory should take into account both what people want (a bottom-up orientation) and cultural constraints, including religious problems, the sexual division of labour and an evaluation of what women already do. IRD's resulting sensitivity should mean that the pace of intended change should not be out of step with wider aspects of social organization.

Kamla Nath (1985) discusses the production of vegetables by women in The Gambia (the vegetable-growing scheme in The Gambia discussed by Morss et al. (1976) appears to have disappeared by

1984 when Nath did her own study). This project is one aspect of an Integrated Rural Development Scheme funded in part by the UK charity Action Aid, and it has meant that the village women have begun to produce vegetables, notably onions, for a buoyant local market. The scheme has enabled women in twenty villages to participate through both direct inputs such as seed and fertilizer and indirectly through the construction of wells for irrigation and help with provision of transport and marketing facilities. Women now get 15–30 *dalasi* (the Gambian currency) per bag of onions, at least twice the price they received when they sold their produce through (male) village intermediaries. Membership of a related rotating credit association means that the women do not have to sell their onions when there is a glut in the local market. However, Nath notes that men are beginning to try to become involved in the scheme as they see its financial advantages, even though, 'traditionally' men played no role in vegetable production. Roberts (1979) also discusses ways in which local men have tried both to benefit from development schemes primarily aimed at women and to undermine women's benefit from them.

However, one of the best-documented schemes of this sort for women is the Women's Programme of the Integrated Rural Development Programme in Bangladesh. This was initiated under the auspices of the Bangladesh Population Planning Project in 1974 and is funded by the World Bank (Abdullah and Zeidenstein, 1979, 1982). Although originally begun as a project to reach rural women directly in terms of providing them with education, health care and family planning, and to improve their chances of earning a cash income, the scheme gradually grew and became associated with the countrywide initiative for IRD.

Tahrunnessa Abdullah and Sondra Zeidenstein (1982) emphasize the necessity for the slow growth of the project. First information on rural women's activities was collected and then rural women's views and attitudes solicited. Because Bangladesh's population is largely Islamic, these exercises had to proceed with great sensitivity: the success of the project depended on the goodwill, not only of the women themselves, but also of their husbands and fathers. In addition project workers, also women, had to be trained and, because in Bangladesh women who work outside the home are often thought to be low-status, planners had to ensure that the project would not be adversely affected by an association with 'low-status women'. Although all this has been extremely time-consuming, Abdullah and Zeidenstein argue that the slow pace is justified by the necessity for lasting and deep-rooted change. One important change as a result of the scheme has been an improvement in women's access to credit for productive ventures together with better access to educational and health services. This has meant greater autonomy for women in a culture which otherwise emphasizes their dependence on men. It is hardly surprising, therefore, that in spite of the deliberately gradual introduction of the project, Abdullah and Zeidenstein found considerable opposition to it from local men as well as from the planners in Dacca (see also Charlton, 1984, pp.181–2).

The IRD project in Bangladesh began as an initiative to improve family planning and health care provision for rural women, and such foci are often incorporated in IRD projects. Apart from controversial features of specific family planning programmes (see, for example, the discussion of family planning programmes in India in Kishwar and Vanita, 1984), projects aimed at women's (and by implication, family) health are deemed 'safe subjects'. They accord with women's image as nurturers and carers and, again, apart from aspects of family planning programmes, are thought unlikely to upset the relations between sexes or instigate change in cultural constructions of gender (see Chapter 9). Mickelwait et al. (1976) identify what they term 'Family Care' projects which may or may not have spin-offs in providing income-generating activities for women. These may be specifically focused on health care or include health education as one component (for example, the Mathata village sub-project in the Leribe Pilot Agricultural Scheme in Lesotho or the Rural Extension of the Mother-Child Service in Bolivia; ibid., pp.156–60). We do not have space to include detailed studies of family planning projects in rural areas here, but the general issues are dealt with in Chapter 8 (see also Anker et al., 1982).

WOMEN AND RURAL DEVELOPMENT IN SOCIALIST COUNTRIES

Since the 1960s several Third World states have elected socialist governments or have had socialist revolutions. It might be imagined

that under socialism class equality would mean gender egalitarianism. However, such an assumption is patently over-optimistic:
indigenous cultural constructions of gender do not disappear with
the advent of socialist policies, nor, where socialist policies have
intervened in existing productive relations, have they necessarily
improved the conditions and status of women. Socialist development policies are in many cases subject to the same kinds of criticism
as the general run of development policies, of assuming the existence
of extra-societal, quasi-'natural' units called households, and the
presence in each of a male 'head' (Croll, 1979, p.5). In the case of
Tanzania (Caplan, 1981, 1984) land reform has detracted from,
rather than enhanced the position of women, and in post-revolutionary Ethiopia, even after land reforms have been instigated, women
in many cases are not entitled to own land (ILO, 1982:46). In theory,
however, as Elizabeth Croll states (1979, p.2):

policies to collectivise fully the means of production should directly affect
the position of peasant women by removing the economic foundations for
the authority of the patriarch or head of household to arrange and supervise
production and control property and labour.

In those areas of Ethiopia where women have been recognized as full
members of collectives, eligible for support and inputs on the same
bases as men, then productivity has improved, a regular supply of
food is produced, and there is hope for the future for those who
would probably otherwise starve in this drought-stricken and war-
torn country (Neustatter, 1988).

  In theory, then, women under socialism should become 'equal'
with men, they should be equally remunerated and the burdens of
their domestic labour should be lightened by using any surplus in the
collective or village community to provide child-care, money for fuel
or piped water and other reproductive tasks. But Croll recognizes
that in practice this is often not the case; domestic tasks remain
largely the responsibility of women and are not assigned a value.
Even though women are enjoined to become 'visible' and to participate fully in production by means of registering as members of
collectives eligible (formally, if not in practice) for land-holding and
agricultural inputs, no account is taken of the domestic work they
already do. The outcome of socialist reforms, as we pointed out in
Chapter 1, may in some cases be detrimental to women's lives.
Where women have been encouraged to participate in productive

work outside the home with no corresponding attempt to socialize their reproductive activities, the 'double burden' has become heavier: women work hard and for longer hours (see McCall, 1987, for a discussion of this process in Tanzania). As the Women in Geography Study Group of the IBG point out: 'New regimes often praise the contributions of women, but are slow to introduce equal rights reforms except where they are necessary to the economic goals of the government' (IBG, 1984, p.107).

Third World socialist governments have varied in the extent to which they have tried to redefine and intervene in 'reproduction'. In Cuba, the 1974 Family Code states that where both partners in a union work, then household tasks must be shared. In contrast, in Tanzania, there has been no attempt to redefine the parameters of the sexual division of labour (Croll, 1979). Villagization, as part of the (*ujamaa*) programme, announced in the Arusha Declaration of 1967 (Mushi, 1981), although emphasizing the significance of both subsistence and export-oriented agricultural production for the national economy, has failed in any effective way to take account of the range of work or 'traditional' rights of women (McCall, 1987). In theory, *ujamaa* embodies participatory ideals, but in practice there are serious problems in implementation (Kitching, 1982). Similarly, in Mozambique and Zimbabwe 'women's issues' are seen to be 'contradictory' (ILO, 1982, p.35), and here, as in other socialist states there is a danger that gender struggles are secondary to the class struggle (Robertson, 1987, p.123). In Zimbabwe where, as in Mozambique and Guinea-Bissau, women were active in the guerrilla movements which preceded political independence, their rights to autonomy and their morals (several had children without marrying during the struggle for independence) are being called into question. Such blatant discrimination, however, has meant that women are now acting as a conscious group both defending and promoting their views (ILO, 1982, p.35).

In Nicaragua and Vietnam women's issues have been recognized as critical by the government and some gender-aware policy measures have been taken. In Nicaragua women have access to land in their own right for the first time (Deighton et al., 1983; Molyneux, 1985b). They may become members of cooperatives on the same bases as men, and where they work for a wage, this is paid directly to them, rather than to the (male) head of household as it was under the previous regime of Anastasio Somoza. However, the national women's organization, AMNLAE (Association of Nicaraguan Women Luisa Amanda Espinoza) while having some 'success' with rural women in introducing cooperative ideas in agriculture and the cultivation of protein-rich soya beans admits that problems remain in the reproductive sphere. As Molyneux (1985a, p.28) states with respect to health, education and employment, 'it is as members of a class that women have benefitted rather than in ways that specifically address gender inequality.' Although the Nicaraguan government is very positive in its attitude to gender issues, there is a huge gap between policy and practice, because of material shortages and the continuing military struggle in the country. In 1982, for example, AMNLAE drafted a new law stipulating that women were entitled to support from the fathers of their children which could be given in three ways: in kind, in labour or in domestic work. There was considerable disquiet in government circles about the implications of this law and AMNLAE was accused of waging a sex war at a time when it was felt that the nation should be unified, it was a law which 'challenges men's irresponsibility and attempts to question the domestic division of labour' (Molyneux, 1985a, p.31). Molyneux, however, questions its effectiveness in the absence of wider campaigns against *machismo* and sexual double standards. Rural women are still expected to shoulder domestic duties and child-care as well as being increasingly active in productive work. Jane Deighton et al. (1983) point to a lack of enthusiasm on the part of agricultural unions and male peasants themselves to change the order. The Roman Catholic Church, in its attitude to contraception and family life, also effectively colludes in women's double burden.

In Vietnam, according to Arlene Eisen (1984), there has also been official recognition of the importance of women and the particular nature of their positions *vis-à-vis* development, but experience here as elsewhere shows that decrees and laws do little on their own to alter the pre-existing forms of gender discrimination (ibid. pp. 90ff).[3] The Women's Union of Vietnam was founded in 1930 but for the first twenty years of its existence faced an uphill struggle. After North Vietnam became a socialist state in 1954 the path of the Women's Union was somewhat easier: its members were active in denouncing violence against women and in promoting land reform. Although the Women's Union was suppressed in the South after 1954, it re-emerged in 1961 and, by 1975 (when the Americans withdrew), is estimated to have had close to two million members.

After the merger of the Northern and Southern Unions in 1976 there was formal representation of women at all levels of national and local government. It must be noted, however, that the Women's Union in Vietnam is an organ of the state, not an independent women's movement. Their brief is to represent:

women to their government and the government depends on the advice of the women to defend women's rights, to design new laws and serve as a watchdog to ensure the implementation of all policies to protect women. (Eisen, 1984, p.124).

Women in Vietnam are members of collectives on the same basis as men, so access to production in rural areas, is in theory similar for both. However, even though there is a formally powerful 'watchdog' here in the shape of the Women's Union to oversee women's rights, the area of reproduction, domestic work, childbearing and rearing is still assumed to be a woman's responsibility. Women's Union officials defend this position arguing their difference from Western feminists (see Chapter 10 for discussion of feminism in the Third World), but the wider issue then remains of how women are 'compensated' or 'remunerated' for time spent on these tasks, and how such tasks are evaluated in the society. Again here, socialism and 'patriarchy' are uneasy partners (see Chapter 1).

All of the socialist countries discussed recognize the crucial significance of education in development, but often resources militate against adequate provision of schools or training facilities on one hand, and even where they are provided, female access on the other (see also Molyneux, 1981 for a fuller discussion of education in Socialist Third World countries). In Tanzania, for example, although the education of women is formally a government priority, in the mid-1970s, 65 per cent of girls in the 15–19 age group were illiterate compared with 38 per cent of boys (Mblinyi, 1972; cited in Croll, 1979). However, Cuba which stressed egalitarian educational provision from the time of the revolution, now has more or less equal proportions of boys and girls in school (Croll, 1979), and in Nicaragua a major literacy campaign launched after the Sandinista Revolution has reached both men and women and has been one of the most significant ways in which women have become involved in post-revolutionary nation-building (Molyneux, 1985). Arlene Eisen (1984) notes, however, that in Ho Chi Minh City, Vietnam, girls from poorer families missed out on education because they had to

look after younger siblings while their parents worked. The government has tried to remedy this by providing evening classes for girls
(and others), but this is hardly adequate: it means that they are again
left with a 'double burden', caring for children by day and studying
at night. A much more logical solution would be to increase the
provision of child-care facilities. In this way, not only could girls go
to school at the normal time, but also a significant move would be
made towards the socialization of reproductive tasks.

Although in theory socialism is predicated on an egalitarian ethic,
in practice issues of gender equality tend to be seen as subordinate to
the class struggle, or even as 'contradictory' (Robertson, 1987,
pp.123-4; ILO, 1982, p.35), in societies which, whatever their links
with the world capitalist system, are still inherently patriarchal.
Thus, here again, as with development in capitalist states, we are
faced with the problem of patriarchy which permeates government
and bureaucratic structures to such an extent that it reinforces the
sources of gender subordination in the reproductive sphere.

CONCLUSION: DEVELOPMENT POLICY AND STATUS

Status is a critical issue in any discussion of women and development
policy, whether in rural or in urban areas, and all so-called gender-
aware development projects have as an ultimate aim an improvement in women's positions in society. Indeed, in some cases, we have
seen that Ahmad and Loutfi's optimism (1985) appears to be
justified, and women's increased access to economic resources
arising from policy interventions or bottom-up initiatives has had
significant effects in improving their status (e.g. Benton, 1987;
Caughman, 1981).

However, on the other hand, in her assessment of four cases of
attempts to initiate officially-sponsored development schemes for
women in South Asia, including the Milk Cooperative discussed
earlier, Ruth Dixon (1978) concludes that it is easier to effect
development in terms of increasing incomes than to improve the
status of women. In all the cases discussed by Dixon, although the
women earn their own money, they are subject to restrictions on
personal freedom of movement if married, and are regarded as low
status if not (in an Agricultural Cooperative in Bangladesh those

women most involved in production are widows and deserted wives who are both low in the status hierarchy; ibid., pp.44–50). Furthermore, even when women achieve success in cash terms, they still have to rely on male members of the cooperative federation to sell their produce and goods. In the cases of the production of handicrafts from jute and of carpet weavers in Nepal (Dixon, 1978), although women earn their own income, they do not necessarily have control over it as we saw in Chapter 3: gender relations in the reproductive sphere, a critical site of cultural status ascription, remain essentially unaltered. Although the Sri Lankan women studied by Rex Casinader et al. (1987) had significantly improved their economic positions in the community, there was much ambivalence from the men towards their new-found power, and accusations of prostitution resulted.

We appear, therefore, to have a double bind: where development schemes are not addressed, either directly or indirectly, to improving women's lot, then women lose out. Where development schemes *do* attempt to improve women's status, then women may also lose out, being accused of being prostitutes (and witches!). In Islamic or Hindu areas, even where women's access to income is improved and they maintain control over at least some of it, then the cultural norms are so strong that women effectively 'opt out' of visibility by going into stricter *purdah* for status reasons. There is no infallible 'recipe' for success when we try to include women in the development process: we can only suggest that some designs and plans are more likely to succeed than others.

Although the range of rural development schemes, philosophies, ideologies and methodologies discussed in this chapter is extremely wide, our task in providing a summarizing conclusion is relatively straightforward. Again and again women's participation in and benefits from development programmes are severely circumscribed by cultural constraints, patriarchal attitudes and assumptions and the weight of women's identification with the 'reproductive' sphere. However, despite the general occurrence of these problems, the diversity of the case studies discussed serves to stress the point that 'women' are not a homogeneous group, either culturally or in class terms. Even where socialist revolution appears to hold out the prospect of an encompassing egalitarianism, culture and forms of patriarchy all too often collude to keep women in subordinate positions. Changes in the reproductive sphere (a vital part of the process of improving women's status) are taking place only very slowly, if at all.

Finally we feel that an indication of the strength of cultural attitudes in suppressing improvements in women's status is given in Casinader et al.'s (1987) case study from Sri Lanka. Here, where women have improved their economic position and standard of living, men are fighting back with cultural ideological weapons, calling successful women 'prostitutes' is not unknown elsewhere in the world. Whether or not women can succeed in society without resorting to culturally defined immorality and (malign) supernatural aid is another issue.[4]

NOTES

1. *Lijjat* is now very widespread and its pappadums marketed in the West, including Britain.
2. Rotating credit associations similar to *bams* are also found in Mexico (the *tanda*), and the institution of *susu/esusu*, originally a Yoruba word (south-western Nigeria) is widespread in southern Nigeria and along the coast at least as far west as Ghana.
3. After independence in 1954 Vietnam was split into two: North Vietnam had a socialist government from this time and the South was capitalist.
4. George Foster (1965, 1972) discusses the ideas of luck and good fortune in peasant communities in terms of a 'limited good': that is, there is only a fixed amount of 'good luck' available to community members. In this context, people appearing to have more than their share of 'good luck' must have resorted to supernatural help, either good (religion) or evil (witchcraft, a form of immorality). These ideas, transmuted to the growth in women's economic power and independence, can be interpreted in such a way that it is only possible for women to 'get ahead' at the expense of men, purloining some of the power and status which formerly 'belonged' to their male counterparts. This is done, in the eyes of the men of the community, by resorting to immorality (prostitution or witchcraft).

5   Gender and Migration

So far we have limited our study to women in rural areas in the Third World, but a study of rural women gives us only half the picture. To complete our overview of gender in Third World countries we not only have to look at urban women, their domestic and productive roles and status, but also at what we might call the interface of the two sectors, the process of migration which has profound consequences for the lives of both rural and urban women. In this chapter we look first at theories which have tried to 'explain' migration as a phenomenon; second, at patterns of migration, that is, who moves (selectivity) and their origins and destinations, and finally, we consider the consequences of population movement.

In general terms, migration is a phenomenon associated with industrialization and urbanization whether in the First or Third Worlds, and relates particularly to spatial differences in employment opportunities: as such, most migration may be characterized as 'labour migration'.[1] If industrialization (generally associated with 'development') is to take place, then a steady supply of labour is needed wherever industries are sited. In general, industries have tended to develop where cities have existed for a long time such as in Latin America, (Butterworth and Chance, 1981), or in areas where there is industry associated with a natural resource such as the Copper Belt of Central Africa (Mitchell, 1987) or at crucial points in a transport network such as ports (Bombay in India or Tema in Ghana are examples here).

Today the population growth of cities is far outstripping that of rural areas, but this precipitate rate of growth is relatively recent: a product of the past 30–40 years. Although massive urban growth is partly due to natural increase (fertility), much of it is the result of in-migration from rural areas.

But if the populations of the Third World were largely rural in the past, why should people want to move to urban areas? We deal with this question in more detail below, but generally speaking, labour

121

migration is generated by a *need* for income (to pay taxes to a colonial or post-colonial state, for example) and also a *desire* for income to buy consumer goods: cloth, bicycles, sewing machines, radios, and so on, and to invest in business and/or education. Migration, ultimately, is the process of the provision of a labour supply for industry with the concomitant supply of labour for a dependent service sector. One further point should be made here: 'industry' does not necessarily have to mean factories or mines. Migrants also go to work on labour-intensive agricultural plantations producing export crops such as tea and bananas, and in parts of Africa there has been considerable population movement associated with peasant cash crop agriculture (cocoa in Ghana, Nigeria and the Ivory Coast, groundnuts in Senegal). However, we are mainly concerned here with rural–urban labour migration and its consequences.

APPROACHES TO LABOUR MIGRATION

Reviewing the migration literature we can see a threefold division in approaches to migration. This is identified very clearly in Thérèse Gerold-Scheepers and Wim van Binsbergen's (1978) discussion with respect to Africa and also emerges both in Douglas Butterworth and John Chance's (1981) book on Latin America and John Connell et al.'s (1976) comparative survey of rural emigration. Very generally, approaches to migration have been either 'individualistic' or 'structural', and structural approaches can be further divided into 'functional' and 'Marxist'. Individualistic approaches to migration are concerned primarily with the reasons why individuals move, with questions of who moves (selectivity) and with individual case histories. Much of the early (1950s and 1960s) anthropological work on migration (for example Mitchell, 1956; van Velsen, 1961), and a study such as Plotnicov's (1967) of male migrants to Jos in Nigeria, adopts this approach. These detailed case studies (which is in effect what such studies are) of migration provide fascinating and useful empirical data, but there are problems when we begin to ask broader, more theoretical questions. We cannot simply sum up numbers of individual responses to questions of why people move and how they have adapted to life in the cities and say that we have a 'theory' of migration (Mitchell, 1959). In order to understand the theoretical basis of migration we have to take structural features into account.

Until the late 1960s most structural studies of migration could be labelled 'functional', that is, they assumed that migration occurred because of forces acting from outside on what was conceived of as a bounded indigenous society. These exogenous forces were derived from the influences of colonial rule and involvement in the world capitalist system. Given this, the emphasis in structural-functional studies was on showing how indigenous societies reacted and adapted to labour migration, and labour migration in itself was seen as a positive force, a force for development, beneficial both to those who migrated to and lived in the cities and, eventually, to those in rural areas. Migrants were seen as innovators, entrepreneurs, some-how more 'developed' or 'modern' than those who did not move and it was assumed that they would act as purveyors of 'modern' society to the 'traditional' rural areas, thus enabling the rural areas to 'develop'. These approaches were generally compatible and closely associated with modernization, 'trickle-down' perspectives on development (Connell et al., 1976; Gerold-Scheepers and van Binsbergen, 1978).

With the emergence of Marxist dependency theories and theories of underdevelopment from the mid-1960s onwards, migration assumed a new status. The question as to whether or not it was 'beneficial' to development was set aside as the Marxist (the term is used here very loosely) theorists saw migration as an important link in the chain of exploitative relations between First and Third Worlds. Labour had to be moved to capital (industrial or agricultural sites) if the economic demands of the First World were to be satisfied. Rather than seeing wages as positive inducements to move to become familiar with modern life, Marxists see the migrant as forced to move to acquire cash to meet the exigencies of the colonial and post-colonial state (taxes), the migrant is victim rather than entrepreneur. Wages paid to migrants are also unfairly low since it is assumed (in the case of men, anyway) either that they are unmarried or, if they are married, that their families can support themselves in the subsistence economy. They are exploited as wage labourers in capitalist relations of production and they are further exploited in that there is no component in their wages for social reproduction (Connell et al., 1976; Gerold-Scheepers and van Binsbergen, 1978).

These, very generally, have been the overall theoretical

approaches to migration in the literature, and more detailed discussions can be found in Connell et al. (1976), van Binsbergen and Meilink (1978), Butterworth and Chance (1981), Fernandez-Kelly (1983), Oberai and Singh (1983) and Bilsborrow et al. (1984). What kind of questions are asked about migration today depends on the orientation of the particular study, and the relevance of an individual or structural approach also varies with the kinds of questions asked, and, often, from what disciplinary perspective.

John Connell et al. (1976) and A. S. Oberai and H. K. Singh (1983) distinguish 'economic' from 'geographical' from 'sociological' and 'anthropological' approaches. Economists tend to view migration as a product of salary differentials and perceived or potential earning opportunities between urban and rural areas, and they have focused on the economic 'pulls' of the cities and the drawback or 'push' features associated with rural life, including landlessness. Geographers have tended to focus on spatial patterns of migration: whether people move short or long distances; whether they tend to make a series of moves, initially to smaller, then to larger towns, and perhaps finally to a primate city (known in the literature as 'step' migration). They are also interested in demographic patterns: perhaps initially one family member moves and once he or she becomes established other relatives may join them, culminating in the move of a whole nuclear or extended family, a process referred to as 'chain' migration (e.g. Bilsborrow et al., 1984; Eades, 1987).

Both geographers and sociologists/anthropologists are also interested in the social concomitants of migration. At the micro-level they ask questions of the context of the decision to migrate, questions of selectivity (dealt with below), and questions of the duration of migration and its social consequences. 'Circular' or 'oscillating' migration means that a migrant has to maintain relationships with a home area and not lose out on any stake in rural production, while longer-term migration perhaps means permanent movement, a complete shift in residence with the severance of ties with the area of origin, or it might mean migration for as long as it takes to acquire enough capital to establish a small business or cash crop farm in the home area, or until a pension enables the migrant to retire to the rural areas and live, relatively comfortably, on the pension together with some farming. This is true for female as well as male migrants (Bujra, 1977). Sociological studies are also concerned with 'push' and 'pull' factors, but the focus tends to be less on economic variables and more on social phenomena: the lure of the 'bright lights' of the city, repressive rural social constraints and so on (Bilsborrow et al., 1984). At the macro-level sociological and anthropological studies in recent years have been concerned with the wider political and economic contexts of migration and here, many studies have focused on the southern African region (e.g. Murray, 1981; Wilkinson, 1987).

Few of these general studies of migration, however, discuss the movement of women in detail. Connell et al. (1976), although the earliest of these general studies, contains the fullest discussion of women's migration. However, more recent studies, (e.g. Fernandez-Kelly, 1983; Sassen-Koob, 1984) which have focused on women and work, see the wider implications of an increasing number of women, both migrant and non-migrant in the world's labour force. They stress the world-wide association among feminization of the workforce, deskilling and devaluation of manufacturing work (see also Chapter 7). In what follows we are particularly concerned with the factors affecting the movement of women, but should also remember that the movement of men has important consequences for women's lives.

WHO MOVES?

Historically, migration in Africa has been largely the movement of men, and where labour migration occurs in South and Southeast Asia, in the past migrant flows have also tended to be male-dominated (Pryor, 1979; Fawcett, Khoo and Smith, 1984). Even in the Caribbean, where women's status is generally assumed to be relatively high and where we might expect women to be enmeshed in the labour market and hence, involved in migration, we find that in the past population movement has been the province of men. In Latin America, however, rural–urban migration has long been dominated by women (Butterworth and Chance, 1981; Gilbert and Gugler, 1982).

To some extent these broad inter-regional differences are related to women's involvement in agriculture. In Latin America, as we saw in Chapter 3, women have relatively low rates of participation in the agricultural labour force (below 20 per cent for most of the continent, Flora and Santos, 1986), whereas in Africa women's involvement in agriculture is high (over 40 per cent, Dixon, 1983; Townsend and Momsen, 1987). Thus *need* for income-earning opportunities is a major reason why women have dominated rural–urban migration flows in Latin America. Indeed, between 1965 and 1975 there were 109 women to every 100 men in Latin American towns compared with only 92 women to every 100 men in African urban areas during the same period (Gilbert and Gugler, 1982: see also Albert, 1982; Radcliffe, 1986).

However, relative lack of female involvement in agriculture is not a valid corollary of women's migration in Southeast Asia, and yet here now women do move to towns. In part, therefore, female migration is also linked to gender-specific patterns of labour demand in cities. In both Southeast Asian and in Latin American cities there are considerable opportunities for women in the service and industrial sectors (especially with the rise of export-processing in these regions: Engracia and Herrin, 1984; Fernandez-Kelly, 1983; Heyzer, 1982; Khoo, 1984; and see also Chapter 7), whereas, in many African, South Asian and Middle Eastern cities, most 'formal' jobs in manufacturing and in the public sector have been reserved for men (Gugler and Flanagan, 1978; Townsend and Momsen, 1987). Only in recent years have there been opportunities for African women to earn in the cities, whether in the formal or informal sectors (Brydon, 1987b; Joekes, 1982).

However, these general observations must be tempered by other aspects of selectivity including age, marital status and education. There are two main categories of younger female migrants: those young girls sent by their families to do domestic work as in Latin America, (Butterworth and Chance, 1981; Lomnitz, 1977b; Smith, 1978; Radcliffe, 1986), or those who work in multinational factories (Heyzer, 1986; Joekes, 1982; Pryor, 1979; Safa, 1986). Many of these young girls receive low wages and often send a proportion of what they have to their families. In Costa Rica, for example, Michelle Albert (1982) sees the migration of large numbers of women as a 'safety valve': changes in land tenure and agricultural modernization mean that there are even fewer wage-earning opportunities for girls in rural areas (see also Radcliffe, 1986). In the case of the export processing zones (where there are world market factories owned by multinational companies) the girls may see little of their wages themselves, the bulk being sent directly to their parents (fathers) in the rural areas (Armstrong and McGee, 1985;

Safa, 1986). Thus, although women move on their own in a demographic sense, patriarchal familial controls are maintained.

In Thailand, Pasuk Phongpaichit (1982) indicates that parents may collude with agents (who may also be family members) and 'sell' their daughters into organized prostitution. In addition to receiving a lump-sum from the agent, parents then expect to receive a proportion of their daughters' earnings. The independent movement of young women in South Asia and the Middle East as labour migrants is very rare and riddled with derogatory status connotations (Connell et al., 1976; Fawcett et al., 1984; Oberai and Singh, 1983). In these two areas the only significant movement of younger women is on marriage, and in accordance with cultural and religious constraints (Townsend and Momsen, 1987). Those women who do work in factories tend to be younger and placed there by parents: unlike their Southeast Asian counterparts, they live with their families rather than in the firm's accommodation (Joekes, 1982, 1985; see also Chapters 6 and 7), and while their parents may have been migrants, they themselves have probably been brought up, if not born, in the cities.

In Africa, women's migration has received little overall attention to date, largely because of the historic dominance of men in the migrant flows. Migration of younger women in West Africa has been confined to sending daughters to older, married women as 'helpers' (Brydon, 1979, 1985a) or maidservants. In this case parents are saved the cost of daughters' education and skill training as the families the girls are sent to are supposed to provide at least a minimum level of these: no wages are sent to the parents. Nici Nelson (1987) discusses the existence of similar practices in Kenya.

We can further divide the migration of older women into two: those who move with their husbands and those who move on their own. Those women who move with their husbands, as an adjunct to marriage, may or may not work in the urban areas to which they move. Whether they do or not is largely dependent on region: in Africa, for example, married migrant women tend to work (Okojie, 1984). If they have education and contacts they may find jobs in the formal sector, but it is more likely that they will become involved in a range of informal occupations such as baking, sewing, laundering, selling cooked food and petty trading (see Chapter 7).

However, as Margaret Peil (1975) notes, it may be more difficult for migrant women to establish themselves in trade if local women already dominate urban trading networks (supply and both market and street retail).

In Latin America, although many married migrant women may be involved in some income-generating activity, they are much more subject to control by their husbands than their (West) African counterparts and the ethos of *machismo* militates against them being very visibly involved in work (Butterworth and Chance, 1981; Chant, 1985a, 1987a). Women in the Middle East and South Asia sometimes move with their husbands, and among the elite, those with educational qualifications and training may work in carefully controlled environments (for example, all-female hospitals or universities). However, most migrant women are not involved in income-generating activities unless they are very poor and must work to survive (Fawcett et al., 1984).

Older women who move on their own initiative, without husbands, and younger women who move without 'family placement' have been treated with great ambivalence in the literature on Africa, as prostitutes or potential prostitutes (Brydon, 1987b; Little, 1973; Obbo, 1980; Sanjek, 1976; Sudarkasa, 1977). However, recent empirical work on African women migrants, and there are increasing numbers of these, indicates that women move for the same reasons as men, to look for work. This work may or may not include prostitution, but it should be remembered that becoming a prostitute is one of a relatively limited range of options, and a lucrative option at that, open to poorly educated or unskilled women (Brydon, 1987b; Bujra, 1977; Nelson 1987). While there may be some organization of prostitution at the level of international hotels on a basis similar to the Southeast Asian 'trade', many of the African women who sell sexual services work on their own account. It remains to be seen what impact AIDS has on prostitution in African states: a study of patients attending a Sexually-Transmitted Diseases Clinic in Nairobi showed that the number of HIV-positive female prostitutes had increased from 4 to 59 per cent between 1980 and 1986 (Panos Institute, 1988).

In the Caribbean, as we mentioned earlier, historically it has been male migration that has been the focus of most discussion, and women have been included as those left behind, as the female *de facto* heads of households whose male *de jure* heads are absent. Where women have moved for work it has been younger women who have left children in the care of their mothers, giving rise in this case not only to female-headed households, but also to 'granny fostering' (see below; Clarke, 1957; Smith, M.G., 1962; Smith, R.T., 1956).

In the literature another prominent feature of 'selectivity' has been the relationship between education and migration. Earlier studies assumed a linear relationship between level of education and tendency to migrate, but from the early 1970s it was shown that this relationship was more often 'J-shaped': that is, those at the ends of the educational spectrum were most likely to move (Conroy, 1976). In addition, migration *for* education, (to go to sixth form, teacher training college, university, and so on) is not insignificant (Gould, 1982). However, much of this literature deals with the relationship between education and the movement of males. Lynne Brydon (1982, 1985a) has pointed out that existing level of education cannot be a reason for migration where women move as wives, or as 'helpers' (in the African case). Evidence from Latin America (Butterworth and Chance, 1981; Smith, 1978) also indicates that girls who go into domestic service often expect, or at least hope, to be able to further their education and so their level of education is probably in no way related to the fact of their migration. It is only when women move for the same reasons as men, to work or to further their education (Brydon, 1987b), that there is any possibility of relating their level of education to the fact that they move.

EFFECTS OF MIGRATION ON RURAL AREAS

In the final section of this chapter we consider the effects of migration on the rural communities people leave, and in particular their implications for gender roles and relations in rural environments. The mass movement of men away from a rural area has consequences both for the rural economy and for rural social organization. Studies from Africa have indicated the existence of a 'feminization' of agriculture when younger men have moved away and the women and older men left behind are unable, both for physical and cultural reasons, to cultivate as much. Women may not be permitted, because of cultural constraints, to plant certain crops, or the work involved in clearing particular types of land may be too heavy for women (Guyer, 1988; Murray, 1981). Consequently, land which does not require much clearing is used over and over again with reduction in the period of fallow in a shifting cultivation system, perhaps leading to loss of fertility. Maila Stivens (1985) shows how male migration in the first instance has led to an almost total neglect of agriculture in some rural communities in Negeri Sembilan, Malaysia, with the consequence that rice (the staple) has to be bought with wages earned in the cities. In the longer term, systematic underproduction of foodstuffs, largely because of migration (which itself results from the cumulative effects of ignoring the rural areas for development) has undoubtedly contributed to the present 'crisis' in African agriculture and urban food supply (Guyer, 1987).

For the majority of migrants, whether male or female, wages must be carefully apportioned between family needs in urban and in rural areas. Even in countries such as Mexico, where a migrant's ties to the home community may lapse after a number of years (Lomnitz, 1977b), in most cases there are links with a rural community and family, and migrants are expected to contribute to the maintenance of the latter. Money is still sent back to villages even if a migrant's spouse and children are in the city. In situations of oscillating migration, male migrants send part of their wage to their rural homes, or save it to bring home at the end of a contract in industrial employment or at the end of a cash crop season. Oscillating (circular) migration is still prominent in southern Africa (Murray, 1981; Qunta, 1987), and increasingly so in the case of (male) migration from sub-Saharan Africa and Asia to the states of the Arabian peninsula and to Libya (Ballard, 1987; Birks and Sinclair, 1980).

In Latin America oscillating migration seems to have occurred in the past, and still does, to some extent where short-term, often agricultural, contract work in the United States is done (Escobar et al., 1987). In Mexican tourist towns, men leave their families in the low season to hire themselves out as day labourers on large farms or to return to their own rural small holdings (Chant, forthcoming). What (relatively scant) information there is from South Asia indicates that remittances are supposed to be sent to wives in rural areas, but that often the man squanders the money on drink or tobacco, and the family, under the headship of the wife, is left destitute (Kishwar and Vanita, 1984). Douglas Butterworth and John Chance (1981) suggest that Latin American parents prefer sending their daughters to work rather than their sons since the former are more conscientious in sending money home to the rural areas, and Connell et al. (1976), in their comparative survey, suggest that this phenomenon is not unique to Latin America.

Where it is largely men who leave, as in Lesotho or Botswana, for example, women tend to take on a much greater share of both agricultural work and decision-making tasks in general (Molapo, 1987; Murray, 1981). Serious problems can arise both in family provision when remittances from male migrants are inadequate for the needs of the family and in status conflicts where women who have grown used to making decisions run up against a male-dominated and oriented judicial system, both in 'traditional' and 'modern' terms. The relatively strong position of women in the Caribbean is perhaps due in part to the fact that women (who are left behind) can engage with the formal bureaucracy and legal system and there is no gender-debilitating set of traditional cultural assumptions to deny them status (Brydon, 1976).

Where both men and women leave rural areas there are further consequences particularly for the organization of child-care. Urban women must be able to reconcile a range of employment activities with child care (see Chapters 6 and 7), and given the fact that most Third World countries do not have provision for free day-care or nursery provision, and even in those (mainly socialist) states that do, there are problems (Chapter 4) in implementation and number of places, urban mothers face problems in this sphere. Mothers who want to work must either have a job such as petty trading with which small child-care can be combined, or they must pay for child-care, either in the form of a 'baby nurse' or sending the child to a day nursery. An additional alternative in some areas such as Africa is that of sending the children to the villages to be looked after by relatives, either the mother's or father's mother, or an older sister or aunt of the parents (Asuni, 1988; Bledsoe, 1980; Bledsoe and Isiugo-Abanihe, forthcoming; Brydon, 1979; 1987b; Isiugo-Abanihe, 1983; Nelson 1987; Page, 1986). This option of 'granny fostering' also has a long history in the Caribbean (Goody, 1975; Brydon 1979).

This kind of phenomenon, concomitant with the movement of women on an increasing scale, has widespread policy implications. Welfare, educational and health-care planners concerned with school placement, immunization programmes, provision of water, and so on need to be able to estimate proportions of the population in rural and in urban areas. A move by parents to a city does not necessarily imply that children will be brought up there and will use urban facilities. On the contrary, schools, childhood vaccination provision, and so on may be even more necessary than ever in the countryside.

It is obvious from what we have said here that, although our substantive chapters are largely concerned either with rural or with urban areas only, there are many links between them. We have already mentioned the flow of money from urban migrants to the villages and discussed the flow of personnel between rural and urban areas. The residence of children is particularly important here since, as women are primarily responsible for the care of infants, they are especially likely to maintain links with rural areas if children are being reared there. But in addition, there are vast networks of transient links between rural and urban areas. Migrants in whatever region, visit their home villages, perhaps only on annual leave, but in some cases more frequently. Having relatives in towns is often a contributory, if not a critical, factor in the decision to leave the rural areas, and often networks of related migrants settle in the same city or area (Doughty, 1979; Lomnitz, 1977a, 1977b; Eades, 1975, 1987). Rural people visit their relatives in the cities; children move backwards and forwards between the country and the town; and although money is sent by urban workers to the villages, foodstuffs, meat, fish, vegetable oils and so on, which are expensive to buy in towns, are sent in the other direction. Links are often so strong that urban migrants from a single village or area form village or ethnic associations in the towns with the aims both of maintaining their identity and links with their home areas and of collecting or raising money for rural improvements (Doughty, 1970; Little, 1965; Mangin, 1959, but see Jongkind, 1986, for an alternative perspective).

CONCLUSION

In this chapter we have given an overview of methodological and theoretical approaches to migration and a description of the migratory process as it affects women, both as migrants themselves and as those left in rural areas. We have highlighted regional variations in the gender composition of migrant flows and have also looked at several aspects of rural–urban interaction. The links between countryside and town serve as a major focus of continuity in rural and urban women's lives. However, residence in towns also brings changes for women, not only in terms of increased opportunities for income-earning, but also with respect to differences in the nature of productive activities, the family and kinship networks within which these activities take place and in the nature of women's reproductive tasks. It is to these issues we now turn in the following chapters on women's lives in Third World cities.

NOTES

1.   Other types of movement, in the Third World and elsewhere, include migration as a result of famine, epidemics, wars, revolutions, and so on.

6 Gender and the Urban Household

Urban households and the roles of women within them have become an important focus of debate in recent years, although as yet there is little comprehensive analysis of their interrelationships through time and across cultures. The difficulties of pointing to potential linkages between emerging urban household forms and gender relations in Third World cities derive not only from a relative paucity of material focusing upon this specific theme, but also from the fact that there is no coherent body of theory which can adequately explain or demonstrate *if*, let alone *how*, household structure itself is modified and transformed with urbanization. Given these difficulties, and the persistent problems of generalizing across different regions, it is only possible to arrive at very tentative conclusions about the relationships between gender and household form in Third World cities.

Having outlined the primary characteristics of kinship systems in Chapter 2, our main focus here is on *households*, i.e. units which may or may not contain kin, although this by no means implies that kinship has no relevance in cities. Discussion is centred on three key questions. First, is the household a relevant concept in urban contexts, and how should it be defined? Second, what evidence, if any, is there to show that urban households differ from rural ones in their composition and basic functions? How is household structure influenced by various aspects of urban life in the Third World, such as migration and poverty? Third, to what extent does urban household structure respond to women's changing roles under economic development and vice versa? In other words, is there any consistent relationship between increased rates of female labour force participation and change in urban household form in developing countries?

URBAN HOUSEHOLD FORMS

Households in Third World cities can generally be grouped into seven main 'types' – five of which consist of kin only, and are thus family-based units. Terminology to describe household form varies widely, especially when it comes to complex extended groupings. Classification is further complicated by the fact that it is difficult to select universally applicable baseline criteria for definition. Even if we take shared residence to be the central variable, to what extent is this relevant when some households also share domestic (i.e. consumption-related) activities and others do not? Moreover, as we pointed out in Chapter 2, household boundaries are sometimes 'permeable'; in certain societies consumption is shared, but not residence. For the purposes of clarity and ease of generalization we construct below a profile of urban households on the basis of those who *share dwellings*, and make subdivisions along the axes of composition, headship and organization of domestic functions. Although the predominant types of urban household, their formation, numbers and dynamics are discussed in detail later in the chapter, we give a brief outline of most of the major forms here for comparative purposes. It is also important to bear in mind that none of the household forms identified is unique to urban areas.

Nuclear Households

The most frequently occurring household in Third World cities appears to be the male-headed *nuclear* or *conjugal* unit. Nuclear households consist of a married or cohabiting couple and their children, who live under the same roof and also form a single unit for consumption. Nuclear households are common in a variety of areas in the Third World. Case studies of Latin American cities, for example, indicate that they predominate in urban areas of Mexico (Chant, 1984a; Gilbert and Ward, 1985; Lomnitz, 1977a), Venezuela (Gilbert and Ward, 1985; MacDonald, 1979) and Brazil (García et al., 1983). This is also the case in various cities of North Africa (Wikan, 1980), West Africa (Skinner, 1974), India (Sharma, 1986) and the Middle East (Gulick and Gulick, 1978).

Women-headed Households

Shared residence and consumption are also applicable to another, less common, but increasingly important household type, the *woman/female-headed* family which consists of a woman living alone with her children. As we pointed out in Chapter 2, it is useful to make a distinction between *de jure* and *de facto* female heads. The former are women who have never set up home with the fathers of their children, or who are legally or permanently separated from them because of divorce, desertion or widowhood; the latter are either women whose spouses are temporarily absent, or those who despite having a co-resident partner, play the dominant economic role in daily family life (Youssef and Hetler, 1983). Female-headed households occur widely in the Caribbean, Latin America and Africa and are discussed more fully later in the chapter.

Extended and Nuclear-compound Households

In addition to the above two types of urban family unit there are two main forms of *extended* household – the extended family proper and the *nuclear-compound* unit. Extended households, sometimes referred to as *joint, stem* or *complex* families, consist of a core nuclear or one-parent family residing with other relatives who share in daily consumption and financial arrangements. Depending on the nature of the core unit the extended family may be male- or female-headed. Households are sometimes 'laterally' extended through the incorporation of kin of the same generation as the household head or spouse, such as siblings, cousins and so on, or they may be 'vertically' extended through the incorporation of older or younger relatives such as parents or grandchildren of the household head or spouse. Vertically extended units may thus consist of three or even four generations. Three-generational extended families are very common in India, North African and Middle Eastern cities where newly-weds frequently begin married life in the home of the groom's parents.

The nuclear-compound household, alternatively, refers to situations where related families share the same plot of land or even living space, but do not share financial resources or basic domestic functions such as cooking or child-care on a regular basis; thus, despite their spatial proximity, they effectively operate as independent units. Nuclear-compound households are often found in Latin American cities where land in low-income neighbourhoods is subdivided between relatives (Chant, 1984a; Gilbert and Ward, 1985). They are also known in Isfahan, Iran and in other Islamic cities where a large percentage of nuclear families opt to live in the same walled compound as their relatives (Gulick and Gulick, 1978; Jeffery, 1979).

Single-sex Households

The fifth type of urban family is the *single-sex* household. This is known in some southern Ghanaian cities and is characteristic of a number of different ethnic groups. For example, among the Ga of Accra, fathers, sons and male relatives live together in separate compounds from mothers, daughters, female kin and very young children. Even though the sexes live apart in *sensu strictu*, residential boundaries are regularly transcended for the purposes of economic, social and sexual interchange (Peil and Sada, 1984; Robertson, 1975; Westwood, 1984). The same is true of the Effutu of Winneba (Hagan, 1983). In the Asante town studied by Katherine Abu (1983) men and women not only live apart from each other, but also sometimes from their children as well.

No-family Households

The sixth main type of unit in Third World cities is the *no-family* household, where unrelated people such as friends or workmates reside in the same dwelling. No-family households may or may not share domestic functions, and may or may not be single-sex units. They are common in places such as Southeast Asia, where young female factory workers lodge together in towns, but continue to maintain strong links with their families of origin in rural areas (Armstrong and McGee, 1985; IBG, 1984; Phongpaichit, 1984; see Chapter 5). They were also common in Nairobi, Kenya earlier this century where two or three men would share a 'bachelor bed-space' (Hake, 1977). The 'no-family' definition can probably also be used to describe households where young men learning a trade are 'fostered' by their employers; some West African apprentices, for example, reside in the homes of their masters until they complete their training (Schildkrout, 1983; Verdon, 1979, 1983). In this latter example, certain household members are related and so households which take in apprentices are not entirely 'no-family' units. Further-more, apprentices are often considered to be 'like children', so in this case they could also be described as extended units. This latter example highlights the difficulties associated with household defini-tion.

Single-person Households

Finally, there are *single-person* households. These again are not unknown in rural areas, but are more likely to occur in cities, especially in recently urbanized areas where insufficient time has elapsed for people to build up a network of relatives in the town, and/or where cheap one-roomed rental accommodation or purpose-built factory lodging is available. Single-person households were very common in African cities from the colonial period onwards, and particularly in the decade after independence when there was a massive increase in urban migration by single males; in Nigeria during the late 1960s and early 1970s, for example, 20.8 per cent of Lagos households consisted of single people, and 20.7 per cent in Maiduguri (Peil and Sada, 1984).

The above typology indicates the complexity and range of urban household forms. Not only is there great variation in the degree and type of functions shared *within* the residential unit, but neither must it be forgotten that *inter*-household networks of reciprocity and exchange among urban groups, especially those on low incomes, are often so strong as to render the idea of the 'independent' household meaningless (Lomnitz, 1977a). The mere fact of separate residence does not imply that households survive entirely through their own means. Nevertheless, as we stressed in Chapter 1, the 'household', especially when it consists of relatives who share residential *and* domestic functions, is still a relevant concept since it usually embo-dies a larger degree of intimacy and interaction than other forms of social unit. Membership of a household requires greater obligation to daily domestic life than when people live apart (García, Muñoz and de Oliveira, 1983). As Peil and Sada (1984, pp.168–9) note, 'Family life is a mixture of consensus, competition and conflict. If there is no consensus or too little, the members usually disperse . . .'. Indeed, Geert Banck (1980) observes for the case of Brazil that it is sometimes extremely difficult for co-resident kin to negotiate satisfactory terms of communal existence. Only when they live apart and mutual assistance remains voluntary, do relatives appear to be committed to helping one another. Shared residence, on the other hand, is often avoided because it implies too much obligation on a regular or daily basis (Banck, 1980).

URBAN VERSUS RURAL HOUSEHOLDS

Household Structure

Having outlined the main types of urban households in Third World countries, we now turn to the question of whether they differ in any systematic way from those of rural areas. Obviously, analysis of this issue is complicated by the fact that great variations exist both between and within different regions of the Third World, and that there is little genuinely comparative historical or contemporary work on households in rural and urban contexts within the same country. All types of household can be found in both rural and urban settings, although relative proportions may differ. Peil and Sada (1984) note that variation in household form is governed both by the domestic cycle (i.e. factors internal to households such as stage in the life-cycle, duration of marriage, and so on) and by economic factors (such as the resources available to support large co-resident households). The forms that urban households take are also linked to the actions of the state, as well as to enduring elements of local kinship patterns (Stivens, 1987). Despite the fact that certain types of household may be more common in urban than in rural areas, there is probably far more continuity than has previously been thought (Peil and Sada, 1984). In this section we concentrate on the most common types of household associated with urbanization, namely 'family units' which fall into the categories of nuclear, extended and woman-headed.

Nuclear and Extended Households

Classical modernization approaches assume that with urbanization and economic development, large, extended rural structures give way to nuclear households (Bock, Iutaka and Berardo, 1980; Brambila, 1986; Durrani, 1976; Goode, 1963). This view is also shared by

Marxian theorists, albeit for different reasons. The modernization school views the trend to nuclearization as an inevitable outcome of a decline in family functions as urban development proceeds, especially in the fields of production and welfare. Marxian authors, alternatively, emphasize how family structure is shaped by wider imperatives of capital accumulation; here the state and the dominant classes collude to encourage nuclearization because of its usefulness to the capitalist mode of production (see below). Whatever the rationale behind each of these theses, their starting and end points are the same: households move from an extended to a nuclear form. Before going on to examine the relevance of this trajectory with reference to empirical examples, we provide a brief summary of the main arguments mounted by various writers in support of the thesis.

Modernization and Marxian theorists alike claim that families tend to be large and extended in pre-industrial situations because the means of production are in the hands of households, rather than those of capitalist producers or the state. Sharing the means of production with kin enables families to amass land and labour power. (Obviously there are significant regional differences in patterns of landholding as we sketched out in our 'rural' chapters, but the key factor here is that land in pre-industrial societies is usually thought to belong to the kin group or lineage.) When 'modern' capitalist economic development occurs, collective and/or subsistence production is replaced by individualized wage-labour, thereby negating the need for large households (Barrett, 1986; Goode, 1963; LACWE, 1980; Leacock, 1972; Peil and Sada, 1984; Seccombe, 1980).

Sharing with kin not only becomes *afunctional* in urbanizing societies, but even *dysfunctional*. Co-residence goes against the ideology of economic individualism fostered by industrial capitalism. Dependent kin are seen to represent a drain on the resources of urban families, and this contributes to a desire to shed, as far as possible, economic obligations to all relatives other than spouses and children (Bock et al., 1980; Carter and True, 1978; Gugler and Flanagan, 1978; Hutter, 1981; Nelson, 1987). This general idea is summarized succinctly by Benetta Jules-Rosette (1985, p.105) who observes on the basis of her work in Lusaka, Zambia, that in cities:

the presence of an extended kin becomes a burden. Family members arrive from the countryside and expect housing and support for indefinite periods of time with minimal household participation. These 'parasites' place a particularly heavy responsibility on the squatter woman whose income and prospects for mobility are already low. The new arrivals also add to the urban adjustment problems of families that are not yet secure in their new environment.

Emerging desires for upward social mobility are accompanied by increased imperatives of spatial mobility; families dependent on waged employment need to be able to move to new sources of work. Small, independent nuclear households are thought to be more adaptable to urban migration than large extended units. This idea, of course, belies a notably ahistorical perspective; over time it is perfectly possible that all members of an original household may re-group in the city. Nevertheless, it is often cited as a contributory factor to the general debate.

Along with the declining economic role of the wider family in urban areas the functions traditionally played by kinship networks in reproduction and socialization are also thought to decrease. Urban residents usually have greater access to state-provided welfare facilities, such as education, health-care and social security, than their rural counterparts. Thus while rural families take on most of the responsibilities for basic welfare provision, the obligation for urban households to provide these services is far less; as a result the necessity of living with kin diminishes in urban settings. It is important to note here, however, that the luxury of minimizing kin ties is only likely to be afforded by middle- and upper-class urban families; poorer people may have no choice but to rely on kinsfolk for most forms of reproductive support (Pine, 1982).

There is too little space here to present a detailed theoretical critique of the basic arguments behind the extended-to-nuclear hypothesis. Nevertheless, in the following paragraphs we draw attention to a range of empirical evidence which suggests that although nuclear households are often prevalent in urban areas, the extended-to-nuclear trajectory is in no way a universal, let alone inevitable outcome of 'urbanization'. On one hand, extended fami-lies are not always found in rural areas, and on the other, they often figure very prominently in cities, as indeed do other types of non-nuclear household as well. As Maila Stivens (1987, p.90) notes: 'the concrete conditions of capitalist development do not in fact pare kinship relations down to a basic elementary family form but tend to produce a range of modified extended family forms which are often female-centred.'

Below we draw attention to a range of evidence about extended families in rural and urban areas, and then go on to look at women headed households.

With regard to the putative dominance of extended households in rural and/or 'pre-industrial' settings, it is clear that this particular conventional wisdom is in need of some revision. As far as historical evidence is concerned, research on pre-industrial family structures in North-West Europe indicates that nuclear households were far more common than was previously thought (see Anderson, 1980; Laslett, 1972; Wall, Robin and Laslett, 1983). Indeed, it is probable that around three-quarters of households in seventeenth and eighteenth century North-West Europe were nuclear, and less than one-tenth extended (Flandrin, 1979; Laslett, 1972; Mitterauer and Sieder, 1982). Low proportions of extended households are sometimes attributed to low life expectancy, early death obviously reduced the possibility of establishing multi-generational households (Flandrin, 1979). Other explanations revolve around issues of land tenure, size of holdings and customary inheritance practices. Here regional variations in property patterns closely mirror regional variations in household form. Where land was equally partitioned between heirs (partible inheritance), as was common in North-West Europe, nuclear families predominated, whereas in cases where primogeniture (transmission of patrimony tò a sole heir) was the norm, as in central and Southern Europe, extended households were more likely, especially where land was transferred during a father's lifetime (Flandrin, 1979; Mitterauer and Sieder, 1982). Aside from dispelling some of the myths concerning the former predominance of extended families, the above work also highlights the importance of regionally specific economic factors in influencing household formation. While Maila Stivens (1987, p.91) cautions us to 'be wary of generalizing from the development of the Western family when discussing the evolution of family patterns in the Third World', in developing countries at present we also find large extended households where local patterns of land tenure and rural family production make them economically advantageous. For example, extended households occur among the Hausa of northern Nigeria because it is beneficial for fathers to retain the manpower of their sons (Peil and Sada, 1984). Alternatively, in Ouagadougou, Burkina Faso, peri-urban cultivators farm small plots and do not expect help from grown sons; in this context, most households are nuclear (Skinner, 1974).

Absence of rigorously verifiable and comparative data about pre-industrial household structures suggests the need to exercise extreme caution in generalizing about the 'rural household', let alone in extrapolating about the transformations in household structure which supposedly occur with urban-economic development. Weight is added to this argument when we find not only that extended households are rarer in rural areas than has previously been thought, but also that nuclear households in developing countries today are often *more* likely to occur in the countryside than in the city. Nuclear households are common, for example, in both Mexican and Peruvian rural communities (Butterworth, 1975; Fromm and Maccoby, 1970; Radcliffe, 1986). In Malaysia, the nuclear household has long been a dominant residential grouping (Stivens, 1987). Amongst the Avatime in Ghana, not only have nuclear households traditionally been the norm, but local processes of economic development and urbanization are actually causing a reverse in the trend ideally supposed to occur: here the stable conjugal household structure is actually giving way to a quasi-extended one where children are fostered out with grandparents to allow their mothers to work in town (Brydon, 1979).

Following on from this, and again contrary to the conventional thesis of family change, several contemporary studies of the Third World have shown that extended households are quite common in cities. Mexican research, for example, reveals that extended households often make up to 25 per cent of households in low-income urban communities (Chant, 1984a; García, Muñoz and de Oliveira, 1982; Gilbert and Ward, 1985). In San Salvador, the capital of El Salvador about 20 per cent of households are extended or multiple units (Thomson, 1986). Extended or joint households also continue to be common in Hindu India, or in Islamic countries in the Middle East and North Africa where young married couples move in with the husband's family, or the husband's mother takes up residence in the newly-weds' home (Caplan, 1985; Mernissi, 1985). In other Third World cities, extended households are even more numerous: a sample survey of urban households in Taiwan, for example, revealed that nuclear families made up only 45 per cent of the total, the remainder consisting of various types of extended structure (Lu,

1984). In Africa, urban extended households are also widespread; in Bo, one of Sierra Leone's largest towns for example, as many as 75 per cent of households are extended (Peil and Sada, 1984).

If extended families are an important household group in Third World cities, the extended-to-nuclear hypothesis is weakened further, and requires us to look for reasons why they might occur in contemporary urban environments. One of the most common arguments supporting a counter-thesis claims that urban household structures are in fact *no* different from their rural counterparts and the only reason why nuclear families *appear* to be in the majority in Third World cities is because most urban-dwellers especially in areas of recent growth, tend to be young, and thus at an earlier stage of the 'development cycle' (see Chapter 2). Extended families are much more likely to obtain when household heads are middle-aged or elderly (Peil and Sada, 1984). Thus in older-established areas, it is likely they will be more prevalent. Another reason why extended households are seen to persist in some cities relates to cultural traditions and the continued value attached to kinship (Cutrufelli, 1983; Gugler and Flanagan, 1978; Peil and Sada, 1984). A further argument holds that extended households occur as a result of rural–urban migration. Migrant relatives are frequently taken in by urban families in their initial period in the city (Arizpe, 1978; Brydon, 1987b; García et al., 1983; Kemper, 1977; Peil and Sada, 1984; Stivens, 1987). Type of migration, whether chain, seasonal, temporary or permanent, is also important here (see Chapter 5). Other discussions revolve around the economic problems of city life; low incomes and housing shortages in urban areas often force people to live together because they cannot afford to establish independent households (García et al., 1983). Moreover, extended families not only reflect short-term crises and the *need* for people to pool incomes and resources, but also mirror rational decisions made by individuals to ameliorate their longer-term prospects of survival: living with kin increases access to multiple sources of earnings, thereby easing the problems associated with underemployment and poverty in Third World cities (Chant, 1985a; Gonzalez de la Rocha, Escobar and de la Peña, 1985). Even if relatives do not actually opt to live under the same roof, several maintain a quasi-extended formation by living nearby and engaging in reciprocal networks of financial and psychological support (Bock et al., 1980; Lomnitz, 1977a; Nelson, 1978; Sharma, 1986; Wikan, 1980).

In the light of the above, we can see that extended households are often likely to be as common in the cities as they are in rural areas, even if the rationale for their formation is somewhat different from that purporting to explain their prevalence in rural areas.

However, one significant difference associated with urbanization is that urban extended households become more contracted than their rural counterparts in terms of overall size and range of kin (Bock et al., 1980; Goode, 1963; Peil and Sada, 1984; Pine, 1982; Skinner, 1974). As Gugler and Flanagan (1978, p.132) point out for West Africa:

the extended family has not remained unchanged in the urban transition. Physical fragmentation is another obvious symptom of this. Where multiple generation or laterally extended units are found in the city, the range of kin is modified, some members are absent and the *domestic* constitutes a subset of the extended family network. (their emphasis, meaning here *consumption*)

In some cases, as we saw in our introductory section, fragmentation of kinship networks is such that people live in no-family households. Another outcome is the rise of the woman-headed unit.

Women-headed Households

As indicated in Chapter 2, post-war economic development seems to be associated with a worldwide increase in women-headed families. Undoubtedly women-headed households are to some extent a by-product of increased labour mobility in the contemporary developing world – a phenomenon which has resulted directly or indirectly from the twin process of industrial and urban development. Rural–urban and/or international labour movements have altered sex ratios in both rural and urban areas and in part the numerical imbalance between men and women has been responsible for contributing to new patterns of household headship and family composition. Female-headed households are usually more common in cities, although they are by no means unknown in rural areas.

As far as the rural context is concerned, women-headed households are often associated with male labour migration (in the Caribbean and in southern Africa, for example; see Chapters 2 and 5), and also with civil wars. High frequencies of both rural and urban female-headed households are found in Nicaragua, for example,

where 48 per cent of all families at a national level are headed by
women because of men killed or fighting against the Contra rebels
(Vance, 1985). In some Central American refugee camps, women-
headed households constitute as much as 90 per cent of the total
(Moser and Levy, 1986). Thus women-headed units are common in a
number of rural areas and/or in certain political contexts, and in
many Third World countries have a long history, however as
Townsend and Momsen (1987:53) point out, 'the *ubiquitous* occurrence of such households *is* new' (our emphasis), and this is clearly
associated with urbanization.

The fact that women-headed households are more likely to occur
in cities is borne out by empirical work in a number of countries.
Jamaican women-headed households, for example, are more often
found in the metropolitan area of Kingston than in rural areas of the
island (Bolles, 1986). In Morocco, where female household headship
is comparatively infrequent due to the traditional control and
protection of women by male kin, as many as 21 per cent of urban
households are headed by women (Joekes, 1985). This is also the
case in Burkina Faso, where Elliott Skinner (1974) makes the
observation that although female-headed households are relatively
rare in the capital, Ouagadougou, they are rarer still in rural areas.

Sex-selectivity of urban migration is a critical factor in understanding the emergence of women-headed units in cities and here
regional variations are paramount. As we saw in Chapter 5, Latin
American women far outnumber men in rural–urban migration
which obviously increases the likelihood that women will head
households (Townsend and Momsen, 1987). In 23 Latin American
countries between 1965 and 1975, there were only 92 men in cities for
every hundred women (Gilbert and Gugler, 1982).

As noted earlier in the book, one reason for the outflow of Latin
American women to towns is that their rural employment opportunities have declined markedly with the capitalization of agriculture
(Butterworth and Chance, 1981; see Chapters 3 and 5). Although
they remain excluded from the best remunerated urban jobs (see
Chapter 7), women's employment prospects are usually far greater
in towns than in the countryside. Openings in domestic service and
other unskilled tertiary occupations permit women's absorption into
the urban workforce, thereby allowing them to settle permanently in
cities (Butterworth and Chance, 1981; Jelin, 1977). While men often
move permanently to towns as well, it is more common for them to

return on a periodic basis to rural smallholdings or to hire themselves out as seasonal workers on large farms. This periodic out-migration of men from cities leads to a situation in which only temporary sexual liaisons are formed in urban areas and women are left to head their households (Rogers, 1980).

Another reason for the high incidence of women-headed households in Latin American cities is women's relatively greater life-expectancy, and hence an excess of women in urban populations (García et al., 1983). The above kinds of process have led to a situation where at least one-fifth of urban women in all parts of Latin America head their own households, ranging from between 20 and 25 per cent in Venezuelan urban communities (Blumberg and García, 1977; MacDonald, 1979; Peattie, 1968), to one-third of households in Honduran towns (Resources for Action, 1982a), to around 50 per cent in Managua, Nicaragua (Vance, 1985). In Belo Horizonte, Brazil, one in four low-income households are headed by women (Merrick and Schmink, 1983).

In addition to demographic factors, cultural traditions of male dominance in Latin America often contribute directly or indirectly to the formation of women-headed units. We noted in Chapter 1 that *machismo* is an enduring feature of social relations in the continent. Men subscribing to this ideology often father children with several women and desert their wives to escape financial obligations and/or to establish other homes, a pattern which is intensified in conditions of urban poverty (Bridges, 1980; Thomson, 1986). Because of a long history of male desertion dating back to the conquest period, women-headed households are probably more widely recognized and accepted in Latin America than in other parts of the world. This relative lack of social stigmatization may contribute to explaining why recent investigation in Latin America has shown that it is sometimes women themselves who decide to establish their own households when they can no longer put up with male infidelity or financial irresponsibility (Chant, 1985b).

As far as Africa is concerned, women-headed households are also quite common in cities, despite the fact that until relatively recently, men were dominant in city-ward migration and far outnumbered women in towns. Between 1965 and 1975, for example, in 22 African countries there were 109 men for every 100 women in urban areas (Gilbert and Gugler, 1982). An excess of men over women, would not, in theory, lead to high numbers of women-headed households, so demographic explanations are inadequate here. Instead, culture and tradition appear to be more relevant factors. One set of explanations, particularly relevant to parts of West Africa, emphasizes the historical weakness of marital unions, and women's preference, in accordance with the norms of traditional kinship, to head their own households or to live with female kin (Etienne, 1983; Vellenga, 1983). Roger Sanjek (1983), for example, found that most women aged 40 or over in the neighbourhood of Adabraka, in the Ghanaian capital, Accra, head their own households or share with other women.

The widespread existence of polygyny in West Africa has also been a major factor in women's resistance to living in their husbands' households; conjugal residence in societies where men are accustomed to taking other wives and lovers is only likely to result in emotional conflict and agonizing jealousies on the part of women (Abu, 1983). Besides the role of custom and culture in favouring the formation of female-headed units in the region, it is also important to bear in mind that sex ratios in most African towns are becoming more balanced over time (Brydon, 1987b; Peil and Sada, 1984).

Greater numbers of single female migrants to cities in the last decade or so are reflected in increased proportions of women-headed units. In Mathare Valley, a Nairobi squatter settlement, for example, over 50 per cent of households are headed by women (Nelson, 1979b). In Lesotho, women now figure so prominently in rural-urban moves that the sex ratio in Maseru, the capital city, is becoming markedly feminine (Wilkinson, 1987). Only about one-quarter of women migrants go to Maseru to join their husbands, the rest are single or heads of household. They remain alone (or with their children) in the city because their partners work elsewhere or because there is little choice of a prospective spouse (ibid.).

Whatever reasons lie behind the formation of women-headed households in various regions, one factor is clear: in most areas of the Third World the emergence of female-headed units is closely linked with poverty (Merrick and Schmink, 1983). Poor men may be simply unable to support their wives or female kin. For example, in Madras, India, where formal divorce and separation are comparatively rare for religious and cultural reasons, low-caste *Adi-Dravida* women are often compelled to head their households because their husbands desert them (Caplan, 1985). In Morocco, widowed or abandoned women have traditionally had the right to return to their paternal or fraternal homes, but increasing financial hardship means their relatives can no longer take them in, thereby forcing them to live alone (Youssef and Hetler, 1983). Since economic development and urbanization often lead to heightened class differentiation and widespread impoverishment, it is perhaps likely that the frequency of women-headed households will continue to increase with urban growth.

The fact that women-headed households are most often found among low-income groups should not, however, give rise to the idea that they are automatically among the poorest of the poor. Given that they tend to occur among the lowest socio-economic strata of society, their composition itself is sometimes seen to be responsible for trapping them in poverty. This idea was particularly common in the 1960s when the 'culture of poverty' thesis of Oscar Lewis was a popular paradigm of urban social deprivation. Women-headed households, through paternal absence and maternal neglect, were thought to diminish severely children's 'life-chances' and thereby perpetuate a 'sub-cultural' form of familial organization (Chester, 1977). Lack of parental discipline and entry into employment at a tender age was seen to lead to a cyclical process of truancy, delinquence, early initiation into sex and perpetual instability in family life (Lewis, 1966).

Women-headed households were also viewed extremely negatively by structural-functionalist sociologists who felt that the nuclear family was the only household ideally suited to urban-economic development (Wilson, 1985). Structural-functionalism had no way of explaining the existence of women-headed households except that they were 'deviant' from the norm and indicative of 'system break-down' (Chester, 1977; Hutter, 1981).

Although several authors have noted that women-headed households tend to arise in situations of poverty and continue to remain poor, they are none the less careful to stress that this is not inevitable. For example, in Southeast Asia, Noeleen Heyzer (1986) recognizes that women household heads suffer hardship on account of their relative lack of access to sources of income, yet she also points out that they are not an undifferentiated group and 'many are not poor when compared to some male-headed households' (Heyzer, 1986, p.7). Susan Joekes (1985) reaches similar conclusions about women-headed households in Moroccan cities. While it is indeed true that women who head households face a range of difficulties due to their

relative lack of education and training, because of social stigmatization or because of discrimination in the labour market, this does not
necessarily mean they are unable to overcome their problems. As
Christine Qunta (1987, p.194) points out for the case of Botswana,
long-term absence of the male is now so common that women have
adjusted admirably to their position as household managers, 'coping
very well indeed without men on both a temporary and permanent
basis'. In Accra, Ghana, living apart from their spouses does not, in
the words of Sanjek (1983, p.343), 'present Adabraka women with
economic catastrophe'. Indeed in many West African towns, such as
Abidjan in the Ivory Coast, women positively resist living with their
partners for fear of being economically constrained (Etienne, 1983).
Having said this, one must also take into account current mounting
pressures on West African women to reside with their husbands. On
the one hand, this is attributable to an historical weakening of
traditional lineage systems dating from colonial times where considerable efforts were made by the British to impose an ideal of the
conjugal family. On the other, it reflects a growing desire on the part
of women to maintain a more watchful eye on their husband's
activities, particularly in order to increase their own income and to
affirm their legal rights to conjugal property; Akan and Ga women
alike are presently showing much more of an interest in strengthen-
ing the marital bond, often in the form of spending more time with
their husbands (Abu, 1983; Vellenga, 1983; Westwood, 1984).

Nevertheless, in Latin America, a possible reverse trend may be
identified. Mexican research has shown that women-headed households are frequently formed as a deliberate strategy on the part of
women to escape the financial and emotional insecurity resulting
from co-residence with an irresponsible male partner (Chant,
1985b). Indeed if one analyses what goes on *inside* male-headed
households, it is often the case that women members are actually
worse-off than their counterparts in female-headed households
(Chant, 1985b). Other authors have noted how growing numbers of
women-headed households in Latin America also have very positive
implications for female autonomy and class-consciousness (Harris,
1982; Safa, 1980).

The message here is that women-headed units should not be
treated as a monolithic category, nor should they necessarily be
construed as 'victims' of 'development' or economic change. Clearly
women household heads face a far greater range of problems than

their male counterparts. but to place undue emphasis on their 'vulnerability' is both pragmatically and ideologically misleading. In several instances, women-headed households are not only established as a result of female initiative and decision-making, but are also eminently capable of gaining a livelihood, even when the odds are weighted heavily against them.

GENDER ROLES, HOUSEHOLD STRUCTURE AND URBANIZATION

Nuclear Families and the Sexual Division of Labour

In addition to observed changes in household form with economic development and urbanization, internal household functions, particularly the responsibilities assigned to men and women, are also seen to alter. Frances Pine (1982, p.402) notes that there are two distinct theoretical trends in the literature on this issue: one which emphasizes how economic development and family nuclearization lead to the breakdown of gender-ascriptive roles and pave the way for female emancipation, the other which points to increasing polarization of men's and women's work and status both within and beyond the household.

The former, 'optimistic', view is characteristic of the work of certain modernization theorists who suggest that nuclear families are conducive to greater equality between the sexes, by releasing women from patriarchal traditions and in particular, by allowing their greater participation in extra-domestic employment (Bridges, 1980; Das, 1980; Goode, 1963; Mitterauer and Sieder, 1982).[1] The latter, more pessimistic, view is usually emphasized by those working within a broad Marxist-feminist framework; here the transition to the 'modern' nuclear family is seen to intensify the sexual division of labour, to confine women to the home and to contribute to a marked loss of female status (Engels, 1972; Leacock, 1972; Nash, 1980). This second view is based on the premise that gender roles in pre-industrial settings were/are *complementary*, if hierarchical, basically because the household combined both production and reproduction in a single spatial unit, thereby uniting the product of male and female labour. Indeed, in rural areas, past and present, where production is carried out on a domestic basis, women are seen to have higher family status than in many urban settings (Elmendorf, 1976; Scott, 1986a; Shapiro, 1980; but see also Rocksloh-Papendieck, 1988).

The advent of industrialization, urbanization and the nuclear family is argued to have upset this essential complementarity of gender relations. The removal of production from the household leads to a spatial divide between remunerated labour and domestic work. Women continue to perform key functions such as housework and child-care in the home, yet men perform their wage-earning activities away from the household. Since capitalism tends to define work only as that which is remunerated, women's unpaid labour becomes progressively undervalued (Huston, 1979; Nash and Safa, 1980; Pahl, 1984). The home-based nature of domestic work and child-care also means that women's becomes less visible to other household members. Male control of the wage leads to a situation where women lose power in family decision-making, their economic dependence is increased, and female subordination becomes ever more entrenched (Seccombe, 1980). Indeed, even in West Africa where women have traditionally retained their economic independence in marriage, there is some evidence to show that urban women are more likely to become economically dependent on their husbands than in rural areas (Cutrufelli, 1983; Etienne, 1983; Oppong, 1974).

Even where women enter the labour market, their position in the workplace is moulded in accordance with their role within the family, and similar patterns of hierarchy and subordination emerge here as they do in the home. (See Chapter 7.)

A critical feature of working women's oppression in contemporary urban families is that they have to take on a 'dual burden' of labour, receiving no reduction in child-care and domestic activities to compensate for increased participation in the workforce (Anker and Hein, 1986). This of course is more likely to be the case in nuclear families than in extended households where female kin may share essential domestic tasks (Durrani, 1976; Liddle and Joshi, 1986).

The tendencies described above are critically important in the analysis of gender and urban households because they show how household structure itself may exacerbate or mitigate wider prescriptions of the sexual division of labour. The isolation of women in nuclear households is argued by many to perpetuate their oppression (Caplan and Bujra, 1978; Huston, 1979; Seccombe, 1980). If the ethos of economic development is built upon a bedrock of nuclear families, then it might also be suggested that it is built upon the economic and social subordination of women. Nevertheless, care must be taken here on two fronts. First, cultural variations need to be borne in mind. As we observed in Chapter 1, Middle Eastern and North African women have traditionally been oppressed by the *extended* family structure, particularly by their mothers-in-law, and here independent nuclear units might contain a seed of liberation (Mernissi, 1985; Minces, 1982). Second, the realities of poverty for many Third Women contradict the tendency observed by several Marxist authors for capitalist development and family nuclearization to confine women to the home. Many low-income women in developing countries show few signs of retreating to the home as development proceeds; on the contrary, they often have little choice but to enter the labour force because their husbands' wages are hopelessly inadequate for household needs (Moser and Young, 1981), although this by no means implies they are absolved from domestic and mothering responsibilities. Chapter 7 deals with women's work in Third World cities in much greater depth, but in the following section we take up this second theme and identify some of the key implications of increased female labour force participation for patterns of household formation among the poor, notably age of marriage, family size and household composition.

Age at Marriage of Urban Women

In areas where demand for female labour is high, as in the zones of multinational export assembly manufacturing in Southeast Asia and Latin America, there is abundant evidence to show that increased employment opportunities for women are resulting in later age of marriage. A study of the Bataan Export Processing Zone in the Philippines, for example, where up to 70 per cent of the factory workforce consists of women, revealed that marriage for girls under the age of twenty has become less frequent since the expansion of industrialization in the area (Zosa-Feranil, 1984). Furthermore, contrary to Philippino social norms, nearly half the women in the above survey had cohabited with their partner prior to formal marriage (ibid.). Later age of marriage has implications both for subsequent size and composition of domestic units, a point we will return to a little further on.

Sometimes, changing marriage patterns in cities represent a response to the difficulties of combining urban employment with the traditional responsibilities of housewifery and motherhood which most women are still expected to perform. In a study of construction workers in Chiang Mai, Thailand's second largest city, it was found that more than two-thirds of female participants in this sector were single, with a mean age of 17.8 years (Singhanetra-Renard, 1984). The fact that few married women form part of the workforce is attributed to the fact that it is difficult to combine productive and reproductive roles in urban areas. While in rural areas of northern Thailand, agricultural work has long been performed by women throughout the life-cycle, in cities, women have to postpone marriage to earn a living (ibid.).

While there is evidence to suggest that the changing extent and nature of women's labour force participation in urban areas raises marrying age, the latter is not wholly attributable to transformations in production and women's role within it. Later age of marriage may also relate to more general processes of social and cultural change. Fatima Mernissi (1985) points to the influence of these kinds of changes on attitudes towards gender roles, marriage and sexual segregation in Moroccan cities. In rural areas, up to 50 per cent of girls marry before they reach puberty, and most of the rest within the first two years after menarche – the object being that illicit sexual encounters between adolescents are prevented. The ideal age of marriage for rural girls remains at around thirteen years. However, in urban Morocco, the corresponding figure is somewhere between seventeen and nineteen (Mernissi, 1985). In addition, in urban environments there is increasing resistance both to arranged marriages among the young and the traditional domination of wives by their mothers-in-law (ibid.). These changes are taking place against a backcloth of relatively low differentials in urban and rural female employment. In 1980, 15 per cent of urban women between the ages of 15 and 69 in Morocco were employed, and 9 per cent of women in rural areas (UNCHS, 1985). Nevertheless, in many countries, increased rates of labour force participation of urban women are undoubtedly playing a significant part in raising marrying age.

Family Size and Female Labour Force Participation

If age of marriage is generally higher for women as urbanization proceeds, then fertility rates show signs of falling, albeit marginally in some areas. Smaller size of urban households may of course be due in part to the younger average age of urban residents, especially in African cities (Peil and Sada, 1984). None the less, lower fertility also relates to fewer child-bearing years within urban marriage, notwithstanding the fact that in several countries childbirth outside of formal marriage or stable partnerships is quite common. Other reasons for falling urban fertility rates include the more 'successful' introduction of state birth control programmes in cities, greater access to education, a re-evaluation of childhood (in the light of reduced use of child labour), greater attention to maternal health, and possibly heightened awareness of women's rights to control their own fertility (Rubin-Kurtzman, 1987). Each of these issues is too complex for in-depth discussion here, and will be followed up in more detail in Chapter 8, but it is probable that varying combinations of the above-mentioned factors contribute to an overall decline in urban birth rates. Having said that, what might be some of the more specific links between female labour force participation and urban family size?

In advanced industrial economies the families of 'working' women tend to be smaller than those of full-time housewives (Papanek, 1976). However, this relationship is by no means clear for less-developed countries (Harkess, 1973). For example, a study carried out in Ibadan, Nigeria by Oladele Arowolo (1978) showed there was no clear pattern of fertility differentials according to female involvement in the labour force or occupational type. Where differences exist, they are often quite marginal. For example, one Mexican study showed that working women have only slightly fewer children (3.8) than non-working women (4.1) (Elú de Leñero, 1980). Sometimes figures even indicate the opposite may be true. For example, Papola's (1986) survey of Lucknow, India, shows that the average size of a woman's family is actually larger (5.11) compared to that of a male worker (4.89), although it is not clear whether the wives of male workers also have employment. Nevertheless, it does indicate that women may still take on remunerated work in spite of having major responsibilities at home. Variations in family size may depend on the kinds of urban employment in which women are involved. For women in 'formal' manufacturing or office work, there is usually an inverse relationship between fertility and labour force participation, as indicated by the case of women factory workers in the Philippines (Zosa-Feranil, 1984). However, this is less true for women in 'informal' employment. The fact that many Third World urban women engage in domestic-based production means that child-care *can* be reconciled with income-generation (Peil, 1975; Smith, 1981). Nevertheless, despite the fact that it is difficult to establish the precise relationship of family size with female labour force participation, especially given that it is only one factor among many which may contribute to lower birth-rates in urban areas, we may assume that urban households are on the whole smaller than their rural counterparts and that women's changing economic and social roles play some part in the process (Caldwell, 1977; Rubin-Kurtzman, 1987).

Household Composition and Women's Work Roles

To conclude this section on gender roles and household structure, we discuss recent evidence which suggests that women's increased labour force participation, may be critical in understanding changing patterns of family composition in cities. This idea is central to both of our current research concerns in Mexico (Chant, 1987a; 1988; 1991) and Ghana (Brydon, 1987a, 1987b). As such we have a strong personal commitment to review this theme, albeit briefly.

Urban women have greater *independent* access to income-earning opportunities than their rural counterparts, and this has several repercussions for household structure. One major implication is that they may head their own households (Blumberg, 1978), and evidence from a number of areas demonstrates a positive link between female employment opportunities and their propensity to play a leading role in household management. In the industrial border towns of northern Mexico, for example, where demand for female labour is very high, not only is it common for women to work, but also to head their own households (Fernandez-Kelly, 1983). This is also true of Morocco where a disproportionate number of women workers in the clothing industry (34 per cent) are heads of one-parent families (Joekes, 1985).

It is also the case that a general rise in women's labour force participation in Third World cities may be related to increasing numbers of *extended* households, basically because the 'dual burden' of working women is virtually unmanageable without assistance. This issue is especially relevant for low-income groups whose wages show little tendency to rise over time, let alone keep apace with inflation. Here, a single wage is not likely to be adequate for household needs and the most effective way of accumulating income is to send other household members into the workforce (Bolles, 1986; Chant, 1985a; Hackenberg, Murphy and Selby, 1981).

Urban nuclear families, consisting in early stages of the developmental-cycle of only two adult members and their children, experience great difficulty in realizing their full wage-earning capacity, especially when they cannot afford domestic help or can no longer rely upon the support of a wide range of female relatives (Anker and Hein, 1986). For example, Tunisian working women in nuclear households face considerable problems in not being able to leave their children with female kin (Durrani, 1976). In West African cities, working urban women are often forced to leave their children in rural areas with grandparents or other relatives in order to circumvent the 'dual burden' (Abu, 1983; Brydon, 1979; Nelson, 1987). In both Mexico and Brazil, where the practice of fostering children out to rural relatives is far less common, nuclear households in a number of cities have very low rates of labour force participation (García et al., 1983). This situation may well exacerbate poverty. Evidence from Brazil, for example, suggests that scarce labour supply and low utilization of 'secondary earners' (i.e. women and children) are dominant characteristics of the poorer urban households (Merrick and Schmink, 1983).

Extended households, on the other hand, have greater flexibility in terms of organizing the family division of labour: many adult members, including women, may be deployed into the labour force because responsibilities for domestic work and child-care are undertaken collectively by female kin or other household members. Several studies have shown that women's labour force participation is higher in extended than in nuclear family units (Chant, 1984a; García et al., 1982, 1983; Sharma, 1986). These findings point, albeit tentatively, to the idea that increased rates of female employment may lead to a shift away from nuclear households in urban areas: women in extended units are able to enlist support in child-care and domestic work thereby freeing them for waged labour; alternatively households may deliberately increase their membership if local economic opportunities favour women's employment. As yet the possible sequence of events between female employment and household change is not well documented, but it is clear that some link is apparent. Indeed the changing economic role of urban women could be a pivotal factor in the analysis of relationships between Third World development and emerging household forms (Chant, 1988; 1991). It is hoped that further research will illuminate the relevance of this point.

Before concluding this discussion, it is important to note that female labour force participation not only appears to favour the extension of male-headed families, but also the even more frequent extension of female-headed units. It is usually imperative that women heads find work when they lack support from a male partner (Blumberg, 1976; Tienda and Ortega, 1982). Women household heads often take in relatives to manage more successfully their multiple responsibilities of wage-earning, domestic work and child-care (Chant, 1985b). Again, this suggests a critical interaction between women's roles and household composition in urban areas, at least in Latin America. (In Africa, as we noted earlier, urban women tend not to *take in* relatives so much as to *send* their children *to them*; these differences are probably attributable to regional variations in culture and kinship.)

Although much evidence here has been drawn from Latin America, Hilary Standing (1985, p.254) writing on Calcutta, feels that there is little doubt that in India as well, 'the entry of women into the labour market appears to be affecting the dynamics of household formation'. In Standing's case this relates to the increasing likelihood of Bengali daughters postponing marriage in order to support their parents, a role traditionally played by their brothers. Nevertheless, her basic premise of a fundamental link between women's work and household structure applies also, as we have seen here, to women as wives, women as mothers and women as household heads. Again we stress the need for further research in other cultures to clarify the relevance of these findings.

CONCLUSION AND IMPLICATIONS FOR FUTURE RESEARCH

In this chapter we have tried to present an overview of the influence of urbanization on household structure, and how this interrelates with the changing roles of women in Third World cities. It has been impossible to cover all the issues relevant to this debate and the wide range of situations identified give some indication of the difficulties associated with generalizing for the Third World as a whole.

However, our main conclusions from each of the three main sections of the chapter are as follows. First, we stress that the urban household is a relevant analytical unit in any study of gender and development. The urban household frequently reflects wider social and economic trends and is meaningful from the point of view of the experiences of its component members. Regardless of the extent to which inter-household ties are maintained between kin and friends, membership of a household still implies more participation in the daily life of the domestic unit than those who live outside it.

Second, conventional wisdoms about urban family structure deriving from both modernization and Marxist theories are in need of revision. While urbanization seems to have led in many cases to the nuclearization of family units, Third World cities often contain considerable numbers of non-nuclear households as well, particularly women-headed and extended structures. These households should not be dismissed as insignificant since there is considerable evidence to show that they are directly related to economic development and urbanization. Another contradiction between the theory and reality of urban family structure emerges in the sphere of roles undertaken by family members. While Marxian analysis has emphasized that development tends to push women into the home and into economic dependence upon their husbands, in many Third World countries women often *have* to participate in the labour force in order to maintain minimum levels of household survival; this in turn has another set of repercussions for gender relations at the household level and is a field which requires detailed empirical work in order to move away from deterministic stereotypes and towards greater understanding of contemporary patterns of Third World social change.

Third, and related to this last point, the general rise in urban women's labour force participation has various consequences for household structure, notably raising age at marriage, reducing family size, and influencing household composition and headship.

In the following chapter we turn to investigate the nature of women's urban labour force participation in more detail, to consider the role that women play in urban production and to examine the extent to which gender inequality is incorporated into urban economic development.

NOTES

1. Classical Parsonian modernization theory regarded women's 'ideal' role in the modern nuclear family as that of mother and housewife. In this sense it differs substantially from the ideas of more 'progressive' modernization theorists such as William Goode who saw the nuclear family as offering greater flexibility in 'traditional' gender roles.

7 Gender and Urban Production

This chapter considers gender and production in Third World cities – production being defined here as activities which directly generate income such as waged work and self-employment. The discussion concentrates on two main issues. First, we look at evidence for men's and women's participation in the urban workforce over time and examine their involvement in various branches of economic activity in different parts of the developing world. To what extent are urban labour markets segregated into 'male' and 'female' sectors, and what are the characteristics of the occupations in which men and women predominate? Second, we try to explain the distribution of men and women in the urban labour market.

GENDER, EMPLOYMENT AND URBANIZATION

In most areas of the world, women's participation in remunerated labour has always been lower than that of men, mainly because of their greater share of reproductive work, particularly domestic labour and child-care. This fundamental aspect of the sexual division of labour has obviously meant that women are far less free than men to engage in wage-earning activity. This is not to say that they do not perform 'productive' work. Indeed, we saw in Chapters 2 and 3 that they not only undertake essential domestic and reproductive tasks which complement and sustain rural production, but also in many areas constitute a large component of the agricultural labour force. However, recent trends towards urban residence in less-developed countries seem to have been accompanied by changes in both the nature and visibility of women's employment. In the first place, the proportion of women in the officially registered labour force has risen, albeit slowly, over the last 30 or so years (Blumberg, 1976). In 1962 only 27 per cent of the world's workforce was made up of women (Pescatello, 1976). By 1980 this figure had crept up to 34 per cent (Castro, 1981).[1] Secondly, over time, women have tended to enter a greater diversity of occupations, even though their opportunities, working conditions and wages are usually far inferior to those of men.

Before turning to evidence for global changes in women's urban labour force participation, it is important to point out that the analysis of general trends is complicated by two major deficiencies in existing data. First, as we have noted in earlier chapters, there are several problems involved with data collection, including sampling procedures, who collects the data and how those data are collected and/or interpreted. Many economic activities, particularly those of women, are often unrecorded because they do not fall neatly into prevailing official perceptions of what constitutes 'employment'. Several part-time, casual, income-generated activities undertaken by women escape the net of national data collection because of their relative invisibility (Townsend and Momsen, 1987; UNCHS, 1985). Secondly, statistical sources of employment often fail to divide the workforce on the basis of rural and urban residence; instead they tend to classify the economically active population by sector: namely the primary or agricultural sector, the secondary or industrial sector and the tertiary or service sector. Thus one is forced to make a series of crude assumptions about the distribution of these activities across national territories – usually that the agricultural sector is located in rural areas and industry and services in cities.

At this stage it is also important to point out that although women's employment has often risen with urban growth, the process is by no means universal throughout the Third World, partly because levels of urbanization vary so widely among major world regions. Another problem is that in some areas, particularly Africa and India, urbanization is actually associated with a decline in overall rates of female labour force participation (Townsend and Momsen, 1987). Obviously we must be cautious in talking about general trends against this backcloth of regional diversity.

Growth in Women's Labour Force Participation

Despite the difficulties of incomplete statistics, differing degrees of urbanization and wide disparities in overall rates of female labour force participation, women's share of urban employment is increasing in many areas of the world, particularly in Southeast Asia and Latin America, the most industrialized regions (Seager and Olson, 1986). In most major Southeast Asian countries, for example, the percentage of women in the urban workforce increased on average by 10–15 per cent in the decade 1970–80. In Taiwan women only made up 17.1 per cent of the urban workforce in 1970, but represented 32.0 per cent of the total in 1980; in Singapore the rate increased from 23.6 per cent to 34.4 per cent over the same period; in Thailand women's labour force participation in cities was already high in 1970 at 39.2 per cent but even this figure had increased to 43.4 per cent by 1980 (Drakakis-Smith, 1987, p.78).

Rates of female participation in the urban workforce tend to be lower in other areas of the world, but similar increasing trends may be perceived, especially for the Latin American case. In the Dominican Republic, women's labour force participation grew five times faster than that of men between 1970 and 1980 (Buvinić, 1984). In Mexico, the percentage of women in the national labour force climbed from only 4.6 per cent in 1930 to 13.6 per cent in 1950 to 19.2 per cent in 1970 (LACWE, 1980). This is largely due to growth in female employment in the cities; with women's share in urban employment being markedly higher than the national average at a figure of around 25 per cent in the early 1980s (Cockcroft, 1983; Pedrero and Rendón, 1982). Census data of intermediate cities in Mexico suggest even greater rises for a variety of different types of labour market: In Puerto Vallarta, a Pacific tourist resort with a large, expanding tertiary sector, the percentage of women in the labour force grew from 24.4 per cent in 1970 to 32.1 per cent in 1980; in León, an industrial city specializing in the small-scale production of footwear and leather goods, women's share of employment rose from 21 per cent in 1970 to 29.2 per cent in 1980; in Querétaro, a heavy, large-scale industrial centre, women's participation in the labour force grew from 21 per cent in 1970 to 28.3 per cent in 1980 (Chant, 1988; 1991). In other rapidly urbanizing countries such as Brazil, Venezuela and Colombia, the proportion of women engaged in economic activity at a national level increased between 1965 and 1975 by 13.9 per cent, 16.3 per cent and 12.5 per cent respectively, no doubt reflecting the greater absorption of women into urban occupations (UNCHS, 1985).

In many African countries figures indicate there was an overall decline in national female activity rates between 1965 and 1975, although it is difficult to ascertain whether this is due to a marginalization of women from productive sectors of the rural economy or their failure to gain entry to economic activities in cities as urban populations have grown. The issue is complicated both by the fact that these trends have to be set against a picture of general economic decline in the post-independence period, and also that data are often inaccurate. Nevertheless, the general consensus is that until the last fifteen years or so, men tended to predominate in urbanward migration in African countries leaving women behind in rural areas, mainly because it was more difficult for women to find urban jobs (Brydon, 1987b; Bukh, 1979; Elkan, 1973; Peil and Sada, 1984; Shields, 1980; Verdon, 1983). Although the number of women moving to cities is now increasing, in many African countries there are still proportionately far higher numbers of women in rural compared to urban areas (see Chapter 3). Nevertheless, the scenario is changing in most of the continent. As we saw in Chapter 5, while in the past women tended to move to towns to join their husbands, there is now considerable evidence to show that several migrate alone and with the specific intention of finding work (Brydon, 1985a; Bryceson, 1985; Peil and Sada, 1984). Whether women will be absorbed into visible areas of the urban economy or not is another question, since evidence from both East and Southern Africa shows they often have to develop their own means of earning an income (e.g. Nelson, 1979b, 1987; Simon, 1984; Wilkinson, 1987). Nevertheless increased migration of African women will undoubtedly have some repercussions on employment patterns in emerging urban labour markets.

PATTERNS OF URBAN WOMEN'S EMPLOYMENT

Having established that women's participation in urban employment is increasing in many parts of the Third World, we now turn to look at the kinds of occupations into which they are being absorbed. First, however, it is important to point out briefly that there is often great variation in the *types* and *scales* of so-called 'urban' occupations, leading many to view urban labour markets as a conjunction of two broad 'sectors' – usually referred to as 'formal' and 'informal' (Hart, 1973).

Dualism in Urban Labour Markets

The 'formal' sector of urban employment describes large-scale, 'modern' urban enterprises such as factories, offices, public services and registered commercial establishments. Formal sector manufacturing enterprises use imported capital-intensive production methods and are often established with foreign investment and technology. Workers in formal sector firms are generally skilled or semi-skilled, are in theory protected by wage and labour legislation and may have membership in officially recognized trade unions. Earnings in this sector are comparatively high and wages are often fixed and regular (Moser, 1978; Raczynski, 1977; Schaefer, 1976).

The urban 'informal' sector, by contrast, is used as a catch-all for economic activities which do not meet the criteria used to define formal sector employment. Informal enterprises are usually small-scale, operate with 'traditional' labour-intensive production methods and rarely have access to foreign capital. Relatives and friends often form the workforce of these informal establishments. Unionization is rare, and earnings tend to be low and irregular (Bromley, 1982; Gilbert and Gugler, 1982; LACWE, 1980; Moser, 1978). Another important feature of informal sector work is that there is no paid holiday, maternity leave, pension or other social security benefits. Some informal workers may pay voluntary contributions to a health or welfare scheme, but usually their earnings are not sufficiently reliable to allow them to commit themselves to regular repayments. Aside from family businesses, other types of informal activity include self-employment, casual work, and long craft or trade apprenticeships.[2] Most types of informal employment operate on the margins of the law, with differing degrees of 'illegality', ranging from working without a licence, to non-payment of taxes, and sometimes to outright criminal offences such as extortion. This finding led Keith Hart (1973) to subdivide the informal sector into two further sectors, the first including 'informal legal' activities such as small-scale commerce and personal services, the second comprising 'illegal' activities such as petty theft and prostitution.

Having perhaps given the impression that informal work is

substantially 'inferior' to that of the formal sector in terms of security, working conditions and remuneration, it is important to note that 'formal' employment is not always a desirable alternative. As Richard Sandbrook and Robin Cohen (1975, pp.3–4) point out for the case of Africa, it should not be assumed that:

'modern' sector workers constitute a privileged group, nor that they have been co-opted by the ruling sectors . . . There are vast income disparities between the political and business classes on the one hand, and the unionized workers on the other, and this economic inequality clearly creates significant differences in life chances between these emergent classes.

Nor, on the other hand, should it be assumed that informal sector work is necessarily easier to obtain. Kenneth King's (1979) research on Nairobi suggests that there are considerable obstacles to entering certain kinds of informal enterprise, as does Margaret Peil's (1975) study of women traders in southern Ghana. Furthermore, mobility between 'sectors' is quite common. For example, a woman may begin life as a seamstress on an informal apprenticeship, then take formal qualifications and work for some time in a factory, and subsequently invest capital in a small business and employ her own apprentices.

The above kinds of observation have lent weight to widespread criticism of the idea that urban labour markets consist of two, or indeed three, distinct sectors. The activities within each vary so widely that there is often as much variation within each sector as there is between them (Connolly, 1981; Sinclair, 1978). Furthermore, it is argued that a dualistic view of urban employment is inappropriate because it obscures an intrinsic interdependence between various economic activities: the formal sector often depends both directly and indirectly on the existence of the informal sector for sources of labour, goods and retail distribution, and therefore the two are very much interrelated (Birkbeck, 1979; Moser, 1978; Raczynski, 1977).

In the light of the above criticisms, a strong case has been made for conceiving of urban production as a *continuum*, whereby small-scale enterprises and independent workers (petty commodity enterprises) are linked through a chain of exploitative activities to large-scale capitalist establishments (Moser, 1978). However, while recognizing that there are obvious linkages between various scales of urban production, it is still useful to refer to the description 'formal' and 'informal' activities in terms of the general kinds of conditions under which different sections of the urban labour force operate. As a rule, women tend to be confined to the informal sector, not only because of discrimination in formal sector recruitment, but also because they have to find ways to balance their involvement in income-generation with domestic labour and child care (Peil, 1975). Nevertheless, the female component of the formal workforce is by no means negligible.

The 'Female Marginalization Thesis'

Before going on to examine the distribution of men and women in Third World urban labour markets, it is also important to consider briefly the 'female marginalization thesis' often used as a framework for the study of women's employment in developing countries. Alison MacEwen Scott (1986b, pp.653–4), while not herself convinced by the 'thesis' (a rather loose collection of ideas and assumptions), identifies four main dimensions of 'marginalization' which have been applied to the analysis of urban women's employment. The first is marginalization as 'exclusion from production' (i.e. women are excluded from employment, or certain types of employment such as manufacturing); the second is marginalization as 'concentration on the margins of the labour market' (i.e. women tend to be confined to marginal occupations, industries, sectors and so on); the third is marginalization as 'segregation and feminization' (i.e. the predominance of women in certain types of jobs leads to the feminization and marginalization of those self-same jobs); the fourth is marginalization as 'economic inequality' (this refers to various forms of economic inequality which accompany occupational differentiation such as wages, working conditions and fringe benefits).

Scott (1986b) points out that there are problems not only in identifying these different aspects of marginalization in empirical work, but also in accounting for them. In the first place, 'marginality' is a relative phenomenon; how does one arrive at a universal, all-encompassing definition of marginalization applicable to different regions and/or to different historical and economic circumstances? Secondly, while the numerous facets of female marginalization are often ascribed to a single causal process, namely capital's concern with keeping wages to a minimum, Scott argues that underlying causes go far beyond economic considerations, and advocates in-depth micro-level analysis in order to refine understanding of gender differentiation in Third World employment.

In light of the above, the following accounts of women and work in urban areas attempt to demonstrate the *breadth* of women's experience in the urban economies of developing countries, and to indicate how various aspects of marginalization may or may not be apparent in both formal and informal sector work. This is followed by a discussion of a range of factors which might help to explain gender differentiation in urban employment.

Gender and 'Formal' Employment

Formal sector employment is that which is most likely to be recorded in official census and survey data, thus here it is relatively easy to establish the proportion of the formal labour force which is made up of women. For analytical and practical purposes, 'formal' urban work is divided into categories of 'industry' and 'services'.

Women in industry

Women's share of industrial work varies greatly throughout the Third World, ranging from between 30 and 40 per cent of the total industrial labour force in Southeast Asia to less than 10 per cent in North Africa, the Middle East and certain Southern African countries such as Namibia and Angola. Women in Latin America, South Asia and East and West Africa have average rates of industrial labour force participation of between 10 and 30 per cent (Townsend and Momsen, 1987). Industry in general tends not to have favoured a female workforce, which to some extent supports one precept of the female marginalization thesis, that women are excluded from certain types of production. Men have usually been recruited into modern industrial activities employing high levels of technology, while women tend to have been left to 'traditional' and/or labour-intensive industries such as textile production, garment-making, food processing and assembly electronics (Aguiar, 1980; Butterworth and Chance, 1981; Cockcroft, 1983; Elmendorf, 1977;

Joekes, 1985; Mukhopadhyay, 1984; Saffioti, 1986). In Mexico, for example, one-third of women industrial workers are employed in the clothing trade, and a further fifth in the food industry (LACWE, 1980). In Morocco, women's share in the clothing industry workforce actually increased from less than half in 1969 to three-quarters in 1980 (Joekes, 1985). Women are also frequently employed as domestic outworkers for industries concerned to escape the legal burdens associated with employing them on a regular basis such as paid maternity leave and legal minimum wages (Nash, 1986). Outwork is generally concentrated in labour-intensive activities requiring a high degree of manual dexterity. In Lahore, Pakistan, for example, women pieceworkers make paper bags out of recycled waste, assemble garments, make trinkets and tinsel garlands, and cut straps for rubber slippers (APHD, 1985). In Southeast Asian cities, women outworkers attach labels to clothes or press out plastic shapes from moulds (Drakakis-Smith, 1987).

Women are not only confined to less dynamic or low-technology industrial sectors, but within those sectors they are also segregated into semi- or unskilled activities where earnings are far less than those of men. Susan Cunningham (1987, p.306) shows for the case of São Paulo state, Brazil, for example, that the percentage of the workforce earning less than the minimum salary is far higher in the female-dominated clothing and food-processing industries than in male-dominated branches of manufacturing such as electrical goods and machinery/metals. Furthermore, within the female-dominated industries, a far greater percentage of women than men earn less than the minimum wage; in the clothing industry, for example, 31.1 per cent of women workers earn under the minimum salary compared with only 17.2 per cent of men. This pattern is repeated in the food and beverages industry where the corresponding figures are 27.5 per cent and 10.1 per cent respectively (Cunningham, 1987). In another study of three electrical plants, two motor component factories, and one manufacturer of toilet products in Brazil by John Humphrey (1985), it was found that women predominated in the lowest-paid jobs, whereas men monopolized higher paid manual posts and supervisory positions. Data for Mexico in the 1970s indicated that women's earnings in industry were generally only 40 per cent of men's (Elmendorf, 1977); in the 1980s data on male and female industrial workers in Querétaro, Mexico showed that the gap had closed slightly, but women were still only earning 47 per cent of male wages in the same sector (Chant, 1987a). Susan Joekes (1985) in her study of the Moroccan clothing industry found that despite women's higher educational qualifications and management's high regard for female productivity, their wages on average are only 72 per cent of those of men. In Sri Lanka, women's average wages in manufacturing in 1982 were 81.9 per cent of men's, and in Singapore the corresponding figure was 63.2 per cent (APHD, 1985). From the above, we may identify further aspects of 'marginalization', namely that women are concentrated on the margins of production, are segregated into 'feminized' jobs, and receive low remuneration.

The reasons for women being segregated into low-paid industrial occupations are manifold. There is undoubtedly a combination of factors involving, on the one hand, decision-making at the level of the industrial plant, and on the other, the way in which women's domestic roles impinge upon their ability to take on certain jobs, especially those that require overtime. Some have suggested that stereotypes of gender aptitude in machine maintenance also relegate women to non-technical, unskilled positions (Saffioti, 1986), although it is not really known how the association between men and machines came about or is sustained (Scott, 1988). Others have suggested that women are paid less because they have lower productivity rates than men owing to their relative lack of physical strength, lack of 'human capital' such as skills, training and education, or because they are likely to have greater rates of turnover and absenteeism, even though there is much evidence to the contrary (Anker and Hein, 1986; Bryceson, 1985; Drakakis-Smith, 1987). There is little doubt that ingrained attitudes of employers regarding gender differences operate to sustain the subordinate position of women in the workplace, however there are several other reasons why industrializing capitalist states would wish men to retain their advantage over women and/or for women to remain in the home – one major rationale being the utility of maintaining a segmented labour market for the purposes of co-opting, controlling and granting minor privileges to the male workforce (Humphrey, 1985; Reich, Gordon and Edwards, 1980). A further reason is that women constitute a cheap, easily manipulable reserve army of labour which may be taken on in boom periods and discarded promptly during slumps (Gordon, 1979; Hartmann, 1979; Nash and Safa, 1980). These reasons, which are discussed in more detail later in the chapter, are often interrelated and have differing degrees of applicability in different situations. As Alison MacEwen Scott (1986b, p.673) notes:

gender plays a role in structuring labour markets, not just as cheap labour, but as subordinate labour, docile labour, immobile labour, sexual labour and so on. Thus it is not just dimensions of marginalization that need to be distinguished, but dimensions of gender. The use made of these different aspects by employers extends far beyond pressure on wages.

Women in 'world market factories'

Expanding on Scott's last point, it is important to document one new area of manufacturing in which women are deliberately sought as workers – this being the multinational assembly firms or 'world market factories' which in the last 10–20 years have been established in special Free Trade or Export Processing Zones (EPZs) in Third World countries, through bilateral agreements between First and Third World governments. Free Trade Zones enable multinational firms to transfer part of the production process – normally that which is labour-intensive to areas where workers are cheap, a process which has become known as the 'new international division of labour' (Elson and Pearson, 1981). Intermediate goods such as circuit boards and partially completed garments are assembled in the EPZs with no tariffs charged on the import of components and no restriction on the subsequent export of the goods. Third World governments in places as far apart as Southeast Asia, Mauritius and northern Mexico have often welcomed the arrival of world market factories in the hope of creating much needed employment and stimulating local enterprise. However it is undoubtedly the multinational firms who are the main benefactors; they frequently pay Third World workers only a fraction (generally 10 per cent or less) of what they would pay for labour in the advanced economies and are thus able to maximize profits. In addition, Third World workers may labour for up to 50 per cent longer than their counterparts in the developed world, and are generally forbidden to form trade unions (Townsend and Momsen, 1987).

A major proportion of the labour force in world market factories is made up of young women which helps to account for the fact that women's share of industrial employment is increasing rapidly in those countries that have established free trade zones. For example, women's participation in the manufacturing sector of peninsular Malaysia rose from 17 per cent in 1957 to 41 per cent in 1976

(Armstrong and McGee, 1985). Of almost 20,000 workers in the Bataan Export Processing Zones in the Philippines, 70 per cent are women (Zosa-Feranil, 1984), and in some electronics factories in Southeast Asia, women constitute between 80 and 90 per cent of the labour force (Drakakis-Smith, 1987). Similar proportions are noted for the world market factories of northern Mexico (Iglesias, 1985), and Mauritius (Hein, 1986). While in some respects the relocation of export-processing to peripheral areas may indicate a widening of opportunities for Third World women, Helen Safa (1981) points out how this is often achieved at the expense of women workers in the advanced economies, who bear a disproportionate amount of job losses. Furthermore, the 'benefits' of assembly employment for Third World women are elusive to say the least.

The rationale for engaging a large proportion of women in world market factories is primarily economic; women may be paid wages that are 20–50 per cent those of men's, in accordance with pre-existing male and female wage differentials in the countries concerned. However, other factors associated with gender differences undoubtedly enter the calculation. For example, women's socialization, training in needlework, embroidery and other domestic crafts, and supposedly 'natural' aptitude for detailed handiwork, gives them an advantage over men in tasks requiring high levels of manual dexterity and accuracy; women are also supposedly more passive – willing to accept authority and less likely to become involved in labour conflicts. Finally, women have the added advantage of 'natural disposability' – when they leave to get married or have children, a factory temporarily cutting back on production simply freezes their posts, thereby avoiding the burden of making compulsory redundancies (Elson and Pearson, 1981; Iglesias, 1985; Safa, 1981).

However, despite this trend towards the absorption of women into world market factories, women's involvement in formally registered work is more often in the service sector, even in areas where export processing has raised the overall participation of women in industrial employment. For example, of all urban women employed in Indonesia in 1980, only 17 per cent were engaged in industry compared with 76 per cent in services. Proportions are similar in Mexico where data for 1973 indicate that 74 per cent of urban women were involved in services, compared with only 23 per cent in industry. In Pakistan in 1973, when only 9 per cent of urban women were employed, the pattern was still the same, with 22 per cent of all employed urban women working in industry and 70 per cent in the service sector (UNCHS, 1985).

Women in services

Services cover a far wider range of *scales* of activity than industry and therefore statistics are less reliable because they often fail to record small-scale operations. Formal sector services also cover different *types* of activity, ranging from construction, commerce, transport, finance, government, and personal and social services. Therefore, at the aggregate level, statistics are perhaps not particularly useful in the analysis of gender and urban occupations, especially as certain service jobs such as government activities and retail distribution are found in rural areas. However, after first considering global variations in women's share of service employment, we shall then attempt to identify the most common occupations for women within the service sector in Third World cities.

Latin American and Southeast Asian women have highest rates of participation in services in the Third World, and make up between 30 and 50 per cent of the total labour force engaged in tertiary activities. In certain West African countries as well, such as Nigeria and Ghana, women represent over 50 per cent of the workforce in services, although in most of sub-Saharan Africa, rates are under 30 per cent. In North Africa and the Middle East, less than 10 per cent of the population employed in services is female. South Asia also displays low levels of women's participation in the service sector at under 20 per cent of the total (Townsend and Momsen, 1987).

In spite of regional variations, there are certain general patterns in the types of service jobs men and women undertake. For example, men tend to dominate construction, transport and finance, although there *are* a few exceptions: for example about 25 per cent of the construction workers in the city of Chiang Mai, Thailand are women (Singhanetra-Renard, 1984). Many women in India are also employed on construction sites where they commonly work up to the ninth month of pregnancy and even to the last day before child-birth (Mukhopadhyay, 1984). However, commerce appears to be the branch of the service sector in which women are most heavily involved. In Indonesia, for example, 45 per cent of all urban women employed in services in 1980 were engaged in wholesale and retail commerce, restaurants and hotels. In Mexico in 1970, nearly one-quarter of urban women in services were employed in the same activities (UNCHS, 1985).

Another important branch of formal service employment for women is in government and public services; 50 per cent of urban women in Indonesia were employed in these services in 1980 and 72 per cent of Mexican urban women (UNCHS, 1985). In Vietnam in 1980, 42.2 per cent of all government workers were women (White, 1981).

As far as clerical occupations are concerned, Third World women are less well represented than they are in industrialized countries. For example, while 30–40 per cent of the clerical labour force is composed of women in Latin America and Southeast Asia, in places like India, office work is regarded as a 'masculine' occupation and women only fill 6 per cent of all clerical positions (Townsend and Momsen, 1987).

However, in general, figures on women's tertiary employment should be interpreted with some caution, since as we have already pointed out, several service activities do not actually enter the net of official data collection, particularly part-time, casual or personal service jobs such as domestic service. One reason for under-recording in this latter case is that employers may not declare that they have a cleaning lady or live-in servant in order to avoid paying social security contributions (where these apply). Nevertheless in-depth case studies of specific cities often indicate that domestic service is a major employer of women; in Querétaro, Mexico for example, a sample survey of three low-income communities showed that 70 per cent of all women household heads engaged in services were domestic servants (Chant, 1987a). In a sense domestic service has 'semi-formal' status since it involves waged employment, usually for women who themselves or through their husbands belong to the 'formal' urban economy. However, since a domestic job is not usually accompanied by an official labour contract, or recorded in labour statistics, it is probably more appropriately described as 'informal' rather than 'formal' (Butterworth and Chance, 1981); as such it will also be discussed in our following section on women's informal employment. The problem of classifying domestic service highlights some of the more general difficulties associated with drawing boundaries between the informal and formal sectors.

Perhaps one major point, to be taken up later in the chapter but worthy of mention at this stage, is that age is often a critical determinant of women's access to different sectors of the labour market. On the whole, the formal sector tends to employ young, single women, generally between the ages of 15 and 25; older married women, on the other hand, are usually forced into the informal sector (Drakakis-Smith, 1987; Heyzer, 1981; Moser and Young, 1981). Older women are not only less likely to be taken on formal sector occupations because of discrimination by employers who prefer recruiting young single girls in the belief that they are more reliable or hardworking, but also because their increased domestic responsibilities make it very difficult for them to engage in full-time work away from the home, unless the composition of their households is such that they may delegate their domestic chores to an older child or to an adult relative. In a sense then we can say that the formal sector is, in many cases, only a transient employer of a minority of women. As Drakakis-Smith (1987, p.80) suggests:

Female participation in the formal wage economy . . . tends to be unstable, short-lived and poorly-paid. It can in no sense be considered to constitute a step-up in the urban socio-economic system. After marriage women often move into the even more unstable condition of petty commodity production.

Women and Informal Employment

Turning now to informal or petty commodity activities in urban areas, here women figure far more prominently than in the formal sector. As stated previously, the informal sector includes a wide range of activities which fall outside the boundaries of social and labour legislation. Informal sector workers include those who own or participate in small-scale manufacturing or commercial concerns, self-employed workers such as itinerant tradespersons, garbage-pickers or stallholders, or people engaged in personal services such as laundrywomen, seamstresses or domestic servants. Many of these informal activities involve more women than men. In Belo Horizonte, Brazil, half of all women workers are self-employed compared to only one-fifth of their male counterparts (Schmink, 1986). It was also established for the same city that 85 per cent of all female household heads were engaged in informal economic activities compared to only 25 per cent of male heads (Merrick and Schmink, 1983).

Wages in informal sector employment vary widely but a common feature of most informal jobs is that profits or earnings are irregular. In cases such as domestic service, wages might be regular, but are still well below the average minimum salary for formal sector workers. Hours in most informal jobs are also highly variable and not always directly related to earnings; for example, ambulant traders in tourist areas of Mexico may see their sales drop by half in the low season, even though they spend the same amount of time working in winter and summer (Chant, 1991).

Throughout the Third World, there is considerable similarity in the areas of informal sector work that women do. First, their activities are usually situated within or very near the home, and second, they tend to be closely associated with the routine domestic activities of women, such as the preparation of food and drink, cleaning, washing, serving, child-care or sexual services (Drakakis-Smith, 1987; Elmendorf, 1977; IBG, 1984; Papanek, 1976). The domestic location of much informal economic activity is a major reason why women have greater access to income-generating opportunities here as opposed to the formal sector. Being tied to the home as mothers and housewives renders women far less flexible and mobile than men, hence they are more likely to be able to tailor their reproductive labour load to a household-based activity than one away from the home (Gilbert and Gugler, 1982; Smith, 1981). When women are unable to pursue informal kinds of income-generation in or near their houses, they opt for jobs where hours are short or flexible, and/or to which they can take their children. In West Africa, for example, where marketing has traditionally been a female occupation and usually involves working from centrally-located market stalls, flexibility of hours and baby-sitting by other market women allows them to combine their productive and reproductive activities (Peil and Sada, 1984; Sudarkasa, 1973).

While the above characteristics of informal employment could be construed as advantageous to women, it is unlikely that their involvement in this kind of work is always governed by choice; in many cases they may wish to enter the formal sector, but are unable to do so because of a lack of education, skills, training and/or insufficient state provision of socialized child-care facilities.

Furthermore, *within* the informal sector itself, there appears to be a further manifestation of the sexual division of labour, with women not only being confined to certain types of jobs, particularly those that are household-based or associated with their traditional domestic skills, but also ones with least status and lowest pay (Chant, 1984a). For example, female traders in many areas such as Mexico, Ecuador and northern Nigeria are prevented by their domestic duties and/or male authority from venturing out of their houses, meaning that their profits in commerce are usually far less than those of men who have a wider market because they may move more freely around the city (Chant, 1987a; Hill, 1969; Moser, 1981). In Kano, Nigeria, because of seclusion, women traders often use their children as intermediaries (Schildkrout, 1978, 1983). Even where women are engaged in street work, they tend to be confined to less profitable, riskier activities than their male counterparts (Bromley, 1982). Amongst the Yoruba of Nigeria, Simi Afonja (1981) notes how there is a clear division in trading, with women generally selling subsistence goods in the open market or from small retail shops, whereas men tend to deal with more valuable consumer products and to own larger stores. In Lima, Peru, low-income women earn only about half the wages of men in their class (Ennew, 1986). The sexual divisions common in formal sector work are thus replicated in the informal sector, with opportunities in the latter often just as restricted as in the former.

In Maseru, Lesotho, for example, migrant women are so disadvantaged with respect to employment opportunities that they are often forced into illegal informal activities such as starting a *shebeen* for the illicit brewing and sale of beer, or into prostitution (Wilkinson, 1987). These activities are also common in low-income settlements in Nairobi, Kenya, where several women brew *buzaa* (maize beer) and have occasional commerical sex with wealthy urban males to supplement their income (Nelson, 1979b). In Katsina City, Nigeria, many single women become *kurawai* (courtesans) and take up residence in a *gidan mata* (house of women) where they support themselves wholly or partially by gifts and payments made for sexual favours (Pittin, 1983). In Bangkok, young female migrants find they can earn seven to eight times as much by working in a massage parlour (which may or may not be a cover for prostitution), than working as a housemaid; since Thai girls often work to support their impoverished rural families, economic pressure and absence of alternative income opportunities turns them towards the sex trade

(Phongpaichit, 1984). Even in countries such as Nicaragua, where prostitution was made illegal within a month of the Sandinista revolution, demand for commoditized sex continues, and in the absence of comparably lucrative alternatives, the activity is still financially attractive for women (Deighton et al., 1983).

Women who are married or have a resident male partner are less likely to be able to engage in prostitution because of male control and surveillance. However, there are several other activities to which they may turn. The preparation and sale of homemade foodstuffs and fruit juices is a common informal occupation for women in Mexico, as are activities such as taking in washing, sewing, or selling sweets and soft drinks from the front room of their shanty dwellings (Arizpe, 1977; Chant, 1987a). In La Paz, Bolivia, women are very actively involved in a range of informal income-earning strategies such as stitching and carding alpaca garments, making wall-hangings and coverlets, and baking bread, cakes and pastries (Beuchler, 1986). In Windhoek, Namibia, low-income women, as their counterparts in other African countries, not only brew beer but also engage in basket-weaving, doll-making and hawking food products (Simon, 1984). In Madras, India, low-caste *Adi-Dravida* women who have been abandoned by their husbands, enter private homes as housemaids where they have to do what is regarded socially as 'defiling work' such as cleaning bathrooms (Caplan, 1985). In Southeast Asian cities women prepare and sell food, take in laundry or charge a fee for looking after other people's children (Drakakis-Smith, 1987).

One obvious conclusion from the above examples of female informal employment is that women demonstrate a considerable resilience and imagination in coping with urban poverty. They often utilize their available time and labour to the full to earn what is usually only a meagre income, but one which helps to maintain their families at or just above subsistence level. However, they are persistently thwarted in their attempts to rise to an equal status with men in the urban labour market by factors ranging from discrimination by employers, to the demands of their domestic roles, and to the attitudes of husbands and fathers who are unwilling to come to terms with female economic independence or autonomy. In the latter half of this chapter we attempt to give an overview of the reasons why women continue to have secondary status within the urban labour market.

EXPLAINING WOMEN'S POSITION IN THIRD WORLD URBAN LABOUR MARKETS

Women's generally subordinate position in the urban labour markets of developing countries is conditioned by a host of different factors (see Scott, 1986b, for a fuller, theoretical discussion). Although it is rather arbitrary to separate out and classify these different influences, broadly speaking the reasons which to date have prevented women from gaining access to male-dominated spheres of employment and from attaining equality of working conditions and wages with the men of their class may be grouped into three main categories. The first set of factors relates to culture and ideology as they influence the normative roles to be played by men and women in a given society. A second set of factors relates to the nature of women's domestic role and a range of practical constraints operating at the level of the household which make it difficult for women to enter the labour market on the same basis as men. The third, and final set of factors relates to the actions and attitudes of employers and the state, who commonly tailor their recruitment practices to the broad requirements of capital accumulation. These may be referred to collectively as the legal or institutional framework of labour relations.

The Role of Culture and Ideology in Influencing Women's Labour

Culture, ideology and gender roles in various regions of the Third World have been discussed in several places in the book (Chapters 1 and 2, for example), so only brief consideration will be made here of their influences on urban female labour force participation.

As we noted earlier, a sexual division of labour by which women have primary responsibility for 'reproductive' work is common throughout the Third World from Latin America, to North Africa to the Middle East, through South and Southeast Asia, the only major exceptions being the Caribbean, and sub-Saharan and particularly West Africa where women do not expect nor want to be dependent upon men, and spend a great deal of time in economic activity (Fapohunda, 1983; Ware, 1983). Nevertheless, even here, women also play a far greater role than men in household management, child-care and domestic labour (Afonja, 1981; Westwood, 1984). These norms are often equally strong in urban as in rural areas and have obvious implications for women's entry into the labour force both from the point of view of supply and demand.

As far as 'supply' is concerned, when the major focus of adult women's roles is child-care and housework, female employment is usually regarded by men and indeed sometimes by women themselves, as peripheral and/or undesirable. The social and cultural importance attached to normative gender roles is such that women are sometimes prevented from working altogether, or at least are channelled into jobs which may be undertaken in conjunction with their domestic responsibilities. Since women are rarely encouraged to invest a great deal of time and effort in waged work or self-employment, it is likely they will opt for part-time work and/or that which is as near to home as possible. It is also usually the case that the content of women's jobs is closely related to their domestic and child-rearing tasks; training for other kinds of employment is viewed as pointless when women's primary allegiance is to the home.

As far as 'demand' is concerned, cultural stereotypes of gender roles are incorporated into the production process itself, influencing employers' attitudes towards the kinds of jobs which are practically, morally and ideologically 'appropriate' for female workers, and frequently resulting in a marked hierarchy of employment along gender lines. 'Supply' and 'demand' factors are undoubtedly inter-related to a very large degree, and as Alison MacEwen Scott (1986a, p.183) points out: 'The gender embeddedness of the division of labour is . . . an outcome of the wider structure of gender inequality and of the institutional linkages which shape the divisions of labour.' Therefore, in the following sections which look more specifically at micro- and macro-level factors, it is important to bear in mind the overarching role played by culture and ideology in determining women's employment patterns.

Women's Domestic Roles and Entry into the Labour Force

Various aspects of women's life at the level of the household contribute to influencing whether or not they enter the labour force, and, if they do, the kinds of jobs they look for. Key issues include age and position within the family unit, educational levels. and male control.

Age and marital status

As we pointed out earlier in the chapter, age and marital status are often critical determinants of women's labour force participation, and evidence from many countries shows that young, single women are far more likely to have paid work than older married women (Jelin, 1980). In Morocco, for exampie, in 1971 21 per cent of urban women between the ages of 15 and 24 were employed, compared to an average of 15 per cent of women between the ages of 25 and 44; in Korea in 1975, 48 per cent of urban women aged 15–24 were employed, compared to 25 per cent of those between 25 and 44; comparable figures for Turkey in 1970 were 15 per cent and 12 per cent respectively (UNCHS, 1985). In Mexico in 1970, 60 per cent of all economically active women were aged between 15 and 29 (LACWE, 1980). Evidently, young single women, or young married women without children, are freer to engage in waged work than those who havc to take charge of housework and child-care. They are also less subject to social taboos. For example, in Malaysia, Islamic women are prevented from taking a job unless they have permission from their husbands and their jobs do not in any way disrupt family life (Siraj, 1984).

At the other end of the spectrum, older widowed and divorced women also have high rates of labour force participation (Youssef, 1982). In Morocco, for example, while married women are frequently discouraged from taking waged employment, abandoned, widowed and divorced women show high rates of economic activity (Joekes, 1985). In Latin American cities, where the incidence of non-marriage and separation is far higher than in North Africa, women's labour force participation tends to be high throughout the life-cycle, except between the ages of 25 and 34 when they are likely to be living with a man (Youssef, 1972).

Notwithstanding regional variations in activity rates in different age groups, we noted earlier that young and older women are likely to enter distinct areas of the urban labour market; increased age is usually associated with a progressive withdrawal and/or exclusion from the formal sector.

Skills and education

Women's relative lack of skills and education is another important factor contributing to their subordinate position in the urban labour force, particularly in terms of access to formal sector work. In most countries in the Third World, female literacy rates and educational levels lag far behind those of men; in 1980, for example, 48.5 per cent of Third World women over fifteen years were illiterate, compared to 32.3 per cent of men (Townsend and Momsen, 1987). While differentials between male and female literacy and educational qualifications tend to be narrowing in urban areas, they are still significant, and lack of education often debars women from some of the better-paid jobs in the urban labour market. In Ghana, for example, although there is a relatively high proportion of girls attending primary school (44 per cent of all school attenders between 1965 and 1975), the number of girls in education fall dramatically at secondary and higher levels (26 per cent between 1970 and 1975); this is significant since it is through higher education that access to the best jobs is achieved (ECA, 1984).

The reasons that men generally have higher educational standards than women relate very much to the sexual division of labour and women's domestic roles. Despite the fact that boys are sometimes needed for farm work, thereby freeing their sisters for school attendance, in most cases girls receive less education than their brothers because it is thought they will end up as wives and mothers and therefore have less need of a formal education (Huston, 1979); this perpetuates the constraints on women's access to work. Nevertheless, even where women are educated to the same level as men, and have access to the same jobs, equality of education 'does not appear to be a sufficient condition for equality of pay' (Anker and Hein, 1986, p.34).

Male control of women's activities

Resistance of husbands and fathers to women working is a final major household-level constraint on the supply of women in the urban labour market. In Latin America, Islamic and South Asian countries for example, despite the fact that extra income is frequently needed by low-income families, men often prevent their wives and daughters from taking jobs. In part this is a question of pride which itself stems from wider cultural and ideological prescriptions. Un- or under-employed men may feel their role of provider is undermined if women begin to contribute to the household budget (Boyle, 1986). In certain countries, such as Mexico, it also relates to male fear that if their wives go out to work, their greater mobility will lead to sexual infidelity (de Barbieri, 1982; Chant, 1987a). In the

Middle East, similar fears about women's potential sexual misconduct encourage men to confine their wives and daughters to the home (Youssef, 1972). In Kano, Nigeria, where Hausa women are secluded after marriage and there is considerable control by husbands over their wives' mobility, women traders are rarely seen in the open market and instead have to set up stalls in their own neighbourhoods (Schildkrout, 1983). In Malaysia, even where Islamic women are allowed out to work in factories, they have to wear loose clothing which covers their limbs and disguises the shape of their bodies (Siraj, 1984). Male insecurity about their wives' involvement in the labour force often means that women are prevented from earning an income at all (Ennew, 1986). The desire to confine women to hearth and home is also a contributory factor to the great majority of women's income-generating work being household-based (Moser, 1981). However, June Nash and Helen Safa (1980) stress that although men often appear to be the most direct oppressors of women, the real source of oppression lies in the structure of the capitalist system, which has a vested interest in maintaining sexual as well as social divisions in the labour force.

The Legal-institutional Framework of Women's Labour Force Participation

Before discussing how the actions of employers and the state influence women's labour force participation in cities, it is important to note some general ways in which capitalism benefits from women's culturally prescribed roles in the structuring of the labour force.

A major advantage of women's roles for capital is that they may be paid less in the workplace than men. Their position in the family as mothers and housewives is often used as a justification for the fact that their earnings are not as central to family welfare as those of the putative male breadwinner; thus, as secondary earners they do not need as large a wage (Heyzer, 1981; Holstrom, 1981). The idea of the 'family wage' by which men have fought for a wage large enough to support their dependants (wives as well as children) is critical here (see Barrett and McIntosh, 1982; Bryceson, 1985).

Capital also benefits from women's family role through the fact that female labour arguably sustains and reproduces the workforce

more cheaply than if capital or the state was to provide essential
social and domestic services such as cooking, cleaning and child-care
– a point we shall return to in more depth in Chapter 8. Women also
provide certain functions that cannot be provided by capital such as
emotional and psychological support to male breadwinners (Jones,
1984; Blumenfeld and Mann, 1980; Seccombe, 1980). In addition,
'housewives' constitute a large reserve of labour that may be drawn
out of the domestic sector in periods of expanded production and/or
labour shortages (Briskin, 1980; Nash and Safa, 1980).

A third way in which capital benefits from the subordinate
position of women is that sexual divisions within the household are
seen to complement class divisions in society. Several authors have
argued that patriarchy aligns male members of society with those in
control of the means of production (Eisenstein, 1979). The fact that
men may exert power and authority within the domestic unit
supposedly compensates for their relative lack of power within the
workplace (Gardiner, 1979; Gissi, 1980; Sacks, 1974). Following the
same line of reasoning, if men are accorded superior status to women
within the labour market itself, the essential verticality of power
relations, and thus the social and political status quo is maintained.
As Alison MacEwen Scott (1986a:157) points out, 'occupational
segregation may be the major mechanism through which gender
affects stratification. It should therefore be considered a central
rather than an incidental aspect of economic inequality.' While
many of the above arguments are speculative and/or based on the
experience of the West, their basic tenets seem to be borne out by the
actions of employers and the state apparatus in many parts of the
developing world.

Dealing with the legislative framework first, in many countries
such as Tanzania and Nigeria, there are *no* laws which guarantee
equal opportunities in employment, and sexual discrimination is
often extremely blatant (Bryceson, 1985; Pittin, 1984). In certain
cases, legislation is even *explicitly sexist*. In Mauritius, for example,
the government has actually established different minimum male
and female wage rates, with women's rates of pay only around half
those of men (Hein, 1986). In Puerto Rico during the 1930s, the
government responded to trade union pressure to curb a mammoth
rise in women's industrial employment by granting preferential
subsidies to firms employing men (Pico, cited in Nash, 1983).
Exclusionary practices by male-dominated trade unions are often

equally important today: in Morocco for example, women's access to certain branches of industrial employment is severely limited by restrictive union policies (Joekes, 1985).

Even where principles of equal pay for equal work and equality of opportunity are officially enshrined in labour law, other forms of legislation often exclude women from key jobs in the formal sector. This is particularly true of laws which are designed to 'protect' women. In Mexico, for example, women are legally barred from doing night work or from undertaking activities which are unduly 'dangerous' or 'arduous' (Canton Moller, 1974; Cobos, 1974; Gonzalez, 1980). In Morocco, prohibition of female night shifts has excluded women from many branches of industry and in others has reserved far greater numbers of jobs for men (Joekes, 1985). These findings display parallels with nineteenth-century Britain, where successive Acts of Parliament restricted the recruitment of women workers in factories and mines on the grounds that it was prejudicial to their health, well-being and ability to carry out domestic duties (Barrett and McIntosh, 1982). While gender-specific protective labour legislation may of course be viewed as desirable in the light of women's weaker physical constitution, it is also important to remember that it usually embodies an implicit moral prescription that women's primary role is to attend to their families. It is also not insignificant that by keeping the numbers of women in industry down, male jobs are thus protected. While the comparative cheapness of women workers may pose a threat to men, legislation requiring the compulsory provision of crêche facilities in factories employing a certain number of women, or paid maternity leave, ensures that their costs are kept high, notwithstanding the fact that several employers do not adhere to these stipulations anyway (LACWE, 1980; Peil and Sada, 1984).

Some of the most radical changes in the legal framework for sexual equality in the labour force have taken place in socialist countries. In Vietnam, for example, equal rights in pay, employment opportunities, and the guaranteed provision of paid maternity leave and crêches have all been written into the state constitution (White, 1981). In Nicaragua, domestic service which has long been a woman's job and unprotected by any form of legislation is now being brought under the control of the state; with the support of the Nicaraguan women's federation, AMNLAE, domestic servants have now become unionized and have managed to reduce their working hours to 10 per day, even though ideally this should be 8, in line with other service workers (Deighton et al., 1983). In Cuba, women not only receive 18 weeks' paid maternity leave, as opposed to a global average of 12, but also the Cuban Family Code stresses that men should share equally in the tasks of housework and child-care; that is, the state recognizes that labour legislation for women alone is not effective but also needs to be complemented by a more egalitarian division of labour in the home. The state has also provided socialized child-care facilities and other services to support families with working women (Communist Party of Cuba, 1981; Stone, 1981). These changes have undoubtedly contributed to the fact that women's share of the Cuban labour force has risen from only 9.8 per cent in 1959 to 32 per cent in 1980, however there is still a long way to go before sexual divisions are eradicated completely (Stone, 1981).

Turning back to the majority of developing economies which operate under a capitalist system, we noted how employers often respond to gender-specific labour legislation by ignoring the law, or avoiding their legal commitments by employing men instead of women. On top of this employers also have their own internal and/ or personal code of practice relating to the recruitment of male and female labour. Here *assumptions* about women are of critical importance. As we noted earlier in the chapter, male employers frequently *assume* that women do not have the technical or educational skills necessary for certain types of mechanical work (Bryceson, 1985; Saffioti, 1986). They also imagine that women are less reliable, less dedicated to their work, and more likely to leave on marriage or childbirth, even though this is often not the case in practice (e.g. Humphrey, 1985; Joekes, 1985). Even where a female workforce is *actively* sought, as in world market factories, the rationale for so doing derives from a set of dubiously 'worthy' assumptions about women: passivity, a capacity to undertake monotonous, repetitive tasks, a willingness to defer to authority and lack of interest in political/union activities (Elson and Pearson, 1981; Harris, 1983; Humphrey, 1985; Iglesias, 1985).

Employers' attitudes therefore interact with state legislation, the domestic circumstances of women and patriarchal culture to force women into the least remunerative and least prestigious corners of the urban labour market. In addition, once certain areas of employment became 'feminized', that is have become dominated by women, they tend to lose their status and are usually transformed into low-paid, low-prestige occupations (Phillips, 1983; White, 1981).

CONCLUSION

In this chapter we have sought to describe and explain women's involvement in urban production. In most Third World cities, women have a very limited range of employment opportunities compared with men, and face severe constraints in overcoming their 'marginalization' in the labour market. One major reason for this phenomenon is the fact that they are forced by culture, the state and their families into spending the greater amount of their time in reproductive activities such as domestic labour and child-care. In the following chapter we look more closely at what these and other aspects of reproduction entail for women in the urban environments of the developing world.

NOTES

1. In reality women's labour force participation is likely to be far higher due to their heavy involvement in unregistered informal occupations.
2. Apprenticeships involve no recognizable formal qualifications and are based on on-the-job training over a number of years. Once an apprenticeship is deemed to have ended (usually with the payment of money to the master), new craftspersons set up on their own (see Verdon, 1979).

8 Gender and Reproduction in Urban Areas

In this chapter three aspects of reproduction are discussed: health care, housing and urban services, all of which represent vital components of household survival in Third World cities and in which women play an extremely important role. Just as the sexual division of labour common in most developing societies assigns men the primary role in production or the direct generation of income, it assigns women the primary responsibility for reproduction, or unwaged activities contributing to the maintenance and welfare of household members. A key difference between rural and urban reproduction is that state intervention plays a far greater role in social welfare in the city than it does in the countryside where as we noted in Chapter 2, many essential reproductive functions are the responsibility of rural families themselves. Although we concentrate primarily in this chapter on selected aspects of urban reproduction, we by no means ignore the rural context, especially in the field of health care, an issue which clearly cross-cuts the urban–rural divide.

Reproduction occupies an ambivalent position in the priorities of Third World governments. On the one hand, developing states have few resources to expend on welfare: faced with a choice of investing in production or reproduction they tend to opt for the former as a means of increasing levels of economic growth. On the other hand, governments must also ensure that the labour force is reproduced at a level sufficient to ensure the continued productivity of workers and to head off political crisis (Roberts, 1978). However sheer lack of resources often means that reproduction is forced to the back of the queue after industrial investment, debt-servicing, defence expenditure and so on; as a consequence, commitment of Third World governments to social expenditure is generally small. For example, in the Latin American region in 1985, only 2.7 per cent of Gross Domestic Product in the Dominican Republic was spent on health, education, social security, housing and other social services; this figure was only 2.2 per cent in Haiti and as low as 2.0 per cent in Guatemala. Even in richer countries such as Mexico and Argentina, investment in social expenditure was only 3.5 per cent and 5.9 per cent respectively in the same year (IDB, 1987, p.64). In the face of this performance, governments implicitly endorse and indeed rely upon the activities of private individuals to reproduce the workforce. Given their responsibilities as mothers and housewives, it is women who usually have to provide essential services for which public finance cannot or will not be found. Because this work is regarded as an extension of their domestic labour – an unwaged activity – women's work enables the state to make substantial savings in social expenditure, and to an extent absolves it of the responsibility for providing economic and infrastructural support for reproduction.

The main objective of this chapter is to examine how state actions interrelate with and capitalize upon women's domestic activities to secure the effective reproduction of the labour force, and to identify the conflicts and contradictions arising from this essentially exploitative set of relations.

GENDER AND HEALTH CARE

The provision of health care in developing countries is usually far from adequate. Investment in health services by Third World governments is rarely more than a minute fraction of GDP, and in 1985, for example, only amounted to 1.0 per cent in the Dominican Republic, 0.7 per cent in Guatemala and 0.3 per cent in Mexico (IDB, 1987, p.68). Although a few countries such as Ghana, and socialist states such as Nicaragua and Cuba, have fairly comprehensive public health programmes, in most places, lack of state provision forces the majority of the population to the private sector, whose services are frequently too costly for low-income groups.[1] Moreover, both state and private medicine tends to be oriented towards cure rather than prevention (Pearson, 1987; Ward, 1987). Citing World Bank data for the mid-1970s, Margaret Hardiman and James Midgley (1982, pp.172–3) draw attention to the fact that in Kenya, El Salvador, Paraguay, Tunisia and Tanzania, over 80 per cent of public health resources are devoted to curative services. The above features make most health systems highly inappropriate for those whose living conditions condemn them to constant risk of disease and malnutrition. Chronic underprovision of inexpensive, preventive public health care is in part offset by the fact that women, in their capacity as wives, mothers and/or carers of dependent kin, take on a range of activities which cushion their families from the worst excesses of government neglect. Women not only tend the sick and aged in the absence of alternatives, but also play a major role in keeping illness at bay in the first place, through their struggle to maintain minimum levels of hygiene in the face of inadequate shelter provision and a lack of essential urban services. In this sense, women's labour is a critical, but unacknowledged resource for the state.

Since disease prevention is so closely associated with the nature of infrastructure and services to be discussed in detail later in the chapter, we shall concentrate on only two aspects of health at this stage; medical care in general, and birth control. These two issues illustrate the generally contradictory position of the state regarding health provision for low-income groups. On the one hand, governments frequently fail to provide the basic means by which the urban poor may be assured of adequate disease prevention or medical care, whereas on the other, it pours huge sums of money into birth control campaigns. Population control programmes are frequently promoted under the banner of an ostensible commitment to improving maternal and child health, where their latent objectives are clearly to solve potential political crises arising from social and economic inequality which population expansion both highlights and intensifies (see Bondestam, 1982, for a fuller discussion of the political ideology of birth control). Not surprisingly the shortcomings of health systems in general often present a major block to the introduction of specific contraception programmes; persistently high rates of infant mortality in several countries are a major reason for the rejection of family planning.

Since birth control represents intervention by the state at the most basic, physiological level of reproduction, we shall first commence with a discussion of tensions and contradictions engendered in the sphere of family planning, both in national territories as a whole as well as more specifically in cities, and then go on to examine health care in general.

Women and Family Planning

One major reason for continued population increase in the developing world is the maintenance of high birth-rates in both rural and urban areas. While fertility rates in cities tend to be slightly lower than in the countryside the effect is offset by the fact that mortality rates are also lower in the former, often by a substantial margin (see Pryer and Crook, 1988). In addition, massive urbanward migration means that most Third World cities are growing at a rate of 3–5 per cent per annum compared with overall national population growth rates of 2–3 per cent (Gilbert and Gugler, 1982). In Brazil, for example, the numbers of people in urban areas leaped from 46 per cent of the national population in 1960, to 65 per cent in 1980; in the Republic of Korea, 55 per cent of the population was urban in 1980 compared with only 28 per cent in 1960, and in the Ivory Coast 38 per cent of the population was urban by 1980 compared with only 19 per cent in 1960 (ibid., pp.6–7).

High rates of urban population growth are a source of considerable concern to Third World governments; not only do they exert pressure on scarce employment and shelter, but they also constitute a starkly visible reminder that the benefits of economic development are reaching comparatively few. Urban labour surpluses produced both by demographic growth and rural out-migration are argued to be far in excess of what is needed to keep wage costs low enough for industry and services to be profitable, and the inability or unwillingness of Third World governments to invest in intermediate technology or labour-intensive forms of industrial manufacturing places the prospects of absorbing increasing urban populations into the productive structure out of reach.

Governments have seen family planning programmes as a way of alleviating the problem of rapid urban population growth and its attendant potential for social and political unrest. Investment in this field has often come from international development agencies, First World governments, and in particular from a range of official and unofficial bodies in the United States (Dickenson et al., 1983; Singh, 1979). Over the last decade in particular, overseas aid for development as a whole has fallen, while funds specifically tied to the expansion of family planning programmes have increased (Drakakis-Smith, 1987). Indeed up to 50 per cent of all population pro-

grammes in developing countries are supported by foreign aid
(Seager and Olson, 1986). The progressive concentration of
resources in population control has no doubt partially contributed to
a decline in the global crude birth-rate from 36.3 per thousand to
28.5 per thousand between 1950 and 1980, and to an overall drop in
population growth rates from 2 per cent per annum in the 1960s, to
1.7 per cent in 1980 (United Nations, 1981). Although global
averages mask disparities between advanced economies and developing countries (the latter on average experience annual national
growth rates of around 2 per cent), the intensification of a commitment to reducing birth-rates has resulted in the establishment of
some form of population control programme in most areas of the
Third World in recent years, and family planning is recognized as
playing a major role in reducing birth-rates alongside other factors
such as increased life expectancy, rising literacy levels and an overall
decline in infant mortality rates, all of which, to a degree, are
associated with economic development (Zaman, 1980).

So far, birth-control programmes have been almost universally
directed at women which presents a cruel and revealing paradox: at
the same time as women are encouraged to remain in the home to
prevent them from swelling the ranks of the un- and underemployed,
and/or to solve problems of inadequate welfare provision, the very
basis of their *raison d'être* in this sphere, motherhood, is being
undermined (see also Chapter 2). As Nash and Safa (1980:26) point
out, 'women . . . being told to have fewer children . . . further
negates their domestic role.'

However, the success of most birth-control programmes in the
Third World to date has been severely hampered by a series of
problems, many of which relate to the conditions of economic
development and welfare provision in general.

Obstacles to the Implementation of Family Planning Programmes

High infant mortality
One major reason for resistance to birth control is that infant
mortality continues to be high in many parts of the developing
world. The death rate is 82 per thousand live births in Kenya and 200
per thousand live births in Sierra Leone, compared with only 10.5 in
countries such as the United States (Helmore, 1986). In poor Third

World communities 10–25 per cent of children die in their first year of life, and 25–33 per cent before they reach five years of age (Pryer and Crook, 1988). High mortality is often related to a lack of protein in the diet of low-income groups, especially in Africa and South Asia (Mountjoy, 1980; Pryer and Crook, 1988). In Niger, Mali and Burkina Faso, average calories available per capita in the early 1970s were less than four-fifths of the estimated requirement, compared to an excess of one-third in the United States, the USSR and most of Europe (Kidron and Segal, 1981). High infant mortality is also linked with the comparatively poor health and nutrition of mothers. Severely malnourished and/or anaemic women are not only likely to deliver low birth weight infants who are vulnerable to death and disease, but are also likely to have lactational deficiencies which also increase the risk of mortality (Pryer and Crook, 1988). In Bangladesh, for example, only 49 per cent of pregnancies actually result in a live birth (MacCormack, 1983). Thus in order to ensure that families are not left childless, people continue to have several children in the hope that some will survive (Hartmann, 1987). Of course there are other reasons for having large numbers of children: in countries such as India and Nepal, for example, sons are considered more prestigious than daughters and women may continue bearing children until a boy is born (Kishwar and Vanita, 1984; Pearson, 1987), although Jack Goody (1976) also notes that in areas where land is scarce, men often try to control the number of male heirs they produce (see Chapter 2). Nevertheless, the spectre of still-birth or infant death is still a significant reason for unwillingness to adopt contraceptive practices.

Infant mortality is generally lower in urban than in rural areas, probably accounting for the fact that family planning programmes are usually deployed more effectively in cities than in the countryside (Drakakis-Smith, 1987). In India in 1979, the urban infant mortality rate was only 69 per thousand live births compared to 139 per thousand in rural areas; in Mexico in 1976–77 the rates were 79 and 97 respectively; and in Iraq in 1975 the rates were 75 and 98 (Gilbert and Gugler, 1982, p.53; see also Pryer and Crook, 1988).

In socialist countries rural–urban differentials in infant mortality rates are narrower, and mortality in general is also lower. For example, in Cuba between 1973 and 1975, the urban infant mortality rate was 26 per thousand, and the rural rate, 31 per thousand (Gilbert and Gugler, 1982, p.53). Life expectancy in Cuba in 1980 was also comparatively high, at 69 for men and 72 for women, about ten years more than some of its neighbours such as the Dominican Republic where rates were 58 and 62 years respectively (Kidron and Segal, 1984). Long life expectancy in Cuba reflects a hugh commitment of investment in health and social welfare and indicates the extent to which mortality levels hinge upon the deployment of public resources in the reproductive sector. In 1981 there were between 401 and 600 hospital beds per 100,000 persons in Cuba, compared to 200 or less in many other developing countries such as Mexico, Colombia, Niger, India, Burma and the Philippines (Kidron and Segal, 1984).

Male control of women's fertility

Another reason for resistance to family planning programmes in the Third World stems from male control over women's fertility. There are two dimensions to this issue. The first is that in many countries a large family is proof of male virility. Second, and perhaps more fundamentally, women's ability to control their own reproductive behaviour smacks of self-determination and freedom from male authority – anathema to men in most societies (Huston, 1979). Male resistance to contraception stems from fears that it will lead to women being sexually permissive, which in turn lessens guarantees of undisputed paternity. These kinds of view have very serious consequences for women, such as physical weakness arising from successive pregnancies and lactation, which men may not appreciate given their lack of personal experience in the physiological aspects of childbirth. Moreover men are not as tied to the domestic sphere as women and may more easily escape their parental duties, consequently they do not suffer to the same extent from overcrowding in the home, a greater burden of domestic labour and the problems of managing scarce economic resources (Robertson, 1984a; Rogers, 1980). Given that men are likely to disapprove strongly of their wives practising birth control, many Indian women resort to injectable contraceptives, which though dangerous, are less traceable than other methods (Savara, 1983; see below).

Religious taboos

Another reason for failure to implement family planning programmes stems from cultural and/or religious considerations, particularly in Roman Catholic countries (Dickenson et al., 1983). For example, in Latin America where Catholicism is practised by the majority of people, the outlawing of contraceptives by the Pope is taken very seriously. In some cases such as Peru in 1977, this has involved the Church actively blocking the introduction of state population programmes (Hartmann, 1987). In other areas, resistance arises out of popular faith itself. Catholic women often stress that children are 'God-given' and are reluctant to interfere with the course of destiny. However, evidence is beginning to suggest this pattern might now be changing. For example, a recent study carried out on Aymara women in the Lake Titicaca region of Bolivia showed that young couples were tending to ignore a Roman Catholic tract which had appeared in 1975, urging people to 'denounce and personally resist all forms of birth control and to submit to the will of God and the needs of Bolivia' (cited in Benton, 1987, p.217).

Wealth flows

The idea of 'wealth flows' developed by John C. Caldwell (1976 and subsequently) also sheds light on the reasons for resisting family planning. Caldwell (1976) has argued for the rationality of the persistence of high fertility in contemporary Third World societies suggesting that average family size will only fall if people perceive that the costs to them of having a large number of children will be greater than those of having fewer children. When, over the period of the life-cycle, wealth flows from children to parents are *greater* than the parents' outlay, then there is no rationale for reducing fertility. Caldwell bases his theories firmly on empirical evidence from Nigeria, where, even if only one child in a family is educated and gains a high government position, or becomes a successful entrepreneur, then the wealth flows to the parents and the rest of the immediate family are vast and easily cover the cost of supporting other family members. Possible differences in wealth flows between rural and urban areas are followed up later in the chapter.

Problems of contraceptive promotion, delivery and methods

Another major source of resistance to birth control is the way in which family planning programmes are introduced and the methods employed. In some areas, family planning is forced upon the population; in Mymensingh, Bangladesh, for example, the army in 1983 organized a campaign of compulsory sterilization on all villagers (mainly women), with three or more children (Hartmann,

1987). Sterilization has also been foisted upon indigenous women in southern Mexico, Peru, Bolivia and other parts of Latin America by American aid organizations such as the Peace Corps, often without their knowledge, let alone their consent (Cubitt, 1988; LACWE, 1980). Sometimes measures are less obviously coercive, but none the less persuasive. In Singapore, for example, families with more than two children receive lower priority on employment, housing and education waiting lists (Drakakis-Smith, 1987); as a result, over the last twenty years Singapore's birth-rate has dropped from 45 to 16 per thousand, and its annual population growth rate has fallen from 4.0 per cent to 1.6 per cent (Dickenson et al., 1983, p.59). In Thailand, a scheme run by the Community Based Family Planning Programme offered women a piglet in return for successful spacing of pregnancies (Hartmann, 1987). In Mexico, persuasion to adopt contraception takes the form of posters prominently displayed in public places, and announcements in the media. Even in cases where family planning is theoretically voluntary, incentives or advertising are such that there is often little effective choice.

Birth-control methods offered to Third World women are generally more limited and inferior to those available in the industrialized nations. Sterilization is often promoted as a relatively cheap once-and-for-all solution to the 'problems' of high fertility. In other cases, drugs which are out-of-date or no longer used by First World Women because of dangerous side-effects are often dumped on Third World markets, or alternatively, new treatments may be 'tested out' on poor women (Savara, 1983; Sen and Grown, 1988). For example, injectable hormonal contraceptives such as *Depo-Provera*, associated with a wide range of problems including menstrual disorders, depression and risk of cancer, and prohibited in most of the West, are widely available in countries such as Thailand and El Salvador (Hartmann, 1987; Thomson, 1986).[2] Problems are also associated with other contraceptive methods which have ended up in less-developed countries, such as high-oestrogen pills, and intra-uterine devices (IUDs) such as the *Dalkon Shield* (Sen and Grown, 1988).[3] It is hardly surprising therefore that Third World women are often reluctant to use Western contraceptive methods or complain of ill-health when they do.

It is rare that family planning programmes encourage men to take precautions, and when they do, they are not likely to be successful. Except in India, where vasectomies have been performed in large 'fairs' or 'camps', and often in return for a cash reward, policies of male sterilization, or even contraception, are rarely pursued. In the Mathare Valley nutrition and family education project in Nairobi, set up by the National Christian Council of Kenya, for example, it was found that the pill and the intra-uterine device were far more popular than condoms and foams (IPPF, 1982). Nevertheless, the lack of promotion of barrier methods such as condoms is not just due to the fact that men are likely to resist contraception more than women, but also because many population agencies dislike methods which remain 'under the user's control' (Hartmann, 1987, p.32).[4]

Another reason for resistance to the introduction of Western contraception, is that traditional forms of birth control are some-times preferred or at least utilized in the absence of alternatives, even if they are sometimes not as effective or clinically safe. At one end of the spectrum this involves the use of natural medicines and methods. These may include herbal prophylactics both to prevent pregnancy and cause abortions, *coitus interruptus*, prolonged breastfeeding and post-partum abstinence (Adeokun, 1982; Bleek, 1976). In Zaire, for example, sperm is expelled by some women via a post-coital scouring of the vagina with either a tobacco-leaf concoction or natural juices; others eject it muscularly, and in some areas sperm is prevented from reaching the cervix by insertion of a rolled-up *nongo* leaf (Cutrufelli, 1983). As far as prolonged breastfeeding on demand is concerned, this is also widely practised in many developing countries, each month of continual breastfeeding being estimated to add three weeks to the interval between births (Hartmann, 1987).[5] Over 50 per cent of Pakistani women, for example, breastfeed for between one and two years in order to reduce fertility (Page et al., 1982). A period of post-partum abstinence from sexual relations is also observed in most developing countries, ranging from 1–3 months in North Africa, Latin America and the Middle East, to 10–15 months in West Africa (Singh and Ferry, 1984; but see also Adeokun, 1982). Abstinence combines with breastfeeding to extend the period between births, which is very important given that infant mortality is far higher when births are closely spaced. In Bangladesh, for example, children born within two years of a previous birth are more than twice as likely to die as those born after a two- or three-year interval (PIP, 1985).

At the other end of the spectrum of 'traditional' methods of birth control, there is infanticide and surgery by unqualified persons. In

Mexico, for example, it is estimated that over one million self-induced or 'backstreet' abortions take place each year, and of this number some 80,000 women die due to insanitary operating conditions (Chant, 1984a; Huston, 1979). In Latin America as a whole it is estimated that about half of all deaths among pregnant women are due to illegal abortion (Wells and Sim, 1987). Spontaneous or induced abortion is also very common in Africa, where women have about a 45 per cent chance of being admitted to hospital at some time during their lives as a result of complications (Rogers, 1980). Seager and Olson (1986, p.105) note that out of every 100,000 abortions performed in less-developed countries, between 50 and 1000 result in death, and suggest that it is infinitely more dangerous to have an abortion than to use any other form of birth control.

India, Cuba and Vietnam are among the few developing countries where abortion is legal on fairly broad grounds, but most Third World states still retain the pro-natalist ideologies of past times and abortion on demand is very rare, limited to cases where there are medical grounds or extreme extenuating circumstances (Rogers, 1980; Seager and Olson, 1986). Even so, in India, for example, it is estimated that only 5 per cent of all abortions taking place are performed legally (Savara, 1983). Nevertheless, in Panama, Indonesia, Somalia, Mauritania, Niger, Burkina Faso, the Central African Republic, Iran, the Dominican Republic and Haiti, there are no legal grounds for abortion at all (Seager and Olson, 1986). However, despite the problems associated with illegal abortion, many 'traditional' methods are not only effective, but also, because they are based on natural rather than synthetic substances, often have fewer side-effects than Western drugs. The main advantage of traditional practices, of course, is that they are usually adopted *voluntarily*; the same cannot often be said of the techniques and treatments imported from the West.

There is no doubt that Western birth control programmes have been significant in reducing levels of population growth in many places. Population experts cite Colombia, Mexico and Thailand as having the most 'successful' government-sponsored 'voluntary' family-planning programmes. Indeed Mexico's birth-rate dropped from 44.9 per thousand in the early 1960s to 32 in 1982; that of Colombia from 44.6 to 28, and that of Thailand from 43.5 to 25 over the same period (Helmore, 1986). Currently 40 per cent of women in Mexico, and 52 per cent of women in Colombia and Thailand use contraceptives, compared with under 15 per cent in most countries in Africa and the Middle East (Seager and Olson, 1986). Nevertheless, the measurement of 'success' is on the part of the agencies, and may have little to do with the lives of the women themselves.

Family Planning in Cities

Before concluding this section, it is important to consider briefly the reasons why family planning schemes have been more effectively introduced in Third World cities than in rural areas. The results of the World Fertility Survey indicate that substantially more urban women are likely to know of contraceptive methods than rural women. For example, in the Yemen Arab Republic, 74 per cent of urban women knew of a contraceptive method as against only 18 per cent of rural women; in Honduras, similar trends are reflected in the fact that the total fertility rate in 1981 was only 4.1 in towns and cities compared with 8.2 in rural areas (PIP, 1985).

Greater knowledge and use of birth control derives from the fact that exposure to the media is generally far greater in towns, as well as the fact that medical facilities in general are also better and more widely available in urban areas. For example, in Papua New Guinea health services tend to be concentrated most heavily in the capital, Port Moresby, and the outer island provinces which have had more exposure to external influence and are more 'developed' (Dickenson et al., 1983). In Mexico, the Federal District has three times as many doctors per capita than elsewhere in the country (Ward, 1986). In Colombia there are 1000 people to every doctor in the towns, while this ratio is 6400 to one in rural areas (Townsend, 1987).

Not only is access to health care (and family planning services) generally greater in towns, but also access to education; this is seen to be associated with the adoption of contraceptive practices (and therefore fertility decline) for two main reasons. First, educated women are more likely to use contraceptives than those with little or no schooling (Dickenson et al., 1983; PIP, 1985; Zaman, 1980).[6] In theory, education raises expectations, tends to postpone marriage (which reduces the number of child-bearing years within marriage), and increases the likelihood of exposure to family planning information (Rubin-Kurtzman, 1987). Indeed Kofi Awusabo-Asare's (1988) study of data from the Ghanaian Fertility Survey suggests that female education is a critical variable in examining patterns of contraceptive use: urban women in Ghana are better-educated and more likely to plan their families than rural women. However, Awusabo-Asare also stresses the need for caution in interpreting responses to questions about contraceptive use. For example, post-partum abstinence, while a very effective form of fertility control, may not be cited as a 'technique' *sensu strictu* in areas where it is an accepted mode of behaviour and way of life. In this way under-recording of fertility control is highly likely in rural areas and may inflate apparent differentials in the use of family planning between countryside and town (Awusabo-Asare, 1988).

The second reason why improved access to education in towns may reduce fertility is associated with the changing economic role of urban children. Since education implies increased costs, or at least foregone earnings, school-age children come to represent a drain on household resources rather than a contribution; as a consequence urban parents have to give more careful consideration to family size (Benton, 1987). For example, a study of the industrializing community of San Cosme Mazatecocho in the central Mexican highlands shows that people are having fewer children nowadays in order to withstand the economic burden of putting them through school (Rothstein, 1986). In terms of Caldwell's (1976) idea of 'wealth flows' discussed earlier in the chapter, the costs of raising and educating children in urban areas are likely to be *higher* than the potential returns; thus wealth flows in cities tend to be greater *from* parents *to* children.

However, the idea that children 'cost' more in urban than in rural areas, and that this automatically leads to lower birth-rates, is by no means clear or general; a large family is still an enormous source of welfare in situations of poverty, and particularly where education is of little consequence in terms of access to local jobs. As Sheila Lewenhak (1980, p.267) notes: 'Among the poor, children as poten-tial workers still seem to carry the best hope of warding off destitution and of help in sickness.' In Mexico, despite government propaganda to promote family planning, summed up in the maxim: 'the small family lives better', the reduction of family size can have very deleterious effects, (Hackenberg et al., 1981). Despite increased opportunities for education, few of the Mexican urban poor attain levels high enough to enable entry into comparatively well-paid jobs; therefore one way of compensating for low earning capacity is to have many children who may then be deployed into the labour force (ibid.).

A final reason why women in many cities may be more disposed to practise birth control relates to increased rates of urban female labour force participation. However, as we noted in Chapter 6, no general pattern between fertility and 'productive' labour is discernible, especially since many low-income women carry out informal work in the home and are thus able to combine child-care with income-generating activities. Whatever, the reasons, however, there is much evidence to support the idea that urban women have been more receptive to family planning techniques than their rural counterparts. Whether or not this is a 'good thing' is another question. While there are many sound reasons why women would wish to reduce fertility, whether to improve their own health and well-being, to reduce their domestic labour load, or to increase financial capacity when children are young, it is undeniable that 'imposed sterility is as oppressive as imposed maternity' (LACWE, 1980, p.13).

Concern for the quality of women's lives or female reproductive freedom is often low on the agenda of population agencies, and many female family planning acceptors continue to have little effective control over their own fertility. As Rogers (1980, p.107) notes:

Population programmes are planned – and organised mainly by men, and aimed almost entirely at women – women as objects whose fertility is to be controlled (hence the phrase 'population control') rather than as people who would wish to control their own fertility. It is assumed that women do not know what is good for them, and that they must be persuaded to become 'family planning acceptors'.

Having looked at some of the issues surrounding fertility itself, we now turn to look at the more general question of maternal and child health. To what degree have the efforts of state and international aid agencies in the field of basic health care matched those which have been dedicated to the prevention of high birth-rates in the first place?

Women and Maternal and Child Health

On the whole, maternal health is poor in most developing countries, and child-birth complications are among the five leading causes of death among Third World women. In 1975, the maternal mortality rate was 123 per 100,000 live births in Mexico, 126 in Chile, 249 in Iran, 370 in India, 570 in Bangladesh and 700 in Afghanistan, compared with a figure of only 12.8 per 100,000 for the United States (Townsend and Momsen, 1987, p.32). In Egypt this figure was between 51 and 100, and in Angola it was over 101 (Seager and Olson, 1986). According to World Bank figures, Third World women face a risk of death in pregnancy 100 times as high as in the developed world and about 1400 women die each day in the course of bearing children or giving birth (Prowse, 1987).

The reasons for high rates of maternal mortality are manifold. Aside from poor diet and unhygienic living conditions, women's general health suffers from repeated pregnancies and/or prolonged breast-feeding (Benería and Sen, 1981; Pearson, 1987). It is also estimated that around two-thirds of pregnant women in developing countries and half of the female population of the Third World as a whole are anaemic; anaemia is closely associated with poverty (particularly poor diet) and is more common in women than in men (MacCormack, 1983; Townsend and Momsen, 1987; Wells and Sim, 1987). It is widely noted that men receive first choice of the family's food in low-income households, and spend much of their earnings outside the family; as a result women have far lower levels of nutritional and calorific intake than their male counterparts (Beuchler, 1986; Kabeer, 1985; Kishwar and Vanita, 1984; Rogers, 1980; Sen and Grown, 1988; Ul Haq and Burki, 1980). Problems associated with general living conditions and diet interrelate with poor standards of maternal health care to produce a very dismal profile of women's health in the developing world.

Many women have little or no access to information or formal medical treatment during childbirth or for peri-natal complications. In Nepal, for example, only one in ten women seeks any medical care during pregnancy and childbirth, and less than 8 per cent use the services of government midwives (Pearson, 1987). Having said this, the majority of women in Africa and rural India are helped by 'traditional' midwives, namely women within the community who have experience and expertise in attending to the needs of pregnant women and in assisting at deliveries (MacCormack, 1982). Nevertheless, the state lags far behind in terms of providing services for women, other than those which reduce their fertility. Barbara

Rogers (1980) points out the irony of the population control programme in Tunisia in 1964–66 where a great deal of effort was spent in persuading women to accept family planning, but woefully little paid to the follow-up care of women who had already accepted contraceptive methods. Indeed, the mantle of women's health donned by so many population agencies in the process of proselytizing the virtues of family planning, is ragged in the extreme; 'improvements' in women's 'health', at the end of the day, come down to gaining acceptors on fertility control programmes, irrespective of whether the methods used to achieve this aim are hazardous, and of whether or not an initial acceptor continues to use contraception.

If public provision of maternal health care is poor, that for infants is also notoriously inadequate. In Nepal, for example, where nearly half the population is rural, over 50 per cent of deaths occur in children under the age of five years, usually from diseases such as diarrhoea, dysentery and gastro-intestinal infections which in other circumstances do not prove fatal (Pearson, 1987). In Mexico, the mortality rate of children under five is five times higher than that of the United States, Canada and Cuba, again as a result of commonplace enteritic infections, or a variety of respiratory diseases such as bronchitis, tuberculosis and pneumonia (Ward, 1987). Of course, infant mortality is also linked to severe malnutrition which in turn lowers the resistance of children to infectious diseases (Pryer and Crook, 1988). In many areas there is little sign of improvement. For example, between 1981 and 1984 only seven out of 23 countries in the Latin American region had succeeded in bringing down their infant mortality rates (IDB, 1987).

An interesting slant on child mortality is presented by a study of the Indian sub-continent which shows that the phenomenon is sometimes sex-selective. Barbara Harriss and Elizabeth Watson (1987) try to explain the anomalous excess of men over women in South Asia, when normally women outnumber men because of a number of innate physiological advantages. The South Asian pattern is related to abnormally high mortality rates for young girls and for women of child-bearing age. High death rates among female children are attributed to two major reasons: first, girls usually receive less in the way of food and nourishment than their brothers, which weakens the body's defences and makes them more vulnerable to infection; second, boys are more likely to receive medical treatment for ill-health than their sisters. Harriss and Watson (1987) tentatively suggest that the masculinization of the South Asian sex ratio over the course of the twentieth century reflects a progressive undermining of female productive roles and status arising from economic and technological change in both rural and urban areas. As Maitrayee Mukhopadhyay (1984, p.25) points out: 'Whatever the final outcome of the present debate, one conclusion is inescapable and unavoidable; women's lives are cheaper and more expendable than men's.'

Health Problems and their Implications for Women

Returning to our initial point about women taking up the slack where government health departments fail to cater adequately for the needs of the poor, it is important to note the extent to which women provide back-up support and/or suffer the consequences of medical neglect through their familial role as carers. An idea of the extent to which women are involved in informal health provision is perhaps indicated by the low figures on consultation of formal medical services. For example, in four rural communities in Nepal, only 20 per cent of the population who had experienced illness had actually consulted a doctor (Pearson, 1987). In these communities women are both 'gatekeepers to' and 'caretakers of' health, detecting and treating symptoms, and making important decisions about whether to consult more specialized experts (ibid., p.126). Obviously in rural areas, distance from health services is a major reason for the low utilization of formal facilities, but even in cities, especially in peri-urban slums, inaccessibility along with high costs mean that many of the poor do not consult a doctor and instead fall back upon women in the household for care, treatment and support.

Of course, in some areas women have traditionally taken on the provision of health care in a more formal capacity. A classic case is that of the Sande Society, a traditional 'secret' women's organization in coastal southern Sierra Leone. Sande has existed since the seventeenth century, and to this day provides a good deal of medical care for the local population, especially in the fields of maternal and child health, nutrition, hygiene and herbal remedies (MacCormack, 1982; Midgley et al., 1986). In Egypt too, local midwives play an extremely important role in their communities, yet in spite of this, they were not employed in the nationwide family planning scheme because the Ministry of Health did not feel their experience had equipped them with the necessary skills (Hartmann, 1987). As Troth Wells and Foo Gaik Sim (1987, p.50) point out: 'Traditional midwives . . . form the crux of health care for pregnant women in large parts of Africa, Asia and South America yet few have had any training to help them perform this role better.' However, negative attitudes towards traditional medicine and women's role within it have recently begun to show signs of change.

New Developments: Primary Health Care and Women

Since 1975 the World Health Organization has stressed the need for a radical restructuring of medical provision along the lines of a primary health care approach (Pearson, 1987). Primary health care involves a decentralization of health services across national territories and calls for local communities to become involved in the delivery of services such as education and information. The primary health care approach is concerned with prevention rather than cure and also recognizes the need for improvements in infrastructure such as sanitation and housing (Tipple and Hellen, 1986; Ward, 1987).

Another hallmark of the primary health care approach is that it recognizes and encourages the role traditionally played by women in their communities by using female workers in local health schemes (WHO, 1979). The inclusion of female community members is expected to improve commitment to projects, as well as their efficiency (MacCormack, 1983). In the Roman Catholic Serabu Village Health Project in Sierra Leone which originated in 1966, the progressive use of traditional female birth attendants (mainly from the Sande Society) in the promotion of tetanus vaccination for example, has resulted in a marked decline of infant morbidity and mortality (Midgley et al., 1986). The Nyeri Women's Project in Kenya, promoted jointly by Planned Parenthood Federation and the Family Planning Association of Kenya, recognized that older women in the community had a special role to play in encouraging the use of family planning through their influence over younger females (IPPF, 1982). The success of family planning programmes in South Korea, Thailand and Nepal is attributed to the fact that women's organizations and midwives have been instrumental in disseminating information, support and appropriate contraception to women. In South Korea, for example, women would only agree to accept IUDs if they were inserted by women and in their own homes (Rogers, 1980).

No doubt the utilization of women in project execution may increase commitment to family planning. However, if primary health care policy is also successful in injecting funds into the improvement of general living standards and infrastructure, it is possible that several families may decide to reduce the number of children they have on a voluntary basis. Obviously nutritional intake needs to be raised, along with improved access to medical facilities. As was found in a study of Narangwal in the Punjab, India, improvement in the delivery of general health services contributed to increases in family planning acceptance (World Bank, 1980). However, a major transformation in the health of low-income groups could also come about through infrastructural improvements to housing and urban services, and it is to these issues we now turn.

WOMEN AND HOUSING: REPRODUCTIVE ISSUES

Most of the urban poor in the developing world lack access to state-built or subsidized housing and are forced to seek their own alternatives. In many African cities, a large supply of cheap rental accommodation houses the majority of residents (Peil and Sada, 1984), and in Singapore, the government has been successful in providing most of the urban poor with public housing (Wong, 1981), however in the bulk of Third World cities, people have been forced to build their own shelter on land acquired illegally around the urban periphery. The illegal acquisition of land generally takes two forms: first, squatting, and second, plot purchase in unauthorized land-sales sponsored by real estate agents and private developers (Gilbert and Ward, 1985). These areas of illegal housing development are collectively referred to as 'irregular' or 'self-help' settlements. Their inhabitants not only lack official title to land, but also basic urban services such as piped water, sewerage, streets, pavements, electricity and rubbish collection (Pryer and Crook, 1988).

Between 1963 and 1973 it was estimated that 33 per cent of the population of Nairobi, Kenya were living in slums and irregular settlements, 43 per cent of the inhabitants of Colombo, Sri Lanka,

50 per cent of the population of Dar es Salaam, Tanzania, 60 per cent of the population of Kinshasa, Zaire and a staggering 90 per cent of the population of Addis Ababa, Ethiopia (Dickenson et al., 1983, p. 186). In 1980, more than half the population of Mexico City lived in self-built low-income settlements (Ward, 1986, p.30); the same is true for 25 per cent of the population of Djakarta and Kuala Lumpur, and 26 per cent of the population of Singapore (Butterworth and Chance, 1981, p.147). Housing in low-income settlements is frequently overcrowded. In irregular settlements in Querétaro, Mexico, the average number of persons per room is 2.5 (Chant, 1984a, p.369). In Greater Bombay it is estimated that 77 per cent of households have an average of 5.3 persons to one room (Misra, 1978, pp.375–6).

Dwellings in irregular settlements are planned, organized and financed by the people themselves. In the early stages particularly, materials consist of anything the settlers can find to hand such as local vegetation, debris, recycled industrial throwaways or extremely cheap products such as corrugated cardboard, tarpaper and tin sheets (Stretton, 1978). As time goes on, families may erect a brick and/or concrete structure, but aside from generating extra material costs, this also often involves the use of paid labour and many cannot afford it – although people organize the building themselves, self-help should not necessarily be equated with self-build (Burgess, 1982). However, if people decide they cannot afford to devote their meagre resources to dwelling improvements, economic savings merely result in an increase in the social costs involved in living in substandard shelter characterized by overcrowding, little protection against the elements, and extreme discomfort (Connolly, 1982). Women bear the brunt of these costs due to their frequent confinement to the home and their responsibility for the bulk of domestic labour (Chant, 1984a, 1987b).

Since the early 1970s, international development agencies and Third World governments have generally begun to play more of a role in promoting the spread of self-help housing as a shelter alternative for the urban poor, recognizing that huge savings may be made by capitalizing on the poor's own initiative and resources. State involvement in self-help housing generally takes one of two forms: first, 'site-and-service schemes', whereby the poor pay for a land plot with legal title and a minimal level of services, on which they build their own dwellings within a stipulated time period, or second, and more commonly, 'squatter upgrading programmes' whereby existing settlements are improved through the regularization of land tenure, the provision of basic services and infrastructure, and sometimes through facilities to obtain credit and/or subsidized building materials.

Women play an important role in both spontaneous and planned self-help housing for a number of reasons; they not only have the extra domestic work which residence in a sub-standard shelter implies, but also devote a considerable amount of time to the actual construction of dwellings and community infrastructure. Some women actively collaborate with their menfolk in skilled building activities such as brick-laying, roofing and laying floors, although more commonly, they assist with various 'secondary' aspects of construction work such as passing tools and materials, mixing cement, providing food and refreshment for male workers and clearing up the debris afterwards (Chant, 1987b; Massolo, 1987; Moser and Chant, 1985; Nimpuno-Parente, 1987). Construction activities, of course, increase the already long hours women devote to their daily work routines.

Poorly consolidated housing is also highly associated with disease, and therefore has a further set of negative implications for women's labour load and general well-being (Savara, 1983). A study of low-income neighbourhoods in Mexico City, for example, showed that cramped and poorly ventilated housing conditions were associated with a high incidence of respiratory infection (Fox, 1972). Indoor cooking on open fires also contributes to chronic lung diseases such as bronchitis (Dankelman and Davidson, 1988; World Bank, 1980). Overcrowding and the forced proximity of various domestic functions such as cooking, eating, sleeping, nappy-changing and caring for the sick means that risk of cross-infection is extremely high (Chant, 1984a); infectious diseases such as measles and whooping cough, for example, are rife in poor and overcrowded slum housing (Pryer and Crook, 1988). Tipple and Hellen (1986) point out for the case of Kumasi, Ghana, that overcrowding not only makes it difficult to avoid or shake off disease, but is also likely to give rise to psychological stress and family tensions. Other environmental health risks include tapeworms or roundworm infections such as *Ascariasis*, which result in gut disorders; these arise where there is inadequate disposal of human waste in the home or where latrines provide a breeding ground for flies and mosquitoes (MacCormack,

1983). In a study carried out in southeastern Mexico it was shown that Chagas disease, an infection attacking the autonomic nerve system and occasionally causing heart failure, was far more likely to occur in houses with thatched roofs than those built of industrialized materials; thatch provides an ideal nesting ground for *Rhodnius prolixus*, an insect which carries the disease pathogen (Prothero and Davenport, 1986). Dirt floors and dust may also lead to the spread of trachoma, a chronic eye infection frequently resulting in blindness (MacCormack, 1983).

WOMEN, REPRODUCTION AND URBAN SERVICES

Evidently, the diseases common in residents of low-income housing are exacerbated by a lack of basic services. World Bank data for 1980 showed that only 25 per cent of urban households in the Third World had a piped water supply, and even fewer had sewerage facilities (Hardiman and Midgley, 1982). In 1984, at least a quarter of the dwellings in most large Mexican cities lacked an interior water source, ranging from 28 per cent of homes in Guadalajara, to 31 per cent in Mexico City and as many as 54 per cent in Tijuana (Ward, 1986, p.88). In 1980, 38.9 per cent of the urban population in the province of Morona Santiago, southern Ecuador, were not served by an electricity supply, and 43.8 per cent had no toilet facility (Armstrong and McGee, 1985, p.126). In urban Malaysia as many as 61 per cent of dwellings do not have a flush lavatory (Wegelin, 1977, p.61).

The problems attached to inadequate water supplies are manifold. Households lacking inside taps have to rely on other sources such as wells, boreholes, rivers, public standpipes and tanker deliveries. One hallmark of these alternatives is that most run far more risk of bacterial contamination than a domestic piped network, due to contact with the open air and vulnerability to interference by animals and insects. Poor water supplies are strongly correlated with the incidence of gastro-enteritic-related infections such as amoebiasis, poliomyelitis and hepatitis A (Elmendorf and Buckles, 1980; Pryer and Crook, 1988), and in Indian urban squatter settlements, there is a high risk of malaria (Prothero, 1987). In order to reduce the risks associated with contamination, women often have to boil water for long periods and take extra care that the vessels which they put them in are freshly cleaned and dried, since dust and rubbish are constantly blown into unprotected shelters, dirtying cooking utensils and other items.

In addition, the work of actually collecting water is extremely time-consuming (see Chapter 2). In some countries it is estimated that women spend up to half their work-time collecting water for household consumption (Dankelman and Davidson, 1988; Ul Haq and Burki, 1980). In Querétaro, Mexico, many irregular settlements are located on steep hillsides with unpaved streets, and a return trip for water to a public standpipe or to a water storage drum may take up to an hour and a half (Chant, 1984b). Sometimes the strain of carrying huge vessels of water on the head or on the shoulders can lead to pelvic deformity and complications in childbirth (IWTC, 1982).

A lack of sewerage also presents women with an intensification of their domestic load, especially if households do not possess their own latrine. This may involve women accompanying their children to suitable spots around the edges of settlements to defecate or collecting up the family's excreta in plastic bags and disposing of it elsewhere. These practices can, of course, have serious supra-local consequences. Tipple and Hellen (1986) note that the emptying of raw faeces into the rivers and streams of Kumasi, Ghana, has exacerbated health problems, especially when the same water source is used for drinking or the preparation of foodstuffs.

Lack of rubbish collection means that women have to burn or dump waste in spots far away from their houses in order to avoid health risks such as lice and flea infestations. Thus when basic urban services such as water, sewerage and rubbish collection are missing, a considerable amount of time and labour is added to women's domestic chores as they attempt to maintain minimum levels of hygiene and welfare (compare 'diaries' in Chapter 2). Another set of problems derives from the fact that most irregular settlements are very poorly served with transport, commerical and educational facilities.

In Mexico, for example, distance between peri-urban settlements and the town centre, and lack of commercial infrastructure in the former, means that low-income women have to make several trips outside their immediate neighbourhood to purchase essentials. In hot climates fresh foods perish quickly – a major problem when many households do not have electricity or refrigerators – and shopping has to be done on a daily basis (Chant, 1984b). This difficulty is compounded by inadequate transport facilities on the urban periphery. Women with children too young to be left with a neighbour or relative have to take babies and toddlers with them, thus increasing travel costs and making shopping extremely burdensome. Many low-income settlements lack primary schools, again involving long trips accompanying young children outside the neighbourhood. It almost goes without saying that there is virtually no public provision of child-care facilities in all except the socialist countries of the Third World. In most cases low-income women contend with a very heavy load of reproductive labour, yet receive virtually no recognition or assistance from the state.

As Manuel Castells (1978, pp.177–8) notes, governments rely heavily on women's unpaid reproductive work in the city:

for it is the subordinate role of women which enables the minimal 'maintenance' of its housing, transport and public facilities . . . because women guarantee unpaid transportation (movement of people and merchandise), because they repair their homes, because they make meals when there are no canteens, because they spend more time shopping around, because they look after others' children when there are no nurseries and because they offer 'free entertainment' to the producers when there is a social vacuum and an absence of cultural creativity . . . if women who 'do nothing' ever stopped to do 'only that', the whole urban structure as we know it would become completely incapable of maintaining its functions.

While the urban structure would also be incapable of maintaining its functions if men withdrew their labour, Castells at least draws attention to the fact that women's critical role in its supporting activity, reproduction, is often overlooked. We hope we have given some idea in this chapter of the importance of numerous reproductive activities undertaken by urban women in developing countries.

As a postscript to this section, it should be noted that women are increasingly displaying a tendency to become involved in organizational and political activity around reproductive issues (Sen and Grown, 1988). For example, in Guayaquil, Ecuador, where many squatter settlements are built on reclaimed swampland, it is women who frequently form the rank-and-file members of settlement committees whose objective is to petition the local authorities for infill and basic services (Moser, 1983). In Tsito, Ghana it was women who mobilized to raise the funds to build a health centre with a maternity wing for their village (Bukh, 1979). In addition, and perhaps in part as a response to these kinds of initiatives, certain community development projects in urban areas are now beginning to devote more of their attention to the 'woman question', and trying to involve women themselves in project execution. It is to these and related issues we turn in the next chapter.

NOTES

1. Despite the fact that Ghana is one of the few Third World countries which has attempted to provide a comprehensive public health service, in 1985 the government was forced to increase hospital fees by a factor of 8–10, and overall the value of per capita expenditure on health in the 1980s was only one-third of its level in the late 1960s and early 1970s (Tipple and Hellen, 1986).
2. *Depo provera* was outlawed in the United States in 1978, but its manufacturers continued to promote it in the Third World (Wells and Sim, 1987).
3. There is strong evidence to show that high oestrogen pills have a number of dangerous side-effects, including the developing of thrombosis. The Dalkon Shield and other IUDs often result in pelvic infection, heavy bleeding and in some cases, sterility (Wells and Sim, 1987).
4. The spread of *Aids* in several Third World countries in recent years may result in greater promotion of the condom as a means of disease- as well as birth-control in the future. Advertising of the condom (as a protective *and* as a contraceptive) has already started in Mexico and Ghana, for example. Having said that, it is also important to note that in some countries such as Brazil, the condom has long been associated with the prevention of venereal disease – one reason why it has rarely been used for the purposes of birth control (Panos Institute, 1988).
5. Breastfeeding on demand causes lactational amenorrhoea which in turn suppresses ovulation and menstruation by release of the hormone prolactin (Hartmann, 1987, p.11).
6. Although education is generally associated with a decline in urban fertility as a result of taking up Western contraceptive methods, in the short run, rates of urban women's fertility may increase due to the abandonment of traditional birth control practices (Mosley et al., 1982; Stewart, 1985).

9 Gender and Urban Planning

In this final chapter on gender in Third World cities, we concentrate upon the experiences of low-income women in urban planning and community development schemes.[1] Many of the problems identified in Chapter 4 of the design of rural programmes, and their frequently unfavourable outcomes for women, are also relevant in urban areas, and the two contexts display several similarities. However, certain features of women's lives in cities and the kinds of project implemented in urban communities are different from those of rural environments, and thus warrant further discussion here. One major difference stems from the fact that women-headed households tend to be more numerous in cities than in the countryside; as a result, the negative consequences of *modernization* and/or gender-blind policies which assume that households are headed by men affect more urban than rural women. A second factor concerns the more frequent physical separation of production from reproduction in the lives of urban women. The expectation that women should perform reproductive activities (housework, child-care and the kinds of task we discussed in Chapter 8 such as health-care), even where they may have jobs outside their homes (factory work, for example), means that deficiencies in particular aspects of planning such as transport may affect urban women to a greater extent than their rural counterparts.

Another major difference between rural and urban areas involves the *types* of projects implemented. Obviously, issues such as access to credit or assistance for agricultural production and marketing, which formed a major focus of our discussion in Chapter 4, are not relevant in cities. Therefore greater emphasis in this chapter is laid on projects concerned with health, housing, transport, the provision of basic services and income-generation in non-agricultural activities.

Another theme taken up in more detail in the present chapter, and of increasing relevance to both rural and urban women, is 'community participation'. While we discuss this in detail later in the chapter we need to have a working definition here: participatory development, now a major component of neighbourhood projects, consists of involving low-income people themselves in the planning, construction and management of their own communities. As such these kinds of scheme are not only important for women in terms of their outcomes, but also in terms of their design, implementation and maintenance. One major focus of this chapter therefore is the nature of women's involvement as *participants* in the community planning process. Community participation is clearly relevant to rural areas as well, and at certain junctures we complement our urban case studies with rural examples.

Other issues broached in this chapter include first, the concept of 'practical' and 'strategic' gender interests (Molyneux, 1984, 1986)[2] as they apply to urban planning, and second, the position of 'women's projects' at the level of the community and the development environment at large.

In the first part of the chapter a broad overview is given of the general types of policies adopted in urban areas, how they affect women and in particular how they address (or do not address) practical and strategic gender interests. The second section looks at a range of gender-aware projects in practice, examining their implementation, and also their standing both within urban communities and in the international planning context. The third section provides a brief outline of community participation and discusses the problems for women as participants and beneficiaries of such projects. The fourth and final section suggests a number of ways in which women's position in urban community development schemes might be improved.

URBAN AND COMMUNITY DEVELOPMENT PLANNING: CONCEPTS AND STRATEGIES

Gender-blind Planning

As in rural areas of the Third World, the bulk of urban development projects take no account of gender differences or women's specific needs and may thus be labelled 'gender-blind' (Moser, 1986). The usual consequence of gender-blind policy approaches, as we saw in

Chapter 4, is that men benefit, while women are excluded or even adversely affected. Typical examples of the failure of planners to recognize the roles and interests of women in the urban context include the case of the Delhi Resettlement Project in India, which took place between 1975 and 1977. The scheme's objective was to relocate 700,000 squatters in inner Delhi to 17 resettlement colonies on the urban fringe. In one such community, Dakshinpuri, women suffered from the move to a far greater degree than men. The new settlement was situated so far from former workplaces that several women through lack of time and cost of travel, could no longer keep their jobs as well as manage their domestic tasks. As a result, the rate of women's labour force participation in Dakshinpuri fell by 27 per cent, compared with a decline of only 5 per cent in male employment (Singh, 1980).

Other examples of gender-blind planning in cities are frequently found with public transport. Marianne Schmink (1982) shows how Brazilian women living in Belo Horizonte's peripheral settlements are severely disadvantaged by the fact that most buses to and from the city centre run at peak hours during the morning and evening to serve the male workforce, but are reduced dramatically during the day. Planners have failed to recognize that women also need transport to get to the shops, to collect their children from school, and to get to their own part-time jobs. The lack of off-peak buses results in women's travel-time being up to three times longer than that of men's (Schmink, 1982). In addition, little is done to protect women from attack or sexual harassment on public vehicles; in Villa El Salvador and Canto Grande, large low-income settlements on the outskirts of Lima, Peru, transport deficiencies and lack of safeguards to physical security, such as adequate street lighting and bus shelters, restrict women's use of all types of transport (Anderson and Panzio, 1986).

Women's access to various types of development schemes is also inhibited by gender-blind planning. One major reason for women's exclusion, as we discussed in Chapter 4, is the misplaced assumption that nuclear households form the vast majority of households in Third World cities (see also Chapter 6). This means that alternative types of family unit such as extended and single-parent households are left out (Chant and Ward, 1987). This is often the case with housing programmes, which recognize only men as household heads and consequently deny women access simply on account of their sex

(Chant and Ward, 1987; Moser, 1987b). Leda Machado (1983), for example, draws attention to the failure of a Brazilian low-income housing programme set up in 1975 to recognize that women-headed households would form an important sub-group of applicants. The programme in question was promoted and financed by the Brazilian National Housing Bank as a sites-and-service operation (see Chapter 8) whereby serviced land plots for self-building were granted to families with between one and three minimum wages. In one of the projects in Vila Velha in south–east Brazil, it was explicitly stated that applicants had to be the *father* of at least two children (Machado, 1983).

Even where women are not explicitly denied access to projects, the need to demonstrate proof of an adequate and regular income to qualify for entry often presents a major obstacle (Moser and Chant, 1985). For example, 46 per cent of women applying to the Solanda site-and-service shelter scheme in Quito, Ecuador, were turned down because their incomes did not reach stipulated levels (Blayney and Lycette, 1983). In the Dandora housing project, Nairobi, several women applicants were not only unable to provide proof of regular income due to their heavy reliance on informal sector occupations, but also had to take out loans or borrow from relatives in order to pay the requisite downpayment (Nimpuno-Parente, 1987).

Apart from the exclusion of women as household heads from certain urban development projects, the reputed benefits of community schemes also fail to reach women *within* male-headed households. To take an example, Fernando Ortiz Monasterio and Marianne Schmink (1986) point out that planners often overlook the fact that women are largely responsible for managing water supplies and sanitation, and instead focus on community leaders who are usually men. Where women are excluded from consultation, discussion and training in this way, they are frequently unable to operate, maintain or repair major items of community infrastructure such as water pumps and sanitation facilities, and the whole community suffers as a result (IWTC, 1982).

In urban housing projects, failure to consult women over dwelling design can also have extremely adverse effects. In the capital of Tunisia, two housing schemes set up by the national government and the United States Agency for International Development (USAID), based their dwelling designs on European models rather than the traditional Tunisian *dar arbi*, a structure which comprises a series of rooms around an internal courtyard. An internal courtyard has long been extremely important for Tunisian women, customarily providing them with a private open space in which they may socialize with female kin and friends. The houses built under the aid programme had only very small courtyards and were totally inappropriate for the needs of women. In many cases there were outbreaks of depression, psychoses and even suicide (Resources for Action, 1982b; see also reference to Lumsden in Chapter 4 for the implications of poor house design in a rural resettlement programme).

However, women are not always passive in the face of these problems: in many areas they have translated concern about homelessness, lack of urban infrastructure and insecurity of tenure into action. In the Mathare Valley squatter settlement in Nairobi, Kenya, for example, Nici Nelson (1978) describes how women have often played a critical role in campaigning for basic services such as water, and to prevent demolition of their homes. In Bombay, India, women from the communities of Rambang, Upnagar and Rajaramwadi formed the majority of participants in a 3000-strong demonstration against slum eviction and poor service provision (APHD, 1985). In Managua, Nicaragua, in 1984, the occupation of lands in the peripheral settlement of Madres Martires de Pantasma was led by a woman (Massey, 1987).

Towards Gender-aware Planning

Recognizing that women in both urban and rural areas play an important role in household survival and *ipso facto*, have a vested interest in improving security and services in their settlements, in recent years governments and agencies have come to adopt a more 'gender-aware' approach to community development, attempting to identify the different needs of men and women, and trying to ensure that women benefit from development schemes as well as their male counterparts (Buvinić, 1983). The commitment to finding women a place in development planning has received considerable impetus from the UN Decade for Women, and is obviously an improvement on earlier modernization-oriented and gender-blind approaches. However, there are still problems, largely due to stereotyped assumptions about what women's roles are and should be. As a result, even women-oriented projects often fail to help the women they are supposed to benefit (see also Chapter 4).

'Family-centred' perspectives, welfare strategies and practical gender needs

Mayra Buvinić (1984) classifies the kinds of perspectives held by planners about women into two main types: 'family-centred' and 'woman-centred'. The former set of perspectives tends to produce projects with a strong welfare element in which women become the recipients of resources aimed at bettering their performance as wives and mothers. Such projects include maternal and child-health, nutrition, hygiene, education and food-distribution schemes, and were especially typical of 'women's' programmes up until 1975 (Moser and Levy, 1986). The important thing about them is that while these kinds of projects may address women's *practical* needs, they do nothing in terms of challenging women's traditional *roles* and the balance of power between men and women (Molyneux, 1984, 1986; Moser, 1986, 1987b). As such, welfare programmes are 'technically simple and politically safe' (Buvinić, 1983, p.25). They do not embody any attempt to tackle the underlying nature of sexual inequality, nor do they bring women into competition with men for the same resources (ibid.). Moreover, as Caroline Moser (1987b, p.29) notes: 'In reality practical needs . . . are required by all the family, especially children, and their identification as "women's needs" serves to preserve and reinforce the sexual division of labour.'

Women-centred perspectives, anti-poverty strategies and practical gender needs

However, even where agencies and governments sympathetic to women have moved away from a family-centred perspective to a woman-centred orientation (which regards women as individuals with needs beyond those they have as mothers and housewives), the tendency is still to leave traditional gender roles intact. The main type of policy stemming from the woman-centred perspective is the 'anti-poverty' strategy (Buvinić, 1984). Anti-poverty strategies work with the assumption that the social relations between men and women are determined above all by poverty (rather than the cultural context of gender differences), and so direct efforts towards improving the material conditions of women, particularly female household heads. Emphasis is focused upon increasing women's income and employment opportunities through skills, training and fund-raising programmes, and through more favourable access to credit (see, for example, Antrobus, 1986). The view that women need some degree of economic autonomy and should be able to fulfil their potential in ways other than those strictly related to marriage and child-rearing has slowly but surely gained greater currency in Third World urban community development planning. Marina Fernando (1987), for example, notes that US Save the Children (SAVE), an organization which has traditionally viewed women as the main vehicle for improvements in child welfare, have over time moved from a welfare to an anti-poverty approach, placing women on training pro- grammes which directly enhance their position in the labour market. However, the main problem with anti-poverty projects is that many of them build upon the skills women already possess in handicrafts, cooking and so forth, and in this way do little to break down gender stereotypes. In addition, little cognisance is made of the fact that in order to take full advantage of employment training schemes, urban women also need some compensation in the reproductive sphere. When skills are provided but neither child-care facilities, nor any attempt to mobilize the participation of men in domestic tasks, it is hardly likely that these schemes will benefit women in any major way. Again a situation emerges in which 'women's projects' do not alter in any substantial way the existing balance of gender roles and relations (Buvinić, 1984). In addition to the above problems, the continued tendency to emphasize the practical needs of women in anti-poverty (as in welfare) programmes not only tends to reinforce women's attachment to their traditional roles, but in so doing also tends to make it difficult for them to discover and formulate their 'strategic' needs (Moser and Levy, 1986).

Women-centred perspectives, equity strategies and strategic gender needs
'Strategic' gender needs/interests are defined by Molyneux (1986: 284) as those which

are derived in the first instance deductively, i.e., from the analysis of women's subordination and from the formulation of an alternative, more satisfactory set of arrangements to those that exist.

In other words strategic gender interests are concerned with chal- lenging the sexual division of labour and bringing about greater equality (Molyneux, 1984, 1986; Moser, 1986). Planners and policy- makers interested in raising not only women's material standards of well-being, but also their status, are in favour of an 'equity' approach (Buvinić, 1984). The equity approach argues for an equal sharing of resources between men and women and the eradication of sexual inequality both at home and in the workplace. Projects emanating from under the umbrella of equity-type policies include awareness or consciousness-raising groups to help women understand the nature of their subordination, sex education, women-only information classes and women-only credit programmes. These kinds of projects theoretically lead women to question their traditional reproductive roles and to demand entry into more 'productive' ones as defined by wider society (see Chapter 1). However, because equity programmes involve governments and international aid agencies in unfamiliar and sensitive areas with obvious implications for the cultural, political and social status quo, and because they require long-term commitment of resources and are therefore expensive, they are rarely desired or implemented by policy-makers (Buvinić, 1984). Besides, it is perhaps doubtful that they would be workable among low-income women; as the Asia Partnership for Human Development (1985, p.103) points out, women from impoverished groups 'have very little time for reflection about themselves and the society they live in'. It is also doubtful, as Buvinić (1984) notes, that many agencies will devote scarce resources to equity-type projects which fundamentally alter existing patterns of sexual inequality. Nevertheless, the issue of breaking down existing gender stereotypes and addressing women's strategic needs is of critical importance if urban development planning is to become truly gender-aware and capable of precipitating fundamental change (Moser, 1987b).

Having discussed the various approaches to women's projects in the Third World, we now go on to look in a little more detail at their practical applications, and the kinds of 'rating' gender-aware projects, policies and policy-makers have in the local community and in the wider development planning context.

WOMEN'S PROJECTS IN PRACTICE: PROBLEMS AND PROSPECTS

One of the major problems with 'women's projects' whether they address practical or strategic gender needs, is that they are often considered to be relatively unimportant and frequently fail to rouse the support or active collaboration of male community members. In part this stems from the fact that the sexual division of labour tends to drive a wedge between the needs and interests of women and those of men. Moreover, because women's activities are so often unacknowledged and/or undervalued, projects evolving around them tend to be seen to be of little consequence to their male counterparts. An example of this is provided by Jette Bukh (1979) in her study of the village of Tsito, Ghana. Here women in the community wished to build a small health clinic with a maternity wing, but failed to get the male chief and elder males interested, largely because of their traditional lack of involvement in health, birth and child-care. Although the women did raise funds, and a handful of men in the community participated in the construction of the clinic, it remained primarily a 'woman's project' and as such was not deemed by the men to be of central importance to the community as a whole (Bukh, 1979).

Women-only Projects

However, sometimes 'women's projects' are deliberately set apart from mainstream community schemes, not just to circumvent the problem of engaging male support for projects directed at women, but also to avoid the conflicts likely to arise when men and women work together. Men are frequently dismissive of women's abilities and resent having to share their skills and expertise with them. For example, in a multi-sectoral community development project in Kirillapone, Sri Lanka, a large squatter settlement on the outskirts of Colombo, project staff employed by US Save the Children had to intervene to persuade male trainers in the community to accept women who had signed up for course in carpentry, masonry, roofing and construction (Fernando, 1987). Similar problems of getting men and women to work together were found in a self-help housing project in San Judas, Managua, Nicaragua (Vance, 1985). Thus women-only projects provide women with a non-competitive (and often non-conflictive) space in which they can acquire skills which are usually the preserve of men.

Sometimes women-only projects have been set up around housing, as in the case of a self-help construction project in Curundu, Panama where 100 houses were built entirely by women (Girling, Lycette and Youssef, 1983). Here institutional back-up included training in construction skills, materials, tools, heavy equipment and supervision. The aim of the project was not only to provide women with housing, but also with skills they could then sell in the labour market (ibid.). A similar project was created in Jamaica, where the Western Kingston Women's Construction Collective trained women in various building skills such as carpentry, electrical installation, masonry, painting and steelwork, and provided them with a loan for the duration of the training period. Once the women had found jobs with their new skills, the loans were repaid and used to train a further group of low-income women (Schmink, 1984).

Women-only projects have also been initiated around credit. Access to finance is usually very difficult for Third World women since not only do they have very restricted access to the earnings and collateral necessary to receive a bank loan, but are also less likely to have essential skills such as literacy, or experience in dealings with formal bodies, to negotiate appropriate fees and interest rate charges (IWTC, 1981). As a response to women's disadvantaged position with respect to access to loans and credit, an idea for a form of women's banking originated in 1975 during International Women's Year based on previous informal credit associations. Women's World Banking was formally founded in 1979 and since then has come to involve over forty countries. Its objectives are to aid women entrepreneurs with small- and medium-scale business ventures by facilitating their access to credit and providing them with information, management, technical assistance and know-how about business development (Helmore, 1986).

An important forerunner of this programme was the Self-Employed Women's Association (SEWA), in Ahmedabad, northern India, initiated in 1972 as a means of protecting the interests of women in informal urban employment such as market-vending, junk collection and cart-pushing. In 1974, SEWA set up their own co-operative bank aiming to provide loans to both low-income urban and rural women. The bank now has over 12,000 members, 90 per cent of whom are illiterate and who would otherwise have been ineligible for financial assistance from formal credit institutions (IWTC, 1981). Other schemes initiated by SEWA include various forms of skills-training programme and income-generating projects. SEWA, which is partly funded by UNIFEM (The United Nations Development Fund for Women), presently has branches in nine

Indian cities (Helmore, 1986). In Ahmedabad alone, it has effectively unionized about one-third of women engaged in petty occupations, a remarkable achievement given that Indian labour legislation has not traditionally legitimized trade associations where there is no identifiable employer (Mukhopadhyay, 1984).

Similar women-only institutions have been founded in other parts of the Third World since the establishment of SEWA and Women's World Banking, such as the Women in Development Incorporated Loan Fund (WID, Inc.) set up in the Caribbean in 1978 and the African Co-operative Savings and Credit Association (ACOSCA) based in Nairobi, Kenya (IWTC, 1981). This growth of women-only projects and programmes at the grass-roots level has been accompanied by, and in part has resulted from certain changes in national bureaucracies, several countries from the mid-1970s onwards having set-up Women's Ministries or Agencies. In other cases, traditional women-only voluntary organizations have extended their influence and power in the national political arena.

Women-only Institutions

An early example of a nationwide women's organization is the Union of Women of Tanzania (UWT) which dates back to 1962 (Mihyo and Rutashobya, 1987). The main aims of the organization are to 'restore the dignity' of Tanzanian women and to cultivate a political consciousness sympathetic to the national ideology of *Ujamaa* and self-reliance (living and working together for the benefit of the whole nation) (see Chapter 4). Their objectives are disseminated through cooperative projects focusing on education, income-generation and services. Education projects include classes and training in nutrition, needlework, gardening and poultry-keeping, as well as literacy. Economic-oriented projects include cooperative enterprise and savings ventures such as handicraft projects. Service-giving projects include the running of day-care, child-health and ante-natal centres (Mihyo and Rutashobya, 1987).

Similar organizations have been established elsewhere in the Third World at a regional level. For example, the Caribbean Women's Association (CARIWA) was set up in 1970 as a regional umbrella institution covering all non-governmental Caribbean women's groups (Antrobus, 1986). Because of lobbying by this association and in response to the general prescriptions of the UN decade, the Secretariat of the Commonwealth Caribbean Governments (CARICOM) established a Women's Desk in 1981. Guyana, also a member of this organization, instigated in 1980 a three-member Women's Advisory Board in the Office of the Prime Minister. In that same year, commitment to gender equality was reinforced by the socialist government's People's New Constitution (Peake, 1987).

Several First World and international development agencies (including USAID, ILO, UNICEF, and the Food and Agriculture Organization (FAO)) now have specific women's bureaux or programmes. Several of the programmes initiated by these organizations try to put women on the agenda of development rhetoric and praxis. For example, in a comprehensive self-help shelter project in Gaborone, Botswana funded by the Foundation for Cooperative Housing International Programme and USAID, single mothers in precarious economic circumstances are especially singled out as potential members of a scheme which not only provides them with housing and water, but also legal services, vocational training and credit (Nieves, 1980).

In addition to gender-aware initiatives in the fields of government and international development planning, the number of women's networks dedicated to the research, analysis and exposure of women's issues at a national, regional or international scale has more than doubled in the last ten years (Davies, 1987). Compared with the past, far greater attention has been paid since 1975 to women's practical needs, and greater pressure has been put on governments and agencies to recognize the systematic disadvantages in women's position in Third World cities. However, there is still a long way to go before urban community development projects are able to focus on women's strategic needs and interests. The difficulties of developing projects which fully incorporate and benefit women are also evident in our following section which looks at community participation.

COMMUNITY PARTICIPATION AND WOMEN

Community Participation as Concept and Practice

'Community participation', otherwise known as 'popular participation', 'grassroots development' or 'development from below', has become increasingly fashionable in recent years as a component of community development schemes in Third World countries. In both rural and urban areas, community participation is broadly speaking a collective form of 'self-help' in which neighbours pool skills, time and resources for various improvements to living conditions in their settlements. Community participation theoretically involves active cooperation between beneficiaries and agencies in three main stages of project execution: design, implementation and maintenance. 'Design' refers to the overall establishment of project goals and objectives; 'implementation' refers to the actual organization and building of projects; and 'maintenance' covers not only the upkeep and repair of community infrastructure, but also the management of repayment (usually beneficiaries are expected to pay back part or all of any loan(s) used to initiate and run projects). Active involvement of local people in community development projects is thought to raise the likelihood of 'success' in a number of ways, primarily in terms of tailoring projects more closely to 'real' needs, and in raising levels of commitment to community activity. This 'bottom-up', grassroots form of planning is widely felt to be more efficient than the 'top-down' method of traditional modernization approaches to development (see discussion of development ideologies in Chapter 4).

The concept of community participation is not new, but has roots and/or parallels in many Third World cultures. For example, in Kenya, *harambee*, a customary practice of community solidarity and self-reliance, was in existence long before the idea of community participation became fashionable among governments and planners (Mbithi and Rasmusson, 1977). In other parts of the world, it is also common for individuals to donate a certain amount of labour each year for community work, expressed in the concept of the *faena* or cooperative work session in Mexico (Algara Cosío, 1981), or the practice of *shramadana* in Sri Lanka (Fernando, 1987). The novelty of community participation as a development initiative, however, derives from the fact that it involves intervention by, and cooperation with, the state and/or other development agencies.

According to the United Nations, one of the organizations most concerned with promoting participatory development, participation is positive for both project beneficiaries and governments alike. For the urban poor, putative advantages include better programme results, the saving of money (because people substitute their own labour for professional hired assistance), and the development of a cooperative and self-enabling spirit within communities (Pasteur, 1979). In addition, through community participation, beneficiaries are able to make planners aware of the real needs of the poor. Above all, it is argued that community participation provides people with the means by which they may exert more fully their democratic rights (Dore, 1981; Hollnsteiner, 1977; Rifkin, 1984; United Nations, 1977). At the same time, improved chances of project success, efficiency and financial savings also benefit governments and agencies. In addition, community participation provides official organizations with considerable political capital, demonstrating to the outside world their willingness to collaborate with the urban poor for social ends (Hollnsteiner, 1977).

However, despite these theoretical advantages for different sets of actors, in practice community participation is rarely an outright success. Usually the poor are expected to participate actively in project implementation and maintenance, but are often left out of the design stage – obviously the most critical phase from the point of view of ensuring that programmes meet 'real' needs. It is hardly surprising that participants often display an apathetic response when asked to give up their free time to work on projects, or default on repayments, when they have had no effective voice in the establishment of project goals. Other problems which hamper the success of community participation include difficulties in building up mutual trust beween agencies and communities, problems of communication, and reluctance on the part of governments to give any substantial power to low-income groups (Hollnsteiner, 1977; Skinner, 1983; UN, 1977).

However, some of the main problems with community participation concern women. One major contradiction stems from the fact that on the one hand, women are often expected to play a major role in project execution on account of their close association with the household and the community, and because they are thought to have more 'free time' than men to devote to voluntary activities (Castells, 1984; Moser, 1984; de la Paz, 1984). On the other hand, although in practice women provide a great deal of the hard labour which goes into community participation schemes, their contributions are probably far less than that of men; second, it means that some women called upon to participate in community efforts may have to take time off work to do so. This is especially serious for women heads of household who may have no other source of income on which to rely.

The fact that women often do make a generally greater contribution to participatory development projects than men by no means signifies that they have more time available, merely that they are possibly willing to make more sacrifices because of vested interests in improving the welfare and living conditions of their families. The fact that this work is unpaid exploits them even more and sets dangerous precedents. Although few people in community participation schemes actually work for money (the whole ethic is voluntary), except perhaps community leaders and those in charge of administering the project at the local level, the fact that women do the bulk of the work and are not remunerated tends to reinforce the idea that their work is 'unproductive' and of little economic value.

Thus, in many cases women undertake a large amount of project work for no payment at all. An example here is a church-initiated primary health care project in Davao City, the Philippines, where community members were encouraged to assist in the management of a clinic and to have a voice in the decision-making and daily running of the centre. When demands on the clinic increased to such a degree that staff resources were stretched to their limit, a programme to train people within the community as voluntary health workers or *katiwalas* was instigated. Most *katiwalas* were women, who remained unpaid despite the fact that their initial work in curative activities expanded over time to include preventive, rehabilitative and promotional functions as well (de la Paz, 1984).

However, certain projects have been more progressive on this front, recognizing that women lose valuable work-time through 'voluntary' activities and trying to reward them for their work. In the Brazilian community of Coque near Recife, for example, an integrated community development project set up by a religious group, a French non-governmental organization and the municipal authorities, pays women residents who work in the community clinic out of the small fees charged to clients (UNICEF, 1983). In another programme known as PROCAPE in Guayaquil, Ecuador, a pre-school project involving a blend of child-care, children's recreation and primary health care, community-recruited staff are paid out of UNICEF funds (UNICEF, 1984).

However, usually there is no finance to pay even nominal wages to participants, and in some of these cases loans have been made available to enable people to take time off work to contribute to the project. This is particularly necessary for women heads of household whose earnings are the mainstay of the household unit. In the Women's Self-Help Construction Project in Panama, participants were paid a stipend during building to free them from their routine income-generating activities (Girling, Lycette and Youssef, 1983). However, the money had to be repaid once the women were housed, so in effect it was only a short-term solution to the problem of giving up their time (Moser, 1987b).

Constraints on Women's Participation

Having identified the fact that women are often expected to donate labour to community projects, it is also important to note that in many cases their full and active participation (in the sense of becoming involved in *all* aspects of project design, implementation and management) is restricted to a far greater degree than their male counterparts by various problems on the ground. The practical constraints on women's participation may reach such a level that they appear not to be making any direct contribution at all, by being relegated to 'invisible', supportive roles characteristic of their routine domestic duties (servicing male participants by providing them with refreshments or clearing up after them, for example). One major limitation to women's active and visible participation is posed by the frequently discriminatory attitudes of male project staff. Another factor is that men within the community often exert a considerable degree of control over the activities of their wives and daughters. A third factor is that traditional community leadership structures are usually dominated by men and thereby inhibit women's potential for exercising control over the design, practice and outcome of participatory projects. The kinds of implication arising from the above constraints may include the fact that women's needs are rarely addressed and/or that project benefits fail to reach them. This, of course, stands in direct contrast to the amount of work they actually do. As Robert Chambers (1974) notes, men often find excuses not to participate in self-help projects, while women still turn out despite the fact that they are rarely involved in project design or decision-making.

Gender composition of project staff
Gender composition of project staff is often a critical determinant of

whether women benefit from community participation schemes. Aside from the fact that the majority of staff are usually male, many may not be sympathetic to female involvement. In some instances men avoid communicating with women altogether: Molapo (1987), for example, discusses how male agricultural extension officers in Botswana rarely take the time and trouble to give advice to women-headed households. When development projects have women female personnel on the other hand, this is usually more favourable to women's full participation, allowing them greater access to information and supply networks and a better degree of trust and cooperation (Rogers, 1980). This also works the other way: UNICEF, for example, has found that women project workers are generally more effective when they work with women in the community rather than with men (Midgley et al., 1986). Female staff or professionals also appear to be more interested than their male counterparts in breaking down gender stereotypes and in getting women into positions of power than their male counterparts. In Southeast Asian cities, for example, groups of élite educated women concerned with increasing the gender-awareness of policy-makers and the general public, are keen to recruit low-income women into action and leadership in their own communities (Heyzer, 1986).

Attitudes of men in the community
In addition to problems encountered with male staff, women may also be prevented from active participation in community development by husbands or fathers unwilling to let them come into close contact with other men (Chant, 1987c; see Abdullah and Zeidenstein, 1982, for rural examples). Other reasons for male resistance to women's participation include resentment that women are spending time away from household duties, or a belief that female involvement in the 'public' world of community development threatens traditional male-dominated power structures. Male resistance may also arise where women enter 'male' spheres of activity. This was the case in Mexico City, in the 'La Tropa' self-help scheme initiated by the ruling political party and the federal agency responsible for housing cooperatives, one-quarter of male beneficiaries refused point blank to allow their wives' participation in any of the construction work (Kusnir and Largaespada, 1986).

Lack of female leadership

Lack of female leadership at the community level is also a major
obstacle to the filtering-through of project benefits to women and/
or their participation itself. Local leaders, either as individuals or as
heads of neighbourhood committees and so on, often play a key role
in communication and brokerage between agencies and residents,
and are usually male (Ward and Chant, 1987). Squatter settlements
in Kenya, for example, are usually presided over by a 'big man'
(Barrows, 1974; Mbithi and Barnes, 1975; Ross, 1973). In India,
leaders also tend to be male (Hale, 1978; Olesen, 1984).

When men are in charge of community organizational structures,
they can sometimes block and/or circumscribe the way in which
agency staff interact with female residents. For example, students
from the African Regional Health Education Centre (ARHEC)
wanting to initiate a project in a neighbourhood of Ibadan, Nigeria
found they could not liaise directly with women on a community
improvement scheme, but instead had to work through the community council of elder males (Brieger and Adeniyi, 1982).

In some Latin American cities women are perhaps a little more
likely to attain leadership posts at the community level, possibly
because several are single or separated, a situation which appears to
grant them greater freedom than marriage. Nevertheless even here
women leaders are still the exception rather than the rule (Ward and
Chant, 1987). Having said this, Moser (1987c) also makes the point
that women might play an important role as leaders but are rarely
recognized as such, simply because they tend to mobilize around
reproductive concerns which, because they are not deemed to be of
central importance to society and/or are the domain of women,
remain less visible (see Chapter 4). This is a critical issue because it
means development agencies may by-pass women leaders through
failing to recognize their contribution to the organization and
improvement of urban settlements.

Women leaders may be ignored not only by development agencies,
but also by men in the community. Indifference or, more often,
resistance to female leadership is likely to emerge in cases where
women leaders pose a threat to traditional patriarchal power structures and to undermine the role of men in local political life. In
Botswana, Lesego Molapo (1987, p.205) notes that Setswana men
find the prospect of women addressing local meetings a 'sacrilege'.
In countries which were former colonies of Britain, such as Nigeria,

women's traditional rights as leaders have declined because the colonists failed to recognize the role that women played in community life (Okonjo, 1976). Evidence also shows that husbands of women leaders face criticism on account of their wives' activities. In Guayaquil, Ecuador, for example, the female leader of Barrio Indio Guayas, a squatter settlement built on reclaimed swampland, failed to persuade her husband to allow her to take on more than a temporary presidency of the Front (a group comprising twenty local committees including her own) (Moser, 1987a). The Asia Partnership for Human Development (1985) cites a case where the husband of a leader of a village women's health movement in southern India threatened to divorce her on account of her involvement. In the Philippines, despite the fact that older women in particular have considerable potential to influence decision-making in their communities, many say they like to make their men feel that they are the ones who take the decisions (APCWD, 1980).

Although women may exercise a degree of informal power within their communities, absence from 'formal' settlement structures such as committees means they are unlikely to have much say in dialogue with project staff. For this reason, women are often left out of consultation on the establishment of project goals and isolated from crucial project stages. As Hollnsteiner (1982) points out, distorted approaches to local decision-making find their

most extreme expression in the passive, non-participatory roles allocated to women. Despite their contributions to the economic and social well-being of the family and community, they rarely occupy formal positions of authority or decision-making on local councils . . . To the explanation frequently given – mostly by men – that women do not want and therefore do not present themselves for these positions one can only cite the many examples of women who do come forward when socio-cultural constraints imposed by male-dominated society are lifted and when incentives encourage them to organize for action on their terms. (Hollnsteiner, 1982, pp.7–8)

WOMEN IN URBAN COMMUNITY DEVELOPMENT: WAYS FORWARD

In the light of what we have discussed in this chapter, it is obvious that there is a major need for the incorporation of women in *all* stages of the development process (Ul Haq and Burki, 1980). However, although this is an easy-to-state solution, we must be aware of the pitfalls. Sometimes, when women are targeted and drawn into participation in urban community development projects, the aim is not so much to improve the situation of women themselves, as to enhance the performance and/or image of governments or agencies. There is now recognition that the participation of women is often a vital ingredient of project success. Not only are women likely to provide considerable amounts of time and labour for project execution, but are also frequently more reliable when it comes to repaying loans. A survey of men and women recipients of mortgage loans from the National Housing Trust (NHT) in Jamaica, for example, found that although both groups were likely to fall into difficulty at some time in meeting regular repayments, women were generally more responsible about their debts than men, and took the trouble to inform office staff when they could not pay (Blackwood, 1986). Therefore, although the increased encouragement for women's participation in some senses facilitates an improvement in women's condition, it is also important to ensure that this participation is not abused and merely exploited for the purpose of agencies or governments wishing to improve their success rates, or to give the impression that they are perhaps more concerned with women than they really are (see also Molyneux, 1986). In the words of Stuart MacPherson and James Midgley (1987, p.191), development must work 'for women', rather than women working 'for development', as has most often been the case. Having said this, what are some more specific issues which should be borne in mind when thinking about future policy which will benefit women?

Women-only versus Integrated Gender Projects

One critical issue in future policy is that of deciding whether women-only or mixed projects are appropriate for the fulfilment of both the practical and strategic needs of women. Do women need space in which they can develop and extend their skills before challenging male domination, or is this space only likely to confine them to their traditional marginalized activities? Both women-only and mixed community development projects have their advantages and disadvantages. Women-only projects allow women to develop skills and resources in an arena where they are not directly competing with men, and also in a sense improve efficiency by streamlining target groups. Target groups including both men and women beneficiaries are likely to be far more heterogeneous than groups consisting of one sex only, therefore making it more difficult to decide on common aims and procedures. This by no means suggests that low-income women form a homogeneous group, indeed as we have seen in this and other chapters, they are differentiated by a whole range of factors, including marital status, religion, age, type of employment, number of children and household structure. However, it is probable that women-only groups feel more identity of interest than those which contain men as well. Women are likely to have certain common shared experiences, not least of which may be some direct contact with gender subordination either at home, in the community or in the workplace, and a commitment to reproductive tasks. Therefore, in women-only groups, interests and needs may converge to a greater extent than in a mixed context. However, women-only projects also have disadvantages, mainly because they are not likely to involve direct confrontation of gender interests, arguably a precursor to frank and honest negotiation between the sexes. Projects prescribing the cooperation of men and women may, if managed sensitively, also set a precedent for improved gender relations over time. However, mixed schemes may too easily come to be male-dominated, thereby depriving women of the benefits arising from participatory experience.

The problems and advantages of women-only versus mixed groups at the project level are likely to be found at other levels of the development hierarchy, notably that of agency structures. Buvinić (1984) points out how the positive aspects of women-only institutions are frequently counterbalanced by their negative ones. According to Buvinić, the main advantages of women-only institutions include their commitment and ability to reach women clients, their role in encouraging greater female participation both at staff and beneficiary level, their scope to approve and act upon the suggestions of individual women, and finally and most importantly, their power in facilitating the entry of women into non-traditional roles, providing them with a vital space in which they can effectively 'catch up' with men in a non-competitive context. However, women-only institutions are frequently plagued by financial constraints and comparatively limited resource networks; they also have limited organizational and technical expertise and frequently become ghettoised within the international development community (Buvinić,

1984; see also Rogers, 1980). Although women-only institutions probably address the issue of strategic gender needs far more profoundly than conventional development organizations, they often do so at the expense of failing to cater for women's practical needs through lack of finance. In fact one important issue for consideration is whether strategic gender needs can be met in the absence of attention to practical gender needs, and what degree of priority should be attached to each of these imperatives.

Gender Composition of Project Staff

Whether the agencies charged with women-oriented community development projects organize mixed or single-sex schemes, it is vital that female personnel are recruited by governments and agencies if project benefits are to reach low-income women. Even where male project staff *are* sensitive to women's needs and concerned that they participate and benefit in projects, in certain cultures it may not be possible for women beneficiaries to deal with men through lack of self-confidence on the part of women, or because they face restrictions from their husbands or male kin (see Abdullah and Zeidenstein, 1982). The employment of female project workers would undoubtedly strengthen the possibilities for dialogue and involvement by women within the community.

In addition, it is important that project organizations do not discriminate against women staff, by segregating them into traditionally 'feminine' areas of project management: frequently female personnel predominate in such areas as community liaison or advisory work, whereas men tend to monopolize legal, financial and technical activities. The movement of female staff away from traditional areas such as mother and child health and nutrition, and into 'non-traditional' areas such as engineering and construction may serve as examples and help to break down existing gender stereotypes within communities.

Changing Leadership Structures

Just as women staff are important if projects are to meet women's needs to a greater degree, so too are female community leaders, as we noted earlier. However, modifying pre-existing male-dominated leadership structures is likely to be extremely difficult; agencies run the risk of alienating communities if they confront and threaten vested interests (Ward and Chant, 1987). One possible method of breaking through male monopoly of power at the community level might be to devise ways in which responsibilities for project organization and execution are dispersed through various sub-committees or multiple leaders, without necessarily impinging upon the interests of existing bodies. However, there is little evidence so far of successful attempts to install women leaders in the face of existing male-dominated gender relations.

Even if women are installed as leaders, it is also important to bear in mind that they might be limited in building up local support, as their social interaction with men is frequently restricted to their male kin or their husband's friends (APCWD, 1980). Given that many women lack experience of formal leadership, they may also need some kind of training in basic skills relating to group management and administration. A programme for training women leaders of self-help groups was set up in Kenya in 1979 by the Women's Bureau of the Ministry of Culture and Social Services in the districts of Kisumu, Kakamega, West Pokot and Kisui. The objective was to provide women leaders with skills such as project planning, human relations and group management in order to raise levels of community participation, to strengthen satisfaction with group activities and to achieve higher rates of successful project completion. While participation did not appear to increase after the training programme, the initiative seemed to have a positive effect on leaders' abilities to manage group conflict, and also resulted in higher numbers of finished projects (Kayongo-Male, 1983).

Paid Community Participation

Another important issue for future policy is that of payment for women participants of community development projects. As we saw earlier, when women provide their time and labour free of charge, they run the danger of reinforcing the idea that their work is 'unproductive' in their own eyes, in those of their menfolk and in those of society at large. Payment of women's work in project execution would not only make their contribution visible, but also would allow those women who cannot otherwise afford to waive routine income-generating activities to become involved in community projects.

However, funds for payment of 'self-help' are likely to be scarce; perhaps the only way to offset the costs involved in sacrificing valuable work-time for community projects is to ensure that in the course of project execution women acquire some skill or expertise which they can later sell in the workplace. In this respect, schemes such as the Panama Women's Self-Help Construction Project, with its twin aims of housing women as well as providing them with training in a wide range of construction skills, may be a useful blueprint for future programmes. If such programmes are backed up with loans or credit to enable women to subsist during the time they participate, this will facilitate the involvement of particularly disadvantaged groups such as women-headed households, who are obviously less able to take time off work.

Awareness Training for Women and Men in Communities

If women's practical interests are to be given more priority in community development programmes in the future, then funding will also have to be set aside for some form of instruction and consciousness-raising on strategic gender interests for both women and men in the community. As Pat Ellis (1986, p.151) suggests:

> If women are to realise their full potential and be free to develop as human beings, then it is important for their men to understand this and to accept that women should not be denied this right. Instead of passively accepting the idea of male dominance and female subordination, women and men need to understand and accept the concepts of interdependence and mutual respect.

The form and content of awareness-raising about the sexual division of labour might take depend heavily on local cultural, political and economic circumstances, but are none the less vital if the issue of strategic gender interests is to be broached.

Integrative Planning

Finally, it is important to point out that women's responsibilities in most low-income communities are manifold, and as Moser and Levy (1986) point out, involve them in domestic labour, productive activities and community managing. Simple attempts at raising women's income-earning opportunities through employment or skills programmes are unlikely to be successful if not backed up by other forms of support to reduce their domestic and community labour loads. For this reason Moser and Levy (1986) draw attention to the need for integrative planning approaches, rather than sectoral ones, in order that women might balance and restructure their large number of jobs (see also Chapter 4). This in turn would help to confront the issue of women's strategic needs. In particular some element of child-care should be provided to release women for other activities (Nieves, 1980; see also section on socialist policies in Chapter 4). This is particularly necessary for those urban women who lack access to kin-based support networks.

CONCLUSION

In this chapter we have tried to present an overview of the way in which current planning responses to urban poverty in the Third World affect women. While in the last ten years women have increasingly appeared on the agenda of urban community development projects, either as participants or beneficiaries, there are still many problems, perhaps, above all, because reproductive work continues to remain undervalued despite its obvious importance for the survival of low-income groups. For the future, we have suggested that programmes trying to attend to women's practical interests should also try to address the question of their strategic interests as well in the hope that ultimately a greater commitment to understanding and equality between poor men and women will lead to a greater sense of solidarity and empowerment among low-income groups.

NOTES

1. Much of the inspiration for writing this chapter derived from a period which the author (Sylvia Chant) spent with Dr Caroline Moser at the Development Planning Unit, University College London in 1985. I was employed to help in the preparation of a training module for the United Nations Centre for Human Settlements (UNCHS, HABITAT), Nairobi

on the participation of women in low-income housing projects, and subsequently became assistant on a short course initiated and directed by Dr Moser entitled 'Planning with Women for Urban Development'. Many of the terms and ideas discussed in the chapter stem from the seminal work undertaken by Dr Moser in the field of gender-aware urban planning and research in developing countries, and a number of the projects cited are taken from the jointly-authored UNCHS draft which was published as a DPU Working Paper (see Moser and Chant, 1985). I am indebted to Caroline for introducing me to this field of enquiry and for providing me, at the time and subsequently, with valuable source material. Responsibility for the contents of this chapter however, is entirely my own.

2. Maxine Molyneux's (1984) distinction between practical and strategic gender interests, developed originally around her work on women in Nicaragua, is critical in the analysis of development policy and planning. (See also Molyneux, 1986 for a more elaborate discussion of the concepts outlined in her earlier article).

    While the nature of these different sets of interests (termed 'needs' by Caroline Moser, 1986, 1987 in her work on gender and urban planning in the Third World) is discussed in the text itself, it is useful to provide a brief resumé here.

    According to Molyneux (1986:284):

Practical gender interests are given inductively and arise from the concrete conditions of women's positioning by virtue of their gender within the division of labor [sic] . . . practical gender interests are formulated by the women themselves who are within these positions rather than through external interventions. Practical gender interests are usually a response to an immediate perceived need and they do not generally entail a strategic goal such as women's emancipation or gender equality.

At the project level, initiatives concerned with practical gender interests would include attempts to meet women's material needs in the roles ascribed to them through the sexual division of labour (as mothers and housewives, for example). Projects addressed to *strategic* gender interests, on the other hand, are more concerned with issues of status and challenging sexual inequality. Their underlying objective might be to abolish the sexual division of labour, to remove the legal barriers to political or economic equality, or to ensure that women are protected from male violence, and so on (Molyneux, 1984, 1986). Strategic gender interests are thus derived deductively, embodying both an analysis of gender inequality and a commitment to changing it (ibid.) In Molyneux's own words:

. . . strategic gender interests . . . are the ones most frequently considered by feminists as women's real interests. The demands that are formulated on this basis are usually termed feminist as is the level of consciousness required to struggle effectively for them (Molyneux, 1986:284).

N.B. Although 'interests' and 'needs' are not theoretical equivalents, the terms are used interchangeably in the present chapter.

10   Conclusion

In this short final chapter we do not intend to draw conclusions in any conventional sense: we do not provide an over-arching summary, nor do we attempt to bring together the main themes of the book. Such an exercise would not only be difficult, given the immense range of Third World women's rural and urban experiences, but would also involve needless repetition of our concluding remarks at the end of each chapter. Instead, we discuss three major topics which have featured in varying degrees in the main body of the text and which are key issues for the future in terms of theory, policy/planning and empirical research: reproduction, the critiques of Western feminism from Third World women, and the general significance of the UN Decade for Women.

REPRODUCTION

In all our chapters, whether referring to rural or to urban women, obstacles to women's 'integration', 'incorporation', 'visibility' or 'de-marginalization' have been shown to derive from the reproductive sphere. This is not necessarily confined to domestic activities, but rather refers to prevailing gender constructions, and is linked, although we cannot say precisely how, with aspects of patriarchy.[1] Constructions of gender and the nature of patriarchy, of course, vary enormously within and between major world regions.

The idea that elucidation ultimately rests with reproduction underlies our discussions of development policy and planning in rural and urban areas (Chapters 4 and 9). In both, we have seen that development programmes, whether or not they were originally designed to include women, fail if they do not take cognizance of assumptions about gender stereotypes (both on the part of local men and project workers), and ignore women's existing responsibilities for reproductive work. These have been identified as critical problems in the current debates on development ideology and methodology: farm systems research (Chapter 4) and the focus on women's practical and strategic needs (Chapter 9). Although the 'double burden' of women's reproductive and productive work is increasingly recognized as an issue for policy and planning, it needs far greater attention if women are to benefit from development interventions. Ideally, in future, Third World women themselves should have a much greater role in defining and acting upon their own needs. Too often the influence of Western ideologies, including the ideas of Western feminists, has turned gender-aware policy into an inadequate instrument for achieving the matrix of social relations in which equitable gender relations might flourish. In addition, the dominance of Western feminists in the sphere of collating, interpreting and distributing information on Third World women sets dangerous and asymmetrical precedents in the relationships and goals of Third World women and their First World counterparts.

THIRD WORLD WOMEN AND FEMINISM

Marta Zabaleta (1986), for example, points out the irony in the fact that Latin American women often read about themselves through the writings of North American academics, and in a language (English) other than their own: they are 'in the strange position of making their own acquaintance through the medium of an internationally-projected, internationally-recognized image of themselves which they played little part in constructing' (ibid. p.97). This phenomenon is, of course, not restricted to Latin America, but is applicable to all women in the Third World.

Furthermore, while First World women have access to and control of information about their Third World counterparts, the reverse is patently not the case. In addition to these aspects of information access and control, the focus of many white/Western feminists (whether socialist or not) on 'patriarchy' as the central variable in women's subordination has been widely criticized by black feminists, whether from the First or Third Worlds.[2] Valerie Amos and Pratibha Parmar (1984) attack white feminists' gross assumption that women's experience everywhere is essentially the same because of their subordination to men. The denial of race as a major parameter in the oppression of Third World women or ethnic minority women in developed states, is, they argue, indicative of white feminists' acceptance of racist and imperialist attitudes and, in turn, continued promulgation of white superiority. Amos and Parmar (1984) criticize both white feminists' attitudes to black women in the First World and their claim to be able to write about, categorize and conceptualize the lives of Third World women without an understanding and acceptance of fundamental differences in the ideologies and contexts which surround them. They are part of a growing movement among black and Third World women for the recognition of differences in women's condition on account of race and ethnicity (Amadiume, 1987; Roberts, 1984; Steady, 1981).[3] In relation to African women, for example, Pepe Roberts (1984, p.182) writes:

there are few grounds for an international feminist agenda dictating the *outcome* of women's personal/political struggles. There are, however, clear grounds for international solidarity in demand of political recognition of these personal/political struggles to enable women to organize collectively around these issues.

THE UNITED NATIONS DECADE FOR WOMEN 1975–85

This search for an 'international feminist agenda' lies behind the initiatives of the UN in its Decade for Women (1975–85), the subtitle of which is 'Equality, Development and Peace'. The Decade itself grew out of a resolution passed at the World Conference in Mexico City in 1975 to mark International Women's Year. International Women's Year, in turn, was the result of the resurgence of the women's movement from the 1960s onwards, together with an increasing acknowledgement on the part of governments and the UN to act positively against the discrimination of women: thus 1967 saw the UN Declaration on the Elimination of the Discrimination Against Women; 1970, the inauguration of the UN Programme of Concerted Action for the Advancement of Women', in 1972, the approval of the UN General Assembly for International Women's Year in 1975; and in 1973 the Percy Amendment to the US Foreign Assistance Act was enacted by Congress. This gave recognition to women's significant roles in production and development in the less

developed countries and stressed the importance of funding programmes designed to integrate women into national economies
(Fraser, 1987). Arvonne Fraser (1987, p.20) goes on to suggest that
the 'integration' of women in development will improve their status
and help development overall. We have seen, however, (Chapters 4
and 9) that not only is the 'integration' of women into development
problematic, but also that their incorporation into (or, more usually
'grafting' on to, see Moser, 1987, pp.29ff), development projects
does not necessarily have beneficial effects on their status.

Planning for International Women's Year began in December
1972 and the official high point of the year was a conference in
Mexico City in the summer of 1975, where the idea of the Decade for
Women was formulated. The Mexico conference produced a 'World
Plan of Action' which projected the aims of the conference into the
'Decade', and included both specific recognition of the problems
faced by women everywhere and plans for their alleviation. The
World Plan of Action emphasized the achievement of equality as its
main target: it recognized the significance of production, but
stressed the point that inequality begins in the home and the family
(that is, in the sphere of reproduction). The Plan's prescription for
achieving equality rested largely on education.

The three 'official' conferences held to mark the Decade (Mexico
City, 1975; Copenhagen, 1980; Nairobi, 1985) were each accompanied by a conference for members of NGOs, academics, 'experts',
bureaucrats and anyone who wanted to take part, and while the
resolutions of the official conferences have had governmental recognition and inspired some action, it was the issues and arguments
discussed at the NGO conferences which attracted most media
attention. This is particularly the case with the Copenhagen Mid-
Decade conference. In 1980 two themes discussed at Copenhagen
held the attention of the press: first, the politicization of the
conference which explicitly recognized an equation between Zionism
and racism (and apartheid), which had been suggested in Mexico in
1975 by the Group of 77;[4] and second, a noticeable divide between
First and Third World women focused on the specific issue of genital
mutilation/clitoridectomy (see Chapter 1), but signifying a more
general resistance on the part of Third World women to the
hegemony/imperialism of First World feminists (Fraser, 1987;
Roberts, 1984).

However, end-of-Decade meetings in Nairobi seemed to be much less contentious than the earlier conferences, focusing on the three 'themes' of the Decade (equality, development, peace), and closing with the publication of the document *Forward Looking Strategies to the Year 2000*. In both 1980 and 1985, the members of the conferences recognized that their earlier prescriptions were over-optimistic, included major revisions of the time-scale for achieving their objectives, and emphasized in their 'strategies' the necessity for men to participate in 'reproductive' responsibilities (including domestic labour and child-care) to the same extent as women. In addition, the Nairobi NGO conference was the only meeting at which peace featured prominently as a theme: a 'Peace Tent' was set up in which women of different views and from opposing sides of military and political disputes could meet and discuss their attitudes publicly. The only 'rules' were 'respect for another's experience and views, openness and a spirit of cooperation, finding common ground for action in a diversity of opinions' (Fraser, 1987, p.210).

CONCLUSION

It is all very well to talk about 'strategies to the year 2000', but we must ask, what impact, if any, the UN Decade has had for women in the Third World? On one hand, in terms of women's visibility to those responsible for development planning in the West, the Decade, as part of the general trend towards awareness of women's exploitation, has been helpful in generating new ideologies and strategies for development and in improving the collection and interpretation of data about women's lives. In addition, Fraser traces the increasing responsibility for the success of the Decade conferences given to women: by 1985 not only the vast majority of delegates, but also the planners and journalists were women. On the other hand, perhaps because of the Decade itself, but possibly also because of the more general change in official attitudes towards women's issues, both in the West and in the Third World, several women's organizations have been founded in various Third World states: WAND in the Caribbean (Ellis, 1986, Massiah, 1986a), GABRIELA (General Assembly Binding Women for Reforms, Integrity, Equality, Leadership and Action), in the Philippines (APHD, 1985), NCWD (the National Council on Women and Development) in Ghana (Oppong, 1987) for example, and also international groups such as DAWN

(Fraser, 1987; Sen and Grown, 1988). The UN Conferences consistently advocated the setting-up of women's bureaux as a key step in improving their status.

Official action in the main body of the UN did not stop with the inauguration of the Decade: in 1979, as the culmination of a long campaign, beginning with the UN Charter itself, the UN ratified the Convention on the Elimination of All Forms of Discrimination Against Women (CEDAW). Subsequently CEDAW has acted as a watchdog, recording progress and asking for specific country reports on discrimination against women. CEDAW has also consistently argued for the formation of national organizations for women's rights as a way forward.

But as we have seen in discussing women's lives in rural and urban areas, old ideologies die hard, and however cautious changes and innovations might be, and however much women themselves want change, we arc still faced with major obstacles in the face of the overwhelming male control of power structures in contemporary Third World societies (see, for example, Abdullah and Zeidenstein, 1982). In one reading of 'equality', men are shown to have more to lose if discrimination against women is eliminated, and so will resist it. We prefer a more optimistic reading, however, in line with the words of Sen and Grown (1988), at the beginning of the book, where gradually, both men and women will come to recognize their real values to each other. The process of change must necessarily be slow, but 'slow and steady wins the race': the allegory of the tortoise and the hare holds good both in the Third World and the First.

NOTES

1. In its general sense, patriarchy may be described as 'the manifestation and institutionalization of male dominance over women and children in the family and the extension of male dominance over women in society in general' (Lerner, 1986, p.239).
2. 'Black' as is used here refers to all women of Third World origin.
3. There is great diversity of approach among these writers themselves.
4. The Group of 77 is a group of women from Third World states (originally 77) formed at the Mexico City conference in 1975, who produced an additional, alternative conference report.

Bibliography

Abdullah, Tahrunnessa and Zeidenstein, Sondra (1979) 'Women's Reality: Critical Issues for Program Design'. In Sondra Zeidenstein (ed.) *Learning about Rural Women*. Special Issue of *Studies in Family Planning*, 10:11/12, 344–52.

Abdullah, Tahrunnessa and Zeidenstein, Sondra (1982) *Village Women of Bangladesh: Prospects for Change*. Pergamon for ILO, Oxford.

Abu, Katherine (1983) 'The Separateness of Spouses: Conjugal Resources in an Ashanti Town'. In Christine Oppong (ed.) *Female and Male in West Africa*. George Allen and Unwin, London, 156–68.

Abu Saud, Abeer (1984) *Qatari Women: Past and Present*. Longman, Burnt Mill, Harlow.

Achebe, Chinua (1958) *Things Fall Apart*. Heinemann, London.

Adeokun, Lawrence (1982) 'Marital Sexual Relationships and Birth Spacing among Two Yoruba Sub-groups'. In *Africa*, 52:4, 1–14.

Adeyemo, Remi (1984) Women in Rural Areas: A Case Study of Southwestern Nigeria. In *Canadian Journal of African Studies*, 18:3, 563–72.

Adlam, Diana (1979) 'Capitalist Patriarchy and Socialist Feminism'. In *M/F*, 3, 83–102.

Afonja, Simi (1981) 'Changing Modes of Production and the Sexual Division of Labor among the Yoruba'. In *Signs: Journal of Women in Culture and Society*, 7:2, 299–313.

Afshar, Haleh (1985) 'The Position of Women in an Iranian Village'. In Haleh Afshar (ed.) *Women, Work and Ideology in the Third World*. Tavistock, London, 66–82.

Afshar, Haleh (1987) 'Women, Marriage and the State in Iran'. In Haleh Afshar (ed.) *Women, State and Ideology: Studies from Africa and Asia*. Macmillan, Basingstoke, 70–86.

Agarwal, Bini (1987) 'Gender Issues in the Agricultural Modernization of India'. In Janet Momsen and Janet Townsend (eds)

Geography of Gender in the Third World. Hutchinson, London, 334-6.

Aguiar, Neuma (1980) 'The Impact of Industrialization on Women's Work Roles in Northeast Brazil'. In June Nash and Helen Safa (eds) *Sex and Class in Latin America*. Bergin, New York, 110-28.

Ahmad, Zubeida and Loutfi, Martha (1985) *Women Workers in Rural Development*. International Labour Office, Geneva.

Albert, Michèlle (1982) *Sex Selectivity in Internal Migration: An Exploratory Study of Costa Rica*. Discussion Paper No. 827, International Development Studies Group, Institute for International Development and Co-operation, University of Ottawa, Ottawa.

Algara Cosío, Ignacio (1981) 'Community Development in Mexico'. In Ronald Dore and Zoe Mars (eds) *Community Development*. Croom Helm, London/UNESCO, Paris, 335-432.

Amadiume, Ifi (1987) *Male Daughters, Female Husbands: Gender and Sex in an African Society*. Zed, London and New Jersey.

Amos, Valerie and Parmar, Pratibha (1984) 'Challenging Imperial Feminism'. In *Feminist Review*, 17, 3-19.

Anderson, Jeanine and Panzio, Nelson (1986) 'Transportation and Public Safety: Services that Make Service Use Impossible'. In Judith Bruce and Marilyn Köhn (eds) *Learning about Women and Urban Services in Latin America and the Caribbean*. Population Council, New York, 246-60.

Anderson, Michael (1980) *Approaches to the History of the Western Family*. Macmillan, London.

Anker, Richard, Buvinić, Mayra and Youssef, Nadia (1982) *Women's Roles and Population Trends in the Third World*. Croom Helm for ILO, London.

Anker, Richard and Hein, Catherine (eds) (1986) *Sex Inequalities in Urban Employment in the Third World*. Macmillan, Basingstoke.

Antrobus, Peggy (1986) 'New Institutions and Programmes for Caribbean Women'. In Pat Ellis (ed.) *Women of the Caribbean*. Zed, London, 131-4.

Ardener, Edwin (1975a) 'Belief and the Problem of Women'. In Shirley Ardener (ed.) *Perceiving Women*. Dent, London, 1-18.

Ardener, Edwin (1975b) 'The "Problem" Revisited'. In Shirley Ardener (ed.) *Perceiving Women*. Dent, London, 19-28.

Ardener, Shirley (1964) 'A Comparative Study of Rotating Credit Associations'. In *Journal of the Royal Anthropological Institute*, 94:2, 201–19.

Arizpe, Lourdes (1977) 'Women in the Informal Labour Sector in Mexico City'. In Wellesley Editorial Committee (eds) *Women and National Development: The Complexities of Change*. University of Chicago Press, Chicago, 24–37.

Arizpe, Lourdes (1978) *Etnicismo, Migración y Cambio Económico*. El Colegio de México, México DF.

Arizpe, Lourdes (1982) 'Women and Development in Latin America and the Caribbean: Lessons from the Seventies and Hopes for the Future'. In *Development Dialogue*, 1/2, 74–84.

Armstrong, Warwick and McGee, T.G. (1985) *Theatres of Accumulation: Studies in Asian and Latin American Urbanization*. Methuen, London.

Arnold, Marigene (1978) 'Célibes, Mothers and Church Cockroaches: Religious Participation of Women in a Mexican Village'. In Judith Hock-Smith (ed.) *Women in Ritual and Symbolic Roles*. Plenum, New York, 45–53.

Arowolo, Oladele (1978) 'Female Labour Force Participation and Fertility: The Case of Ibadan City in the Western State of Nigeria'. In Christine Oppong, G. Adaba, M. Bekombo-Priso and J. Mogey (eds) *Marriage, Fertility and Parenthood in West Africa*. Australian National University, Canberra, 533–64.

Asian and Pacific Centre for Women and Development (APCWD) (1980) *Participation of Women in Decision-Making: Some Guidelines*. APCWD, Bangkok.

Asia Partnership for Human Development (APHD) (1985) *Awake: Asian Women and their Struggle for Justice*. APHD, Sydney.

Asuni, Judith Burdin (1988) 'Changing Patterns of Egba Childrearing'. Unpublished PhD dissertation. Centre of West African Studies, University of Birmingham.

Awusabo-Asare, Kofi (1988) 'Education and Fertility in Ghana'. PhD dissertation. Unpublished. Department of Geography, University of Liverpool.

Babb, Florence (1986) 'Producers and Reproducers: Andean Marketwomen in the Economy'. In June Nash and Helen Safa (eds) *Women and Change in Latin America*. Bergin and Garvey, Massachusetts, 53–64.

Ballard, Roger (1987) 'The Political Economy of Migration: Pakistan, Britain and the Middle East'. In Jeremy Eades (ed.) *Migrants, Workers and the Social Order*. Association of Social Anthropologists Monograph No.26, Tavistock, London, 17–41.

Banck, Geert (1980) 'Survival Strategies of Low-Income Urban Households in Brazil'. In *Urban Anthropology*, 9:2, 227–42.

de Barbieri, Teresita (1982) 'Familia y Trabajo Doméstico'. Paper presented at seminar 'Domestic Groups, Family and Society'. El Colegio de México, México DF. 7–9 July 1982.

Barrett, Michèle (1986) *Women's Oppression Today: Problems in Marxist Feminist Analysis*. Verso, London (fifth impression).

Barrett, Michèle and McIntosh, Mary (1982) 'The "Family Wage" '. In Elizabeth Whitelegg et al (eds) *The Changing Experience of Women*. Martin Robertson, Oxford, 71–87.

Barrow, Christine (1986) 'Finding the Support: A Study of Strategies for Survival'. In *Social and Economic Studies*, 35:2. Institute of Social and Economic Research, University of the West Indies, 131–76.

Barrows, Walter (1974) 'Comparative Grassroots Politics in Africa,' *World Politics*, 26, 283–97.

Bascom, William (1952) 'The Esusu: A Credit Institution of the Yoruba.' In *Journal of the Royal Anthropological Institute*, 82:1, 63–9.

de Beauvoir, Simone (1953) *The Second Sex*. Penguin, Harmondsworth.

Beechey, Veronica (1979) 'On Patriarchy'. In *Feminist Review*, 3, 66–82.

Benería, Lourdes and Sen, Gita (1981), 'Accumulation, Reproduction and Women's Role in Economic Development'. In *Signs: Journal of Women in Culture and Society*, 7:2, 279–98.

Bennholdt-Thomsen, Veronika (1981) 'Subsistence Production and Extended Reproduction'. In Kate Young, Carol Wolkowitz and Roslyn McCullagh (eds) *Of Marriage and the Market*. CSE, London, 16–29.

Benton, Jane (1987) 'A Decade of Change in the Lake Titicaca Region'. In Janet Momsen and Janet Townsend (eds) *Geography of Gender in the Third World*. Hutchinson, London, 215–21.

Beuchler, Judith-Maria (1986) 'Women in Petty Commodity Production in La Paz, Bolivia'. In June Nash and Helen Safa (eds) *Women and Change in Latin America*. Bergin and Garvey, Massachusetts, 165–88.

Bhaduri, Amit and Rahman, Anisur Md. (eds) (1982) *Studies in Rural Participation*. Oxford and IBH Publishing Co. for ILO, New Delhi.

Bilsborrow, Richard E., Oberai, A.S. and Standing, Guy (1984) *Migration Surveys in Low-Income Countries: Guidelines for Survey and Questionnaire Design*. Croom Helm for the International Labour Office, London and Sydney.

van Binsbergen, Wim and Meilink, Henk A. (eds) (1978) *Migration and the Transformation of African Society (African Perspectives 1)*. Afrika-Studiecentrum, Leiden, Netherlands.

Birkbeck, Chris (1979) 'Garbage Industry and the "Vultures" of Cali, Colombia'. In Ray Bromley and Chris Gerry (eds) *Casual Work and Poverty in Third World Cities*. John Wiley, Chichester, 161–83.

Birks, J.S. and Sinclair, C.A. (1980) *International Migration and Development in the Arab Region*. International Labour Office, Geneva.

Blackwood, Florette (1986) 'The Performance of Men and Women in Repayment of Mortgage Loans in Jamaica'. In Judith Bruce and Marilyn Köhn (eds) *Learning about Women and Urban Services in Latin America and the Caribbean*. Population Council, New York, 101–15.

Blayney, Robert and Lycette, Margaret (1983) *Improving the Access of Women-Headed Households to Solanda Housing: A Feasible Down-Payment Assistance Scheme*. International Center for Research on Women, Washington DC.

Bledsoe, Caroline (1980) *Women and Marriage in Kpelle Society*. Stanford University Press, Stanford, California.

Bledsoe, Caroline and Isiugo-Abanihe, Uche C. (forthcoming.) 'Strategies of Child-Fosterage among Mende Grannies in Sierra Leone'. In Ronald Lesthaeghe (ed.) *Reproduction and Social Organization in Tropical Africa*. University of California Press.

Bleek, Wolf (1976) *Sexual Relationships and Birth Control in Ghana: A Case Study of a Rural Town*. Antropologisch-Sociologisch Centrum, Universiteit van Amsterdam, Amsterdam.

Blomström, Magnus and Hettne, Björn (1984) *Development Theory in Transition*, Zed, London.

Blumberg, Rae Lesser (1976) 'Fairy Tales and Facts: Economy, Family, Fertility and the Female'. In Irene Tinker, Michèle Bo Bramsen and Mayra Buvinić (eds) *Women and World Develop-*

ment. Praeger, New York, 12–21.

Blumberg, Rae Lesser (1978) 'The Political Economy of the Mother-Child Family Revisited'. In André Marks and René Römer (eds) *Family and Kinship in Middle America and the Caribbean*. University of the Netherlands Antilles and the Department of Caribbean Studies, Royal Institute of Linguistics and Anthropology, Leiden, Netherlands, 526–75.

Blumberg, Rae Lesser with García, María Pilar (1977) 'The Political Economy of the Mother-Child Family: A Cross-Societal View'. In Luis Leñero-Otero (ed.) *Beyond the Nuclear Family Model: Cross-Cultural Perspectives*. Sage, London, 99–163.

Blumenfeld, Emily and Mann, Susan (1980) 'Domestic Labour and the Reproduction of Labour Power: Towards an Analysis of Women, the Family and Class'. In Bonnie Fox (ed.) *Hidden in the Household: Women's Domestic Labour under Capitalism*. The Women's Press, Toronto, 267–307.

Bock, E. Wilbur, Iutaka, Sugiyama and Berardo, Felix (1980) 'Urbanization and the Extended Family in Brazil'. In Man Singh Das and Clinton Jesser (eds) *The Family in Latin America*. Vikas, New Delhi, 161–84.

Bolles, A. Lynn (1986) 'Economic Crisis and Female-Headed Households in Urban Jamaica'. In June Nash and Helen Safa (eds) *Women and Change in Latin America*. Bergin and Garvey, Massachusetts, 65–83.

Bondestam, Lars (1982) 'The Political Ideology of Population Control'. In Hamza Alavi and Teodor Shanin (eds) *Sociology of Developing Societies*. Macmillan, London and Basingstoke, 252–9.

Boserup, Ester (1970) *Woman's Role in Economic Development*. George Allen and Unwin, London. Reprinted 1986, Gower: Aldershot.

Boyle, Catherine (1986) 'Images of Women in Contemporary Chilean Theatre'. In *Bulletin of Latin American Research*, 5:2, 81–96.

Brambila, Carlos (1986) *Migración y Formacion Familiar en México*. El Colegio de México/UNAM, México DF.

Bridges, Julian (1980) 'The Mexican Family'. In Man Singh Das and Clinton Jesser (eds) *The Family in Latin America*. Vikas, New Delhi, 295–334.

Brieger, William and Adeniyi, Joshua (1982) 'Urban Community

Health Education in Africa'. In *International Quarterly of Community Health Education* 2:2, 109–21.

Briskin, Lina (1980) 'Domestic Labour: A Methodological Discussion'. In Bonnie Fox (ed.) *Hidden in the Household: Women's Domestic Labour under Capitalism.* The Women's Press, Toronto, 135–72.

Bromley, Ray (1982) 'Working in the Streets: Survival Strategy, Necessity or Unavoidable Evil?'. In Alan Gilbert in association with Jorge Hardoy and Ronaldo Ramírez (eds) *Urbanization in Contemporary Latin America: Critical Approaches to the Analysis of Urban Issues.* John Wiley, Chichester, 59–77.

Brown, Judith K. (1970) 'A Note on the Division of Labor by Sex'. In *American Anthropologist*, 72, 1073–8.

Bryceson, Deborah Fahy (1985) 'Women's Proletarianization and the Family Wage in Tanzania'. In Haleh Afshar (ed.) *Women, Work and Ideology in the Third World.* Tavistock, London, 128–52.

Brydon, Lynne (1976) 'Status Ambiguity in Amedzofe-Avatime: Women and Men in a Changing Patrilineal Society'. Unpublished PhD dissertation. Department of Social Anthropology, University of Cambridge.

Brydon, Lynne (1979) 'Women at Work: Some Changes in Family Structure in Amedzofe-Avatime, Ghana'. In *Africa*, 49:2, 97–111.

Brydon, Lynne (1981) 'Rice, Yams and Chiefs in Avatime: Speculations on the Development of a Social Order'. In *Africa*, 53:2, 659–77.

Brydon, Lynne (1985a) 'The Avatime Family and Migration 1900–1977'. In R. Mansell Prothero and Murray Chapman (eds) *Circulation in Third World Countries.* Routledge and Kegan Paul, London, 206–25.

Brydon, Lynne (1985b) 'The Dimensions of Subordination: A Case Study from Avatime, Ghana'. In Haleh Afshar (ed.) *Women, Work and Ideology in the Third World* Tavistock: London, 109–127.

Brydon, Lynne (1987a) 'Women in the Family: Cultural Change in Avatime, Ghana; 1900–1980'. In *Development and Change*, 18, 251–69.

Brydon, Lynne (1987b) 'Who Moves? Women and Migration in West Africa in the 1980s'. In Jeremy Eades (ed.) *Migrants,*

Workers and the Social Order. Association of Social Anthropologists Monograph No.26, Tavistock, London, 165–80.

Buenaventura-Posso, Elena and Brown, Susan (1980) 'Forced Transition from Egalitarianism to Male Dominance: The Bari of Colombia'. In Mona Etienne and Eleanor Leacock (eds) *Women and Colonisation.* Praeger, New York, 109–33.

Buenaventura-Posso, Elena and Brown, Susan (1987) 'Westernisation and the Bari of Colombia'. In Eduardo Archetti, Paul Cammack and Bryan Roberts (eds) *Sociology of Developing Societies: Latin America.* Macmillan, Basingstoke, 321–328.

Bujra, Janet (1977) 'Production, Property and Prostitution: Sexual Politics in Atu'. In *Cahiers d'Études Africaines*, 65 (17:1), 13–39.

Bukh, Jette (1979). *The Village Woman in Ghana.* Scandinavian Institute of African Studies, Uppsala.

Burton, Michael L. and Reitz, Karl (1981) 'The low, female contribution to agricultural subsistence and polygyny: A log linear analysis'. In *Behavior Science Research*, 16, 275–305.

Burton, Michael L. and White, Douglas, R. (1984) 'Sexual division of labor in agriculture'. In *American Anthropologist*, 86, 568–83.

Butterworth, Douglas (1975) *Tilantongo: Comunidad Mixteca en Transición.* Instituto Nacional Indigenista y Secretaría de Educación Pública, México DF.

Butterworth, Douglas and Chance, John (1981) *Latin American Urbanization.* Cambridge University Press, Cambridge.

Buvinić, Mayra (1983) 'Women's Issues in Third World Poverty: A Policy Analysis'. In Mayra Buvinić, Margaret Lycette and William McGreevey (eds) *Women and Poverty in the Third World.* Johns Hopkins University Press, Baltimore, 13–31.

Buvinić Mayra (1984) *Projects for Women in the Third World: Explaining their Misbehaviour.* International Center for Research on Women, Washington DC.

Caldwell, John C. (1976) 'Towards a Restatement of Demographic Transition Theory'. In *Population and Development Review*, 2:3/4, 321–65.

Caldwell, John C. (1977) *Population Growth and Family Change in Africa.* C. Hurst and Company, London.

Canton Moller, Miguel (1974) 'Equality of Employment Opportunities in Mexico'. In International Labour Office, *Equality of Opportunity in Employment in the American Region: Problems and Policies.* ILO, Geneva, 50–60.

Caplan, Patricia (1981) 'Development Policies in Tanzania: Some Implications for Women'. In Nici Nelson (ed.) *African Women in the Development Process*. Frank Cass, London, 98–108.

Caplan, Patricia (1984) 'Cognatic Descent, Islamic Law and Women's Property on the East African Coast'. In Renée Hirschon (ed.) *Women and Property – Women as Property*. Croom Helm/St Martins, London/New York, 23–43.

Caplan, Patricia (1985) *Class and Gender in India: Women and their Organisations in a South Indian City*. Tavistock, London.

Caplan, Patricia and Bujra, Janet (eds) (1978) *Women United, Women Divided: Cross-Cultural Perspectives on Female Solidarity*. Tavistock, London.

Carter, William and True, William (1978) 'Family and Kinship Among the San José Working Class'. In André Marks and René Römer (eds) *Family and Kinship in Middle America and the Caribbean*. University of the Netherlands Antilles and the Department of Caribbean Studies of the Royal Institute of Linguistics and Anthropology. Leiden, Netherlands, 227–50.

Casinader, Rex, Fernando, Sepalika and Gamage, Karuna (1987) 'Women's Issues and Men's Roles: Sri Lankan Village Experience'. In Janet Momsen and Janet Townsend (eds) *Geography of Gender in the Third World*. Hutchinson, London, 309–322.

Castells, Manuel (1978) *City, Class and Power*. Macmillan, London.

Castells, Manuel (1984) *The City and the Grassroots*. Edward Arnold, London.

Castro, Fidel (1981) 'The Revolution within the Revolution'. In Elizabeth Stone (ed.) *Women and the Cuban Revolution*. Pathfinder Press, New York, 48–54.

Caughman, Susan (1981) *Women at Work in Mali: The Case of the Markala Cooperative*. Boston University African Studies Center Working Paper No. 50, Boston.

Cecelski, Elizabeth (1985) *The Rural Energy Crisis, Women's Work and Basic Needs: Perspectives and Approaches to Action*. Rural Employment Policy Research Programme, Technical Cooperation Report, International Labour Office, Geneva.

Chagnon, Napoleon A. (1968) *Yanomamo: The Fierce People*. Holt Rinehart and Winston, New York.

Chambers, Robert (1974) *Managing Rural Development: Ideas and Experience from East Africa*. Scandinavian Institute of African

Studies, Uppsala.

Chambers, Robert (1983) *Rural Development: Putting the Last First.* Longman, London.

Chant, Sylvia (1984a) '"Las Olvidadas": A Study of Women, Housing and Family Structure in Querétaro, Mexico'. Unpublished PhD dissertation. Department of Geography, University College, London.

Chant Sylvia (1984b) 'Household Labour and Self-Help Housing in Querétaro, Mexico'. In *Boletín de Estudios Latinoamericanos y del Caribe*, 37, 45–68.

Chant, Sylvia (1985a) Family Formation and Female Roles in Querétaro, Mexico'. In *Bulletin of Latin American Research*, 4:1, 17–32.

Chant, Sylvia (1985b) 'Single-Parent Families: Choice or Constraint? The Formation of Female-Headed Households in Mexican Shanty Towns'. In *Development and Change*, 16, 635–56.

Chant, Sylvia (1987a) 'Family Structure and Female Labour in Querétaro, Mexico'. In Janet Momsen and Janet Townsend (eds) *Geography of Gender in the Third World*. Hutchinson, London, 277–93.

Chant, Sylvia (1987b) 'Domestic Labour, Decision-Making and Dwelling Construction: The Experience of Women in Querétaro, Mexico'. In Caroline Moser and Linda Peake (eds) *Women, Human Settlements and Housing*, Tavistock, London, 33–54.

Chant, Sylvia (1987c) 'Gender and Leadership in Low-Income Communities'. Paper presented at seminar 'Local Leaders and Community Development and Participation'. Fitzwilliam College, Cambridge 28–30 September 1987.

Chant, Sylvia (1988) 'Women, Households and Urban Labour Markets in Mexico'. Paper presented at workshop 'Household Income and Resource Management', London Third World Economic History Group, School of Oriental and African Studies, University of London, 12 January 1988.

Chant, Sylvia (1991) *Women and Survival in Mexican Cities: Perspectives on Gender, Labour Markets and Low-income Households.* University of Manchester Press, Manchester.

Chant, Sylvia and Ward, Peter (1987) 'Family Structure and Low-Income Housing Policy'. In *Third World Planning Review*, 9:1, 5–19.

Chapman, Murray and Prothero, R. Mansell (eds) (1985) *Circula-*

tion in the Third World. Routledge and Kegan Paul, London.

Charlton, Sue Ellen (1984) *Women in Third World Development*. Westview Press, Boulder, Colorado.

Chester, Robert (1977) 'The One-Parent Family: Deviant or Variant?' In Robert Chester and John Peel (eds) *Equalities and Inequalities in Family Life*. Academic Press, London, 149–61.

Chimedza, Ruvimbo (1987) 'Women and Decision-Making: The Case of District Councils in Zimbabwe'. In Christine Qunta (ed.) *Women in Southern Africa*. Allison and Busby, London, 135–45.

Clarke, Colin (1986) *Livelihood Systems, Settlements and Levels of Living in 'Los Valles Centrales de Oaxaca', Mexico*. Research Paper 37, School of Geography, University of Oxford.

Clarke, Edith (1957) *My Mother who Fathered Me: A Study of the Family in Three Selected Communities in Jamaica*. George Allen and Unwin, London.

Cloudsley, Anne (1981) *Women of Omdurman: Victims of Circumcision*. London (private publication).

Cobos, B. (1974) 'Mexico'. In International Labour Office, *Equality of Opportunity in Employment in the American Region: Problems and Policies*. ILO, Geneva, 66–73.

Cockcroft, James (1983) *Mexico: Class Formation, Capital Accumulation and the State*. Monthly Review Press, New York.

Communist Party of Cuba (1981) 'Thesis: On the Full Exercise of Women's Equality'. In Elizabeth Stone (ed.) *Women and the Cuban Revolution*. Pathfinder Press, New York, 74–105.

Connell, John, Dasgupta, Biplab, Laishley, Roy and Lipton, Michael (1976) *Migration from Rural Areas*. Oxford University Press, Delhi.

Connolly, Priscilla (1981) 'El Desempleo, Subempleo y la Pauperización Urbana: Crítica a las Interpretaciones Corrientes'. Paper presented at the third reunion of the Grupo Latinamericano de Investigación, México DF, 23–31 July 1981.

Connolly, Priscilla (1982) 'Uncontrolled Settlement and Self-Build: What Kind of Solution? The Mexico City Case'. In Peter Ward (ed.) *Self-Help Housing: A Critique*. Mansell, London, 141–74.

Conroy, J.D. (1976) *Education, Employment and Migration in Papua New Guinea*. Development Studies Centre Monograph No. 3, The Australian National University, Canberra.

Conti, Anna (1979) 'Capitalist Organization of Production through Non-Capitalist Relations: Women's Role in a Pilot Resettlement in Upper Volta'. In *Review of African Political Economy*, 15/16, 75–92.

Coontz, Stephanie and Henderson, Peta (1986) 'Introduction'. In Stephanie Coontz and Peta Henderson (eds) *Women's Work, Men's Property*. Verso, London, 1–42.

Coulson, Noel and Hinchcliffe, Doreen (1978) 'Women and Law Reform in Contemporary Islam'. In Lois Beck and Nikki Keddie (eds) *Women in the Muslim World*. Harvard University Press, Cambridge, Massachusetts, 37–51.

Coward, Rosalind (1983) *Patriarchal Precedents*. Routledge and Kegan Paul, London.

Crehan, Kate (1984) 'Women and Development in North Western Zambia: From Producer to Housewife'. In *Review of African Political Economy*, 27/28, 51–66.

Croll, Elizabeth (1979) *Socialist Development Experience: Women in Rural Production and Reproduction in the Soviet Union, China, Cuba and Tanzania*. IDS Discussion Paper No. 143, University of Sussex, Sussex.

Crow, Ben and Thomas, Alan with Jenkins, Robert and Kimble, Judy (1983) *Third World Atlas*. Open University Press, Milton Keynes.

Cubitt, Tessa (1988) *Latin American Society*. Longman, London.

Cunningham, Susan (1987) 'Gender and Industrialization in Brazil'. In Janet Momsen and Janet Townsend (eds) *Geography of Gender in the Third World*. Hutchinson, London, 294–308.

Cutrufelli, Maria Rosa (1983) *Women of Africa: Roots of Oppression*. Zed, London.

Dankelman, Irene and Davidson, Joan (1988) *Women and Environment in the Third World: Alliance for the Future*. Earthscan Publications, London.

Das, Man Singh (1980) 'Introduction to Latin American Family and Society'. In Man Singh Das and Clinton Jesser (eds) *The Family in Latin America*. Vikas, New Delhi, 1–11.

Das, Man Singh and Jesser, Clinton (eds) (1980) *The Family in Latin America*. Vikas, New Delhi.

Davies, Miranda (ed.) (1983) *Third World – Second Sex*. Zed, London.

Davies, Miranda (ed.) (1987) *Third World – Second Sex, Volume 2*. Zed, London.

Davis, Susan Schaefer (1978) 'Working Women in a Moroccan Village'. In Lois Beck and Nikki Keddie (eds) *Women in the Muslim World*. Harvard University Press, Cambridge, Massachusetts, 416–33.

Deere, Carmen Diana (1977) 'Changing Social Relations of Production'. In *Latin American Perspectives*, IV: 1/2, 48–69.

Deere, Carmen Diana (1986) 'Rural Women and Agrarian Reform in Peru, Chile and Cuba'. In June Nash and Helen Safa (eds) *Women and Change in Latin America*. Bergin and Garvey, Massachusetts, 189–207.

Deere, Carmen Diana and Leon de Leal, Magdalena (1981) 'Peasant Production, Proletarianization and the Sexual Division of Labour in the Andes'. In *Signs: Journal of Women in Culture and Society*, 7:2, 338–60.

Deere, Carmen Diana and Leon de Leal, Magdalena (1982) *Women in Andean Agriculture*. International Labour Office, Geneva.

Deighton, Jane, Horsley, Rossana, Stewart, Sarah and Cain, Cathy (1983) *Sweet Ramparts: Women in Revolutionary Nicaragua*. War on Want/Nicaragua Solidarity Campaign, London.

Dey, Jennie (1981), 'Gambian Women: Unequal Partners in Rice Development Projects?'. In Nici Nelson (ed.) *African Women in the Development Process*. Frank Cass, London, 109–22.

Dickenson, John et al. (1983) *A Geography of the Third World*. Methuen, London.

Dinan, Carmel (1983) 'Sugar Daddies and Gold-Diggers: The White Collar Single Women in Accra'. In Christine Oppong (ed.) *Female and Male in West Africa*. George Allen and Unwin, London, 344–66.

Divale, William and Harris, Marvin (1976) 'Population, Warfare and the Male Supremacist Complex'. In *American Anthropologist*, 78:3, 521–38.

Dixon, Ruth (1978) *Rural Women at Work*. Johns Hopkins Press for Resources in the Future, Baltimore.

Dixon, Ruth (1983) 'Land, Labour and the Sex Composition of the Agricultural Labour Force: An International Comparison'. In *Development and Change*, 14, 347–72.

Dixon-Mueller, Ruth (1985) *Women's Work in Third World Agriculture: Concepts and Indicators*. Women, Work and Development 9, International Labour Office, Geneva.

Dore, Ronald (1981) 'Introduction: Community Development in the 1970s'. In Ronald Dore and Zoe Mars (eds) *Community Development*. Croom Helm, London/Unesco, Paris, 13–46.

Doughty, Paul (1970) 'Behind the Back of the City: "Provincial" Life in Lima, Peru'. In William Mangin (ed.) *Peasants in Cities:*

Readings in the Anthropology of Urbanization. Houghton and Mifflin, Boston, 30–46.

Drakakis-Smith, David (1987) *The Third World City.* Methuen, London.

Draper, Patricia (1975) '!Kung Women: Contrasts in Sexual Egalitarianism in Foraging and Sedentary Contexts'. In Rayna R. Reiter (ed.) *Toward an Anthropology of Women.* Monthly Review Press, New York and London, 77–109.

Durrani, Lorna Hawker (1976) 'Employment of Women and Social Change'. In Russell Stone and John Simmons (eds) *Change in Tunisia.* State University of New York Press, Albany, 57–72.

Eades, Jeremy (1975) 'The Growth of a Migrant Community: The Yoruba of Northern Ghana'. In Jack Goody (ed.) *Changing Social Structure in Ghana.* International African Institute, London, 37–58.

Eades, Jeremy (1980) *The Yoruba Today.* Cambridge University Press, Cambridge.

Eades, Jeremy (1987) 'Prelude to an Exodus: Chain Migration, Trade and the Yoruba in Ghana'. In Jeremy Eades (ed.) *Migrants, Workers and the Social Order.* Association of Social Anthropologists Monograph No.26, Tavistock, London, 199–212.

Economic Commission for Africa (ECA) (1984) *Law and the Status of Women in Ghana.* ECA, United Nations, Addis Ababa.

Edholm, Felicity, Harris, Olivia and Young, Kate (1977) 'Conceptualising Women'. In *Critique of Anthropology*, 3: 9/10, 101–30.

Edholm, Felicity, Harris, Olivia and Young, Kate (1982) 'La Conceptualización de la Mujer'. In Secretaría de Programación y Presupuesto (SPP) (ed.) *Estudios Sobre la Mujer 1. El Empleo y la Mujer. Bases Teóricas, Metodológicas y Evidencia Empírica.* SPP, México DF, 349–73.

Eisen, Arlene (1984) *Women and Revolution in Viet Nam.* Zed, London.

Eisenstein, Zillah (ed.) (1979) *Capitalist Patriarchy and the Case for Socialist Feminism.* Monthly Review Press, New York.

Ekejiuba, Felicia (1984) 'Contemporary Households and Major Socio-Economic Transitions in E. Nigeria'. Paper given at Workshop 'Conceptualising the Household: Issues of Theory, Method and Application'. Harvard University, Cambridge, Massachusetts, 2–4 November, 1984.

Elkan, Walter (1973) 'Circular Migration and the Growth of Towns in East Africa'. In Richard Jolly, Emanuel de Kadt, Hans Singer and Fiona Wilson (eds) *Third World Employment: Problems and Strategy*. Penguin, Harmondsworth, 106–14.

Ellis, Pat (ed.) (1986) *Women of the Caribbean*. Zed, London.

Elmendorf, Mary (1976) 'The Dilemma of Peasant Women: A View from a Village in Yucatan'. In Irene Tinker, Michèle Bo Bramsen and Mayra Buvinić (eds) *Women and World Development*. Praeger: New York, 88–94.

Elmendorf, Mary (1977) 'Mexico: The Many Worlds of Women'. In Janet Zollinger Giele and Audrey Chapman Smock (eds) *Women: Roles and Status in Eight Countries*. John Wiley, New York, 127–72.

Elmendorf, Mary and Buckles, Patricia (1980) *Appropriate Technology for Water Supply and Sanitation: Socio-Cultural Aspects of Water Supply and Excreta Disposal*. World Bank, Washington.

Elson, Diane (1982) 'The Differentiation of Children's Labour in the Capitalist Labour Market'. In *Development and Change*, 13:4, 479–97.

Elson, Diane and Pearson, Ruth (1981) '"Nimble Fingers Make Cheap Workers": An Analysis of Women's Employment in Third World Export Manufacturing'. In *Feminist Review*, 7, 87–107.

Elú de Leñero, María del Carmen (1980) 'Women's Work and Fertility'. In June Nash and Helen Safa (eds) *Sex and Class in Latin America*. Bergin, New York, 46–68.

Ember, Carol R. (1983) 'The Relative Decline in Women's Contribution to Agriculture with Intensification'. In *American Anthropologist* 85, 285–305.

Engels, Frederick (1972) *The Origin of the Family, Private Property and the State*. Lawrence and Wishart, London. (Originally published in 1884).

Engracia, Luisa and Herrin, Alejandro (1984) 'Employment Structure of Female Migrants to the Cities in the Philippines'. In Gavin W. Jones (ed.) *Women in the Urban and Industrial Workforce: Southeast and East Asia*. Development Studies Monograph No.33, Australian National University, Canberra, 293–304.

Ennew, Judith (1978) 'The Material of Reproduction'. In *Economy and Society*, 7:1, 99–124.

Ennew, Judith (1986) '*Mujercita* and *Mamacita*: Girls Growing up in Lima'. In *Bulletin of Latin American Research*, 5:2, 49–66.

Escobar, Agustín, González, Mercedes and Roberts, Bryan (1987) 'Migration, Labour Markets and the International Economy'. In Jeremy Eades (ed.) *Migrants, Workers and the Social Order*. Association of Social Anthropologists Monograph No.26, London, 42–64.

Etienne, Mona (1983) 'Gender Relations and Conjugality among the Baule'. In Christine Oppong (ed.) *Female and Male in West Africa*. George Allen and Unwin, London, 303–19.

Europa (1987) *Africa South of the Sahara*. Europa Publications, London.

Fapohunda, Eleanor 1983. 'Female and Male Work Profiles'. In Christine Oppong (ed.) *Female and Male in West Africa*. George Allen and Unwin, London, 32–53.

Fawcett, J.T., Khoo, S. and Smith, P.C. (1984) (eds) *Women in the Cities of Asia: Migration and Urban Adaptation*. Westview Press, Boulder, Colorado.

Feldman, Rayah (1984) 'Women's Groups and Women's Subordination: An Analysis of Policies towards Rural Women in Kenya'. In *Review of African Political Economy*, 27/28, 67–85.

Fernandez-Kelly, Maria Patricia (1981) 'Development and the Sexual Division of Labor: An Introduction'. In *Signs: Journal of Women in Culture and Society*, 7:2, 268–78.

Fernandez-Kelly, Maria Patricia (1983) 'Mexican Border, Industrialization, Female Labour Force Participation and Migration. In June Nash and Maria Patricia Fernandez-Kelly (eds) *Women, Men and the International Division of Labour*. State University of New York Press, Albany, New York, 205–23.

Fernando, Marina (1987) 'New Skills for Women; A Community Development Project in Colombo, Sri Lanka'. In Caroline Moser and Linda Peake (eds) *Women, Human Settlements and Housing*. Tavistock, London, 88–112.

Flandrin, Jean-Louis (1979) *Families in Former Times: Kinship, Household and Sexuality*. Cambridge University Press, Cambridge.

Flora, Cornelia Butler and Santos, Blas (1986) 'Women in Farming Systems in Latin America'. In June Nash and Helen Safa (eds) *Women and Change in Latin America*. Bergin and Garvey, Massachusetts, 208–28.

Fortes, Meyer (1958) 'Introduction'. In J.R. Goody (ed.) *The

Developmental Cycle in Domestic Groups. Cambridge University Press, Cambridge, 1–14.

Fortes, Meyer (1970) 'Time and Social Structure'. In Meyer Fortes (ed.) *Time and Social Structure and Other Essays.* Athlone Press, London, 1–32.

Fortes, Meyer (1980) 'Informants'. In *L'uomo*, IV:2, 363.

Foster, George (1965) 'Peasant Society and the Image of the Limited Good'. In *American Anthropologist*, 67, 293–315.

Foster, George (1972) 'A Second Look at the Limited Good'. In *Anthropological Quarterly*, 45, 57–64.

Fox, David (1972) 'Patterns of Morbidity and Mortality in Mexico City'. *Geographical Review*, 62, 151–86.

Fraser, Arvonne S. (1987) *The UN Decade for Women: Documents and Dialogue.* Westview Special Studies on Women in Contemporary Society, Westview, Boulder and London.

Freund, Bill (1984) *The Making of Contemporary Africa.* Macmillan, London and Basingstoke.

Fromm, Erich and Maccoby, Michael (1970) *Social Character in a Mexican Village: A Sociopsychoanalytic Study.* Prentice Hall, Englewood Cliffs, New Jersey.

Fuller, C.J. (1976) *The Nayars Today.* Cambridge University Press, Cambridge.

García, Brígida, Muñoz, Humberto and de Oliveira, Orlandina (1982) *Hogares y Trabajadores en la Ciudad de México.* El Colegio de México/UNAM, México DF.

García, Brígida, Muñoz, Humberto and de Oliveira, Orlandina (1983) Familia y Trabajo en México y Brasil. *Estudios Sociológicos*, 1:3 El Colegio de México, México DF, 487–507.

Gardiner, Jean (1979) 'Women's Domestic Labour'. In Zillah Eisenstein (ed.) *Capitalist Patriarchy and the Case for Socialist Feminism.* Monthly Review Press, New York, 173–89.

Geertz, Clifford (1962) 'The Rotating Credit Association: A "Middle Rung" in Development'. In *Economic Development and Cultural Change*, 10:3, 241–63.

Gerber, Stanford and Rasmussen, Knud (1978) 'Further Reflections on the Concept of Matrifocality and its Consequences for Social Science Research'. In André Marks and René Römer (eds) *Family and Kinship in Middle America and the Caribbean.* University of the Netherlands Antilles and the Department of Caribbean Studies, Royal Institute of Linguistics and Anthropology, Leiden,

Netherlands.

Germani, Gino (1970) 'Mass Immigration and Modernisation in Argentina'. In Irving Horowitz (ed.) *Masses in Latin America*. Oxford University Press, New York, 289–330.

Germani, Gino (1981) *The Sociology of Modernisation: Studies on its Historical and Theoretical Aspects with Special Regard to the Latin American Case*. Transaction, New Brunswick, New Jersey.

Gerold-Scheepers, Thérèse and van Binsbergen, Wim (1978) 'Marxist and Non-Marxist Approaches to Migration in Tropical Africa'. In Wim van Binsbergen and Henk Meilink (eds) *Migration and the Transformation of African Society* (*African Perspectives* 1). Afrika-Studiecentrum, Leiden, Netherlands, 21–36.

Ghai, Dharam and Radwan, Samir (1983) *Agrarian Policies and Rural Poverty in Africa*. International Labour Office, Geneva.

Gilbert, Alan and Gugler, Josef (1982) *Cities, Poverty and Development: Urbanization in the Third World*. Oxford University Press, Oxford.

Gilbert, Alan and Ward, Peter (1985) *Housing, the State and the Poor: Policy and Practice in Three Latin American Cities*. Cambridge University Press, Cambridge.

Girling, Robert, Lycette, Margaret and Youssef, Nadia (1983) *A Preliminary Evaluation of the Panama Women's Self-Help Construction Project*. International Center for Research on Women, Washington DC.

Gissi, Jorge (1980) 'Mythology about Women, with Special Reference to Chile'. In June Nash and Helen Safa (eds) *Sex and Class in Latin America*. Bergin, New York, 30–45.

Gonzalez, Gloria (1980) 'Participation of Women in the Mexican Labour Force'. In June Nash and Helen Safa (eds) *Sex and Class in Latin America*. Bergin, New York, 183–201.

González de la Rocha, Mercedes, Escobar, Agustín and De la Peña, Guillermo (1985) 'Crisis Económica y Pobreza, Vecindad y Organizaciones Populares en Guadalajara en los Años 1981–1985'. Research project presented by the Centro de Estudios Regionales, Colegio de Jalisco in collaboration with the Centro de Estudios Superiores en Antropología Social (CIESAS), México DF.

Goodale, Jane (1971) *Tiwi Wives*. University of Washington Press, Seattle.

Goode, William (1963) *World Revolution and Family Patterns*. The Free Press, New York.

Goody, Esther (1971) 'Forms of Pro-Parenthood: The Sharing and Substitution of Parental Roles'. In Jack Goody (ed.) *Kinship*. Penguin, Harmondsworth, 331–45.

Goody, Esther (1975) 'Delegation of Parental Roles in West Africa and the West Indies'. In Jack Goody (ed.) *Changing Social Structure in Ghana*. International African Institute, London, 137–66.

Goody, J.R. (ed.) (1958) *The Developmental Cycle in Domestic Groups*. Cambridge University Press, Cambridge.

Goody, J.R. (ed.) (1971) *Kinship*. Penguin, Harmondsworth.

Goody, Jack (1976) *Production and Reproduction: A Comparative Study of the Domestic Domain*. Cambridge University Press, Cambridge.

Goody, J.R. and Buckley, J. (1973) 'Inheritance and Women's Labour in Africa'. In *Africa*, 43, 108–21.

Gordon, Linda (1979) 'The Struggle for Reproductive Freedom: Three Stages of Feminism'. In Zillah Eisenstein (ed.) *Capitalist Patriarchy and the Case for Socialist Feminism*. Monthly Review Press, New York, 107–32.

Gould, W.T.S. (1982) 'Education and Internal Migration: A Review and Report'. In *International Journal of Educational Development*, 1:3, 103–27.

Graham, Ronald (1982) *The Aluminium Industry and the Third World*. Zed, London.

Gugler, Josef and Flanagan, William (1978) *Urbanisation and Social Change in West Africa*. Cambridge University Press, Cambridge.

Gulick, John and Gulick, Margaret (1978) 'The Domestic and Social Environment of Women and Girls in Isfahan, Iran'. In Lois Beck and Nikki Keddie (eds) *Women in the Muslim World*. Harvard University Press, Cambridge, Massachusetts, 501–21.

Guyer, Jane (1980) 'Food, Cocoa and the Division of Labour by Sex in Two West African Societies'. In *Comparative Studies in Society and History*, 22, 355–73.

Guyer, Jane (1981a) *The Raw, the Cooked and the Half-Baked: A Note on the Division of Labor by Sex*. Boston University African Studies Center Working Paper No.48, Boston.

Guyer, Jane (1981b) 'Household and Community in African Studies'. In *African Studies Review*, 24:2/3, 87–137.

Guyer, Jane (1984a) *Family and Farm in Southern Cameroon*. African Research Studies 15, Boston University African Studies Center, Boston.

Guyer, Jane (1984b) 'Naturalism in Models of African Production'. In *Man*, 19, 371–88.

Guyer, Jane (ed.) (1987) *Feeding African Cities*. Manchester University Press, Manchester.

Guyer, Jane (1988) 'The Multiplication of Labor'. In *Current Anthropology*, 29:2, 247–72.

Guyer, Jane and Peters, Pauline (1987) 'Introduction'. In *Conceptualising the Household: Issues of Theory and Policy in Africa*. Special issue of *Development and Change*, 18:2, 197–214.

Hackenberg, Robert, Murphy, Arthur and Selby, Henry (1981) The Household in the Secondary Cities of the Third World. Paper prepared for Wenner-Gren Foundation Symposium 'Households: Changing Form and Function'. New York, 8–15 October 1981.

Hagan, George Panyin (1983) 'Marriage, Divorce and Polygyny in Winneba'. In Christine Oppong (ed.) *Female and Male in West Africa*. George Allen and Unwin, London, 192–203.

Hake, Andrew (1977) *African Metropolis: Nairobi's Self-Help City*. Sussex University Press published by Chatto and Windus, London.

Hale, Sylvia (1978) 'The Politics of Entrepreneurship in Indian Villages'. In *Development and Change*, 9, 245–75.

Hardiman, Margaret and Midgley, James (1982) *The Social Dimensions of Development: Social Policy and Planning in the Third World*. John Wiley, Chichester.

Harkess, Shirley (1973) 'The Pursuit of an Ideal: Migration, Social Class and Women's Roles in Bogotá, Colombia'. In Ann Pescatello (ed.) *Female and Male in Latin America*. University of Pittsburgh Press, Pittsburgh, 231–54.

Harris, Nigel (1983) *Of Bread and Guns: The World Economy in Crisis*. Penguin, Harmondsworth.

Harris, Olivia (1978) 'Complementarity and Conflict: An Andean View of Women and Men'. In J.S. La Fontaine (ed.) *Sex and Age as Principles of Social Differentiation*. Association of Social Anthropologists Monograph No. 17, Academic Press, London, 21–40.

Harris, Olivia (1980) 'The Power of Signs: Gender, Culture and the Wild in the Bolivian Andes'. In Carol MacCormack and Marilyn

Strathern (eds) *Nature, Culture and Gender*. Cambridge University Press, Cambridge, 70–94.

Harris, Olivia (1981) 'Households as Natural Units'. In Kate Young, Carol Wolkowitz and Roslyn McCullagh (eds) *Of Marriage and the Market*. CSE, London, 48–67.

Harris, Olivia (ed.) (1982) *Latin American Women*. Minority Rights Group, London.

Harris, Sonia (1986) 'An Income Generating Project for Women in Rural Jamaica'. In Pat Ellis (ed.) *Women of the Caribbean*. Zed, London, 135–46.

Harrison, Paul (1979) *Inside the Third World*. Penguin, Harmondsworth.

Harriss, Barbara and Watson, Elizabeth (1987) 'The Sex Ratio in South Asia'. In Janet Momsen and Janet Townsend (eds) *Geography of Gender in the Third World*. Hutchinson, London, 85–115.

Hart, Keith (1973) 'Informal Income Opportunities and Urban Employment in Ghana. In Richard Jolly, Emmanuel De Kadt, Hans Singer and Fiona Wilson (eds) *Third World Employment: Problems and Strategy*. Penguin, Harmondsworth, 66–70.

Hartmann, Betsy (1987) *Reproductive Rights and Wrongs: The Global Politics of Population Control and Contraceptive Choice*. Harper and Row, New York.

Hartmann, Heidi (1979) 'Capitalism, Patriarchy and Job Segregation by Sex'. In Zillah Eisenstein (ed.) *Capitalist Patriarchy and the Case for Socialist Feminism*. Monthly Review Press, New York, 206–47.

Harvey, Penelope (1988) 'Muted or Ignored? Questions of Gender and Ethnicity in the Politics of the Southern Peruvian Andes'. Paper presented at the XIV International Congress of the Latin American Studies Association, New Orleans, Lousiana, 17–19 March, 1988.

Hein, Catherine (1986) 'The Feminisation of Industrial Employment in Mauritius: A Case of Sex Segregation'. In Richard Anker and Catherine Hein (eds) *Sex Inequalities in Urban Employment in the Third World*. Macmillan, Basingstoke, 277–311.

Helmore, Kristin (ed.) (1986) *The Neglected Resource: Women in the Developing World*. Christian Science Monitor Special Report.

Heyzer, Noeleen (1981) 'Towards a Framework of Analysis'. In

Bulletin, 12:3 Institute of Development Studies, University of Sussex, 3–7.

Heyzer, Noeleen (1982) 'From Rural Subsistence to an Industrial Peripheral Work Force: An Examination of Female Malaysian Migrants and Capital Accumulation in Singapore'. In Lourdes Benería (ed.) *Women and Development*. Praeger for the International Labour Office, New York.

Heyzer, Noeleen (1986) *Working Women in South-East Asia: Development, Subordination and Emancipation*. Open University Press, Milton Keynes.

Hill, Polly (1969) 'Hidden Trade in Hausaland'. In *Man*, 4:3, 392–409.

Hirashima, S. (ed.) (1977) *Hired Labour in Rural Asia*. Institute for Developing Economies, Tokyo.

Hirschfeld, Lawrence A. et al. (1978) 'Warfare, Infanticide and Statistical Inference: A Comment on Divale and Harris'. In *American Anthropologist*, 80, 110–15.

Hollnsteiner, Mary Racelis (1977) 'People Power: Community Participation in the Planning of Human Settlements'. In *Carnets de l'Enfance*, 40, 11–47.

Hollnsteiner, Mary Racelis (1982) 'People-Powered Development: Thoughts for Urban Planners, Administrators and Policy Makers'. Paper presented at the Regional Congress of Local Authorities for Development of Human Settlements in Asia and the Pacific, Yokohama, Japan, 9–16 June 1982.

Holstrom, Nancy (1981) '"Women's Work", The Family and Capitalism'. In *Science and Society*, 45, 186–211.

Hoogvelt, Ankie (1976) *The Sociology of Developing Societies*. Macmillan, London and Basingstoke.

Horowitz, Berny and Kishwar, Madhu (1984) 'Family Life: The Unequal Deal'. In Madhu Kishwar and Ruth Vanita (eds) *In Search of Answers: Indian Women's Voices from Manushi*. Zed, London, 69–103.

Hugh-Jones, C. (1978) 'Food for Thought – Patterns of Production and Consumption in Pirá-Paraná Society'. In J.S. La Fontaine (ed.) *Sex and Age as Principles of Social Differentiation*. Association of Social Anthropologists Monograph No.17, Academic Press, London, 41-66.

Hugh-Jones, C. (1979) *From the Milk River*. Cambridge University Press, Cambridge.

Humphrey, John (1985) 'Gender, Pay and Skill: Manual Workers in Brazilian Industry'. In Haleh Afshar (ed.) *Women, Work and Ideology in the Third World*. Tavistock, London, 214–31.

Huston, Perdita (1979) *Third World Women Speak Out*. Praeger, New York.

Hutter, Mark (1981) *The Changing Family: Comparative Perspectives*. John Wiley, New York.

Hyden, Goran (1980) *Beyond Ujamaa in Tanzania: Underdevelopment and an Uncaptured Peasantry*. Heinemann, London.

Hyden, Goran (1986a) 'The Anomaly of the African Peasantry'. In *Development and Change*, 17, 677–705.

Hyden, Goran (1986b) 'The Invisible Economy of Smallholder Agriculture in Africa'. In Joyce Lewinger Moock (ed.) *Understanding Africa's Rural Households and Farming Systems*. Westview Press, Boulder, Colorado, 11–35.

Ifeka, Caroline (1982) 'The Self Viewed from "Within" or "Without": Twists and Turns in Gender Identity in a Patrilineal Society'. In *Mankind*, 13:5, 401–15.

Ifeka-Moller, Caroline (1975) 'Female Militancy and Colonial Revolt: The Women's War of 1929, Eastern Nigeria'. In Shirley Ardener (ed.) *Perceiving Women*. Malaby, London, 127–58.

Iglesias, Norma (1985) *La Flor Mas Bella de la Maquiladora: Historias de Vida de La Mujer Obrera en Tijuana, Baja California Norte*. SEP/CEFNOMEX, México DF.

Ingrams, Doreen (1983) *The Awakened: Women in Iraq*. Third World Centre for Research and Publishing, London.

Institute of British Geographers Women and Geography Study Group (IBG) (1984) *Geography and Gender: An Introduction to Feminist Geography*. Hutchinson, London.

Inter-American Development Bank (IDB) (1987) *Economic and Social Progress in Latin America: Special Section – Labour Force and Employment*. IDB, New York.

International Labour Office (ILO) (1977) *Poverty and Landlessness in Rural Asia*. ILO, Geneva.

International Labour Office (ILO) (1982) *Rural Development and Women in Asia*. ILO, Geneva.

International Labour Office (ILO) (1984) *Rural Development and Women in Africa*. ILO, Geneva.

International Planned Parenthood Federation (IPPF), Evaluation Department (1982) *Planned Parenthood – Women's Develop-*

ment. IPPF, London.

International Women's Tribune Center (IWTC) (1981) *Newsletter No. 15: Women, Money and Credit*. IWTC, New York.

International Women's Tribune Center (IWTC) (1982) *Newsletter No. 20: Women and Water*. IWTC, New York.

Isbell, Billie-Jean (1976) 'La Otra Mitad Esencial: Un Estudio de Complementariedad Sexual en los Andes'. In June Nash (ed.) *La Mujer en los Andes*. Special issue of *Estudios Andinos* 5:1, Center for Latin American Studies, University of Pittsburgh, 37–56.

Isbell, Billie-Jean (1978) *To Defend Ourselves: Ecology and Ritual in an Andean Village*. University of Texas Press, Austin.

Isiugo-Abanihe, Uche C. (1985) 'Child Fosterage in West Africa'. In *Population and Development Report*, 11:1, 53–73.

Jain, Devaki (1980) *Women's Quest for Power*. Vikas, Sahibabad, India.

Jayawardena, Kumari (1986) *Feminism and Nationalism in the Third World*. Zed, London.

Jeffery, Patricia (1979) *Frogs in a Well: Indian Women in Purdah*. Zed, London.

Jelin, Elizabeth (1977) 'Migration and Labour Force Participation of Latin American Women: The Domestic Servants in the Cities'. In Wellesley Editorial Committee (eds) *Women and National Development: the Complexities of Change*. University of Chicago, Chicago, 129–41.

Jelin, Elizabeth (1980) 'The Bahiana in the Labor Force of Salvador, Brazil'. In June Nash and Helen Safa (eds) *Sex and Class in Latin America*. Bergin, New York, 129–46.

Joekes, Susan (1982) *Female-led Industrialisation: Women's Jobs in Third World Export Manufacturing*. Institute of Development Studies Research Report No.15, University of Sussex, Falmer, Sussex.

Joekes, Susan (1985) 'Working for Lipstick? Male and Female Labour in the Clothing Industry in Morocco'. In Haleh Afshar (ed.) *Women, Work and Ideology in the Third World*. Tavistock, London, 183–213.

Jones, Gavin W. (ed.) (1984) *Women in the Urban and Industrial Labour Force: Southeast and East Asia*. Development Studies Centre Monograph No. 33, The Australian National University, Canberra.

Jongkind, Fred (1986) 'Ethnic Solidarity and Social Stratification: Migrant Organisations in Peru and Argentina'. In *Boletín de Estudios Latinoamericanos y del Caribe*, 40, 37–48.

Jules-Rosette, Benetta (1985) 'The Women, Potters of Lusaka: Urban Migration and Socioeconomic Adjustment'. In Beverly Lindsay (ed.) *African Migration and National Development*. Pennsylvania State University, Pennsylvania, 82–112.

Kabeer, Naila (1985) 'Do Women Gain from High Fertility?' In Haleh Afshar (ed.) *Women, Work and Ideology in the Third World*. Tavistock, London, 83–106.

Kahl, Joseph (1968) *The Measurement of Modernism: A Study of Values in Brazil and Mexico*. University of Texas Press, Austin.

Kamugisha, Stephanie (1986) 'Violence against Women'. In Pat Ellis (ed.) *Women of the Caribbean*. Zed, London, 74–9.

Kayongo-Male, Diane (1983) 'Helping Self-Help Groups Help Themselves: Training of Leaders of Women's Groups'. In *Journal of Eastern African Research and Development*, 13, 88–103.

Keesing, R. M. (1975) *Kin Groups and Social Structure*. Holt, Rinehart and Winston, New York.

Keesing, Roger M. (1985) *Cultural Anthropology*. CBS College Publishing, Japan, New York, Toronto, London, Madrid.

Kemper, Robert (1977) *Migration and Adaptation: Tzintzuntzan Peasants in Mexico City*. Sage, Beverly Hills, California.

Khatib-Chahidi, Jane, (1981) 'Sexual Prohibitions, Shared Space and Fictive Marriages in Shi'ite Iran'. In Shirley Ardener (ed.) *Women and Space: Ground Rules and Social Maps*. Croom Helm, London, 112–35.

Khoo, Siew-Ean (1984) 'Urbanward Migration and Employment of Women in Southeast and East Asian Cities: Patterns and Policy Issues'. In Gavin W. Jones (ed.) *Women in the Urban and Industrial Workforce: Southeast and East Asia*. Development Studies Centre Monograph No. 33, Australian National University, Canberra, 277–92.

Kidron, Michael and Segal, Ronald (1981) *The State of the World Atlas*. Pan, London.

Kidron, Michael and Segal, Ronald (1984) *The New State of the World Atlas*. Pan, London.

King, Kenneth (1979) 'Petty Production in Nairobi: The Social Context of Skill Acquisition and Occupational Differentiation'. In Ray Bromley and Chris Gerry (eds) *Casual Work and Poverty in Third World Cities*. John Wiley, Chichester, 217–28.

Kishwar, Madhu and Vanita, Ruth (eds) (1984) *In Search of Answers: Indian Women's Voices from Manushi.* Zed, London.

Kitching, Gavin (1982) *Development and Underdevelopment in Historical Perspective.* Methuen, London and New York.

Kusnir, Liliana and Largaespada, Carmen (1986) 'Women's Participation in Self-Help Housing Projects in Mexico City'. In Judith Bruce and Marilyn Köhn (eds) *Learning about Women and Urban Services in Latin America and the Caribbean.* Population Council, New York, 84–100.

Ladipo, Patricia (1981) 'Developing Women's Cooperatives: An Experiment in Rural Nigeria'. In Nici Nelson (ed.) *African Women in the Development Process.* Frank Cass, London, 123–36.

La Fontaine, J. S. (ed.) (1978) *Sex and Age as Principles of Social Differentiation.* Association of Social Anthropologists Monograph No. 17, Academic Press, London, New York, San Francisco.

Laguerre, Michel (1978) 'The Impact of Migration on the Haitian Family and Household Organisation?' In André Marks and René Römer (eds) *Family and Kinship in Middle America and the Caribbean.* University of the Netherlands Antilles and the Department of Caribbean Studies at the Royal Institute of Linguistics and Anthropology, Leiden, Netherlands, 446–81.

Lancaster, Chet and Beckman Lancaster, Jane (1978) 'On the Male Supremacist Complex: A Reply to Divale and Harris'. In *American Anthropologist*, 80, 115–17.

Laslett, Peter (1972) *Household and Family in Past Time.* Cambridge University Press, Cambridge.

Latin America Bureau (LAB) (1983) *Grenada: Whose Freedom?* Latin America Bureau, London.

Latin American and Caribbean Women's Collective (LACWC) (1980) *Slaves of Slaves: The Challenge of Latin American Women.* Zed Press, London.

Leach, Edmund (1982) *Social Anthropology.* Fontana, Glasgow.

Leacock, Eleanor (1972) 'Introduction to *The Origin of the Family, Private Property and the State*'. In Frederick Engels, *The Origin of the Family, Private Property and the State.* Lawrence and Wishart, London, 7–67.

Leacock, Eleanor (1978) 'Women's Status in Egalitarian Society'. In *Current Anthropology*, 19:2, 247–76.

Lee, Richard B. (1968) 'What do Hunters do for a Living, or How to Make Out on Scarce Resources'. In Richard B. Lee and Irven DeVore (eds) *Man the Hunter*. Aldine, Chicago, 30–48.

Lerner, Gerda (1986) *The Creation of Patriarchy*. Oxford University Press, New York and London.

Lévi-Strauss, Claude (1969) *The Elementary Structures of Kinship*. Eyre and Spottiswoode, London.

Lévi-Strauss, Claude (1972) *Structural Anthropology*. Penguin, Harmondsworth.

Lewenhak, Sheila (1980) *Women and Work*. Fontana, Glasgow.

Lewis, Oscar (1966) 'The Culture of Poverty'. In *Scientific American*, October 1966, 19–25.

Liddle, Joanna and Joshi, Rama (1986) *Daughters of Independence: Gender, Caste and Class in India*. Zed, London.

Little, Kenneth (1965) *West African Urbanization: A Study of Voluntary Associations in Social Change*. Cambridge University Press, Cambridge.

Little, Kenneth (1973) *African Women in Towns*. Cambridge University Press, Cambridge.

Llewelyn-Davies, Melissa (1978) 'Two Contexts of Solidarity'. In Patricia Caplan and Janet Bujra (eds) *Women United, Women Divided*. Tavistock, London, 206–37.

Llewelyn-Davies, Melissa (1981) 'Women Warriors and Patriarchs'. In Sherry B. Ortner and Harriet Whitehead (eds) *Sexual Meanings*. Cambridge University Press, Cambridge, 330–58.

Lomnitz, Larissa (1977a) *Networks and Marginality – Life in a Mexican Shanty Town*. Academic Press, New York.

Lomnitz, Larissa (1977b) 'Migration and Network in Latin America'. In Alejandro Portes and Harley Browning (eds) *Current Perspectives in Latin American Urban Research*. Institute of Latin American Studies, University of Texas at Austin, Austin, 133–50.

London Iranian Women's Liberation Group (LIWLG) (1983) 'Iranian Women: The Struggle Since the Revolution'. In Miranda Davies (ed.) *Third World – Second Sex: Women's Struggle and National Liberation*. Zed, London, 143–58.

Lu, Yu-Hsia (1984) 'Women, Work and the Family in a Developing Society: Taiwan'. In Gavin Jones (ed.) *Women in the Urban and Industrial Workforce: Southeast and East Asia*. Development Studies Centre Monograph No. 33, Australian National University, Canberra, 339–67.

Lumsden, D. Paul (1975) 'Resettlement and Rehousing: Unintended Consequences among the Nchumuru'. In Jack Goody (ed.) *Changing Social Structure in Ghana*. International African Institute, London, 201–28.

Lycette, Margaret and Jaramillo, Cecilia (1984) *Low-Income Housing: A Women's Perspective*. International Center for Research on Women, Washington DC.

MacCormack, Carol (1977) 'Wono: Institutionalised Dependency in Sherbro Descent Groups (Sierra Leone)'. In Suzanne Miers and Igor Kopytoff (eds) *Slavery in Africa*. University of Wisconsin Press, Madison and London, 181–204.

MacCormack, Carol (ed.) (1982). *Ethnography of Fertility and Birth*. Academic Press, London.

MacCormack, Carol (1983) *Minimum Planning and Evaluation Guidelines for Women, Health and Development*. Report prepared for World Health Organisation, Division of Family Health. Evaluation and Planning Centre, London School of Hygiene and Tropical Medicine.

MacCormack, Carol and Strathern, Marilyn (eds) (1980) *Nature, Culture and Gender*. Cambridge University Press, Cambridge.

MacDonald, John Stuart (1979) 'Planning Implementation and Social Policy: An Evaluation of Ciudad Guayana. In *Progress in Planning*, Vol. 11, Parts 1/2, 1–211.

Machado, Leda (1983) 'Low-Income Housing in Brazil and Women: Evaluation of the PROFILURB Project in Terms of its Capacity to Define and Reach Female-Headed Households as a Target Group'. Masters Dissertation, Development Planning Unit, University College, London.

Mackintosh, Maureen (1979) 'Domestic Labour and the Household'. In Sandra Burman (ed.) *Fit Work for Women*. Croom Helm, London, 173–91.

Mackintosh, Maureen (1981) 'Gender and Economics: The Sexual Division of Labour and the Subordination of Women'. In Kate Young, Carol Wolkowitz and Roslyn McCullagh (eds) *Of Marriage and the Market*. Conference of Socialist Economists, London, 1–15.

MacPherson, Stuart and Midgley, James (1987) *Comparative Social Policy and the Third World*. Wheatsheaf, Sussex.

Maher, Vanessa (1974) *Women and Property in Morocco*. Cambridge University Press, Cambridge.

Maher, Vanessa (1978) 'Women and Social Change in Morocco'. In Lois Beck and Nikki Keddie (eds) *Women in the Muslim World*. Harvard University Press, Cambridge, Massachusetts and London, 100–23.

Maloney, K. (1986) 'More than a Parley'. In *Community Development Journal*, 21:1, 52–8.

Mangin, William (1959) 'The Role of Regional Associations in the Adaptation of Rural Populations in Peru'. In *Sociologus*, 9, 21–36.

Manushi (1983) 'Indian Women Speak Out Against Dowry'. In Miranda Davies (ed.) *Third World – Second Sex: Women's Struggles and National Liberation*. Zed, London, 201–13.

Marshall, Lorna (1960) '!Kung Bushmen Bands'. In *Africa*, 29, 335–65.

Marshall, Lorna (1961) 'Sharing, Talking and Giving'. In *Africa*, 32, 231–52.

Martin, Susan (1988) *Palm Oil and Protest: An Economic History of the Ngwa Region, South-Eastern Nigeria, 1800–1980*. Cambridge University Press, Cambridge.

Massey, Doreen (1987) *Nicaragua*. Open University Press, Milton Keynes.

Massiah, Joycelin (1986a) 'Women in the Caribbean Project: An Overview. *Social and Economic Studies*, 35:2. Institute of Social and Economic Research, University of the West Indies, 1–29.

Massiah, Joycelin (1986b) 'Work in the Lives of Caribbean Women'. In *Social and Economic Studies*, 35:2. Institute of Social and Economic Research, University of the West Indies, 177–239.

Massolo, Alejandra (1987) 'Por Esas Cuatro Paredes'. In *Fem* (México DF), 52, 19–24.

Mather, Celia (1985) '"Rather than make trouble, its better just to leave": Behind the lack of industrial strife in the Tangerang region of West Java'. In Haleh Afshar (ed.) *Women, Work and Ideology in the Third World*. Tavistock, London, 153–82.

Mazumdar, Vina (1979) 'From Research to Policy: Rural Women in India'. In Sondra Zeidenstein (ed.) *Learning About Rural Women*. Special issue of *Studies in Family Planning*, 10:11/12, 353–8.

Mbithi, Philip and Barnes, C. (1975) *Spontaneous Settlement*

Problem in Kenya. East African Literature Bureau: Nairobi.

Mbithi, Philip and Rasmusson, Rasmus (1977) *Self-Reliance in Kenya: The Case of Harambee.* Scandinavian Institute for African Studies: Nairobi.

Mblinyi, M. (1972) 'The State of Women in Tanzania'. In *Canadian Journal of African Studies*, 2, 371-2.

McCall, Michael (1987) 'Carrying Heavier Burdens but Carrying Less Weight: Some Implications of Villagization for Women in Tanzania'. In Janet Momsen and Janet Townsend (eds) *Geography of Gender in the Third World.* Hutchinson, London, 192-214.

McLean, Scilla (ed.) (1985) *Female Circumcision and Infibulation: The Facts and Proposals for Change.* Minority Rights Group, London.

Mernissi, Fatima (1985) *Beyond the Veil: Male–Female Dynamics in Modern Muslim Society.* Al Saqi Books, London.

Merrick, Thomas and Schmink, Marianne (1983) 'Households Headed by Women and Urban Poverty in Brazil'. In Mayra Buvinić, Margaret Lycette and William McGreevey (eds) *Women and Poverty in the Third World.* Johns Hopkins, Baltimore, 244-71.

Mickelwait, Donald, Riegelman, Mary Ann and Sweet, Charles (1976) *Woman in Rural Development.* Westview, Boulder, Colorado.

Midgley, James with Hall, Anthony, Hardiman, Margaret and Dhanpaul, Narine (1986) *Community Participation, Social Development and the State.* Methuen, London and New York.

Mies, Maria (1982) 'The Dynamics of the Sexual Division of Labor and Integration of Rural Women into the World Market'. In Lourdes Benería (ed.) *Women and Development.* Praeger, New York, 1-28.

Mies, Maria (assisted by Lalita K. and Krishna Kumari) (1986) *Indian Women in Subsistence and Agricultural Labour.* International Labour Office, Geneva.

Mihyo, Zuky and Rutashoba, Letticia (1987) 'The Role of Women in Liberation Struggle and Reconstruction: Tanzanian Experiences'. In Christine Qunta (ed.) *Women in Southern Africa.* Allison and Busby, London, 217-25.

Mikell, Gwendolyn (1984) 'Filiation, Economic Crisis, and the Status of Women in Rural Ghana'. In *Canadian Journal of*

African Studies, 18:1, 195–218.

Milton, Kay (1979) 'Male Bias in Anthropology'. In *Man*, 14:1, 40–54.

Minces, Juliette (1982) *The House of Obedience: Women in Arab Society*. Zed, London.

Misra, R. P. (ed.) (1978) *Million Cities of India*. Vikas, New Delhi.

Mitchell, J. Clyde (1956a) *The Yao Village*. Manchester University Press, Manchester.

Mitchell, J. Clyde (1956b) *The Kalela Dance*. Rhodes Livingstone Paper No. 27. Manchester University Press, Manchester.

Mitchell, J. Clyde (1959) 'The Causes of Labour Migration'. In *Bulletin of Inter-African Labour Institute*, 6, 12–46.

Mitchell, J. Clyde (1987) *Cities, Society and Social Perception: A Central African Perspective*. Clarendon Press, Oxford.

Mitchnik, David A. (1978) *The Role of Women in Rural Zaire and Upper Volta: Improving Methods of Skill Acquisition*. Working Paper No. 2. Oxfam, Oxford.

Mitterauer, Michael and Sieder, Reinhard (1982) *The European Family*. Basil Blackwell, Oxford.

Molapo, Lesego (1987) 'Women and Agriculture in Botswana'. In Christine Qunta (ed.) *Women in Southern Africa*. Allison and Busby, London, 204–6.

Molyneux, Maxine (1977) 'Androcentrism in Marxist Anthropology'. In *Critique of Anthropology*, 3:9/10, 55–81.

Molyneux, Maxine (1981) 'Women's Emancipation Under Socialism: A Model for the Third World?' In *World Development*, 9:9/10, 1019–37.

Molyneux, Maxine (1984) 'Mobilisation without Emancipation? Women's Interests, State and Revolution in Nicaragua'. In *Critical Social Policy*, 10, 4:7, 59–75.

Molyneux, Maxine (1985a) 'Nicaragua: The Position of Women after the Revolution'. In Gordon White and Kate Young (eds) *Nicaragua after the Revolution: Problems and Prospects*, Institute of Development Studies Discussion Paper No. 200. University of Sussex, 28–31.

Molyneux, Maxine (1985b) 'Women'. In Thomas Walker (ed.) *Nicaragua: The First Five Years*. Praeger, New York, 145–62.

Molyneux, Maxine (1986) 'Mobilisation without Emancipation? Women's Interests, State and Revolution in Nicaragua'. In Richard Fagan et al. (eds) *Transition and Development:*

Problems of Third World Socialism. Monthly Review Press, New York, 280–302.

Momsen, Janet Henshall (1987) 'The Feminisation of Agriculture in the Caribbean'. In Janet Momsen and Janet Townsend (eds) *Geography of Gender in the Third World*. Hutchinson: London, 344–7.

Momsen, Janet Henshall and Townsend, Janet (eds) (1987) *Geography of Gender in the Third World*. Hutchinson, London.

Moock, Joyce Lewinger (ed.) (1986) *Understanding Africa's Rural Households and Farming Systems*. Westview Press, Boulder, Colorado.

Moore, Henrietta and Vaughan, Megan (1987) 'Cutting Down Trees: Women, Nutrition and Agricultural Change in the Northern Province of Zambia, 1920–1986'. In *African Affairs*, 86 (345), 523–40.

Morss, Elliott, Hatch, John, Mickelwait, Donald and Sweet, Charles (1976) *Strategies for Small Farmer Development* (2 volumes). Westview Press, Boulder, Colorado.

Moser, Caroline (1978) 'Informal Sector or Petty Commodity Production: Dualism or Dependence in Urban Development?' In *World Development*, 6:9/10, 1041–64.

Moser, Caroline (1981) 'Surviving in the Suburbios'. In *Bulletin*, 12:3. Institute of Development Studies, University of Sussex, 19–29.

Moser, Caroline (1984) *Residential Level Struggle and Consciousness: The Experiences of Poor Women in Guayaquil, Ecuador*. Working Paper No. 15, Development Planning Unit, University College, London.

Moser, Caroline (1986) 'Women's Needs in the Urban System: Training Strategies for Gender Aware Planning'. In Judith Bruce and Marilyn Köhn (eds) *Learning About Women and Urban Services in Latin America and the Caribbean*. Population Council, New York, 40–61.

Moser, Caroline (1987a) 'Gender: The Experience of Poor Women in Guayaquil'. In Eduardo Archetti, Paul Cammack and Bryan Roberts (eds) *Sociology of Developing Societies: Latin America*. Macmillan, Basingstoke, 305–20.

Moser, Caroline (1987b) 'Women, Human Settlements and Housing: a Conceptual Framework for Analysis and Policy-Making'. In Caroline Moser and Linda Peake (eds) *Women, Human*

Settlements and Housing. Tavistock, London, 12–32.

Moser, Caroline (1987c) 'Are There Women Leaders, or Are They Just Invisible?'. Paper presented at seminar 'Local Leaders and Community Development and Participation'. Fitzwilliam College, Cambridge, 28–30 September, 1987.

Moser, Caroline and Chant, Sylvia (1985) *The Participation of Women in Low-Income Housing Projects.* Gender and Planning Working Paper No. 5, Development Planning Unit, University College London (Final draft of training module commissioned by the United Nations Centre for Human Settlements (HABITAT) Nairobi).

Moser, Caroline and Levy, Caren (1986) *A Theory and Methodology of Gender Planning: Meeting Women's Practical and Strategic Needs.* Gender and Planning Working Paper No. 11, Development Planning Unit. University College, London.

Moser, Caroline and Young, Kate (1981) 'Women of the Working Poor'. In *Bulletin*, 12:3. Institute of Development Studies, University of Sussex, 54–62.

Mosley, W. Henry, Werner, Linda and Becker, Stan (1982) *The Dynamics of Birth Spacing and Marital Fertility in Kenya.* Scientific Reports No. 30. International Statistical Institute, Voorburg, Netherlands.

Mountjoy, Alan (1980) 'World Food Supply: Protein Intake'. In *Third World Quarterly*, II, 3, 555–6.

Mukhopadhyay, Maitrayee (1984) *Silver Shackles: Women and Development in India.* Oxfam, Oxford.

Murdock, G. P. and Provost, C. (1973) 'Factors in the Division of Labor by Sex: A Cross-Cultural Analysis'. In *Ethnology*, 12, 203–5.

Murdock, G. P. and White, Douglas R. (1969) 'Standard Cross-Cultural Sample'. In *Ethnology*, 8:4, 329–69.

Murray, Colin (1981) *Families Divided: The Impact of Migrant Labour in Lesotho.* Cambridge University Press: Cambridge.

Murray, Colin (1987) 'Class, Gender and the Household: The Developmental Cycle in Southern Africa'. In *Development and Change*, 18, 235–49.

Mushi, Samuel (1981) 'Community Development in Tanzania'. In Ronald Dore and Zoe Mars (eds) *Community Development.* Croom Helm, London/UNESCO, Paris, 139–242.

Nadel, S. F. (1952) 'Witchcraft in Four African Societies: An Essay in Comparison'. *American Anthropologist*, 54, 18-29.

Nash, June (1980) 'A Critique of Social Science Roles in Latin America'. In June Nash and Helen Safa (eds) *Sex and Class in Latin America*. Bergin, New York, 1-21.

Nash, June (1983) 'The Impact of the Changing International Division of Labour on Different Sectors of the Labor Force'. In June Nash and Maria Patricia Fernandez-Kelly (eds) *Women, Men and the International Division of Labour*. State University of New York Press, New York, 3-38.

Nash, June (1986) 'A Decade of Research on Women in Latin America'. In June Nash and Helen Safa (eds) *Women and Change in Latin America*. Bergin and Garvey, Massachusetts, 3-21.

Nash, June and Safa, Helen (eds) (1980) *Sex and Class in Latin America*. Bergin, New York.

Nash, June and Safa, Helen (eds) (1986) *Women and Change in Latin America*. Bergin and Garvey, Massachusetts.

Nath, Kamla (1985) *Women and Vegetable Gardens in the Gambia: Action Aid and Rural Development*. Boston University African Studies Center Working Paper No. 109, Boston.

Nelson, Nici (1978) 'Women Must Help Each Other': the Operation of Personal Networks among Buzaa Beer Brewers in Mathare Valley, Kenya'. In Patricia Caplan and Janet Bujra (eds) *Women United. Women Divided: Cross-Cultural Perspectives on Female Solidarity*. Tavistock, London, 77-98.

Nelson, Nici (1979a) *Why Has Development Neglected Rural Women: A Review of the South Asian Literature*. Pergamon, Oxford.

Nelson, Nici (1979b) 'How Women and Men Get By: The Sexual Division of Labour in the Informal Sector of a Nairobi Squatter Settlement'. In Ray Bromley and Chris Gerry (eds) *Casual Work and Poverty in Third World Cities*. John Wiley, Chichester, 283-302.

Nelson, Nici (1981) 'Mobilizing Village Women: Some Organizational and Management Considerations'. In Nici Nelson (ed.) *African Women in the Development Process*. Frank Cass, London, 47-58.

Nelson, Nici (1987) 'Rural-Urban Child Fostering in Kenya: Migration, Kinship Ideology and Class'. In Jeremy Eades (ed.) *Migrants, Workers and the Social Order*. Association of Social

Anthropologists Monograph No. 26. Tavistock, London, 181–98.

Neustatter, Angela (1988) 'The Cooperative Way Ahead'. In *The Guardian*, 23 February 1988.

Nieves, Isabel (1980) 'Beyond Survival Skills: Providing Basic Services to Satisfy the Needs of Poor Women'. In International Center for Research on Women (ICRW) (ed.) *Priorities in the Design of Development Programmes: Women's Issues*. ICRW, Washington, 97–121.

Nimpuno-Parente, Paula (1987) 'The Struggle for Shelter: Women in a Site and Service Project in Nairobi, Kenya'. In Caroline Moser and Linda Peake (ed.) *Women, Human Settlements and Housing*. Tavistock, London, 70–87.

Obbo, Christine (1980) *African Women: Their Struggle for Economic Independence*. Zed, London.

Oberai, A. S. and Singh, H. K. (1983) *Causes and Consequences of Internal Migration*. Oxford University Press for the International Labour Office, Delhi.

Odie-Alie, Stella (1986) 'Women in Agriculture: The Case of Guyana'. In *Social and Economic Studies*, 35:2. Institute of Social and Economic Research, University of the West Indies, 241–85.

Okali, Christine (1983) *Cocoa and Kinship in Ghana*. Routledge for the International African Institute, London.

Okali, Christine and Kotey, R. A. (1971) *Akokoaso: A Resurvey Report*. Institute for Social, Statistical and Economic Research, University of Ghana, Legon.

Okeyo, Achola Pala (1979) 'Women in the Household Economy: Managing Multiple Roles'. In Sondra Zeidenstein (ed.) *Learning About Rural Women*. Special issue of *Studies in Family Planning* 10:11/12, 337–43.

Okojie, Christina E. E. (1984) 'Female Migrants in the Urban Labour Market: Benin City, Nigeria'. In *Canadian Journal of African Studies*, 18:3, 547–62.

Okonjo, Kamene (1976) 'The Dual-Sex Political System in Operation: Igbo Women and Community Politics in Midwestern Nigeria'. In Nancy Hafkin and Edna Bay (eds) *Women in Africa: Studies in Social and Economic Change*. Stanford University Press, Stanford, 45–58.

Okonjo, Kamene (1979) 'Rural Women's Credit Systems: A Nigerian Example'. In Sondra Zeidenstein (ed.) *Learning About Rural Women* Special Issue of *Studies in Family Planning*, 10:11/12, 344-52.

Olesen, Adolf (1984) *A Study of Slums and Slum Improvement in Madras.* Report of a study period in Madras. Institute of Development and Planning, Aalborg, Denmark (mimeo).

Oppong, Christine (1974) *Marriage among a Matrilineal Elite.* Cambridge University Press, Cambridge.

Oppong, Christine (1980) *A Synopsis of Seven Roles and Statuses of Women: An Outline of a Conceptual and Methodological Approach.* International Labour Office Working Paper No. 94, Geneva.

Oppong, Christine (ed.) (1983) *Female and Male in West Africa.* George Allen and Unwin, London.

Oppong, Christine (ed.) (1987) *Sex Roles, Population and Development in West Africa.* Heinemann, London: James Carry, Portsmouth, New Hampshire.

Oppong, Christine and Abu, Katherine (1985) *A Handbook for Data Collection of Seven Roles and Statuses of Women.* International Labour Office, Geneva.

Oppong, Christine and Abu, Katherine (1987) *Seven Roles of Women: Impact of Education, Migration and Employment of Ghanaian Mothers.* International Labour Office, Geneva.

Organization of Angolan Women (OAW) (1984) *Angolan Women: Building the Future.* Zed, London.

Ortiz Monasterio, Fernando and Schmink, Marianne (1986) 'Women and Waste Management in Urban Mexico'. In Judith Bruce and Marilyn Köhn (eds) *Learning about Women and Urban Services in Latin America and the Caribbean.* Population Council, New York, 163-83.

Ortner, Sherry (1974) 'Is Female to Male as Nature is to Culture?' In Michelle Zimbalist Rosaldo and Louise Lamphere (eds) *Woman, Culture and Society.* Stanford University Press, Stanford, California, 67-88.

Ortner, Sherry and Whitehead, Harriet (1981) 'Introduction: Accounting for Sexual Meanings'. In Sherry Ortner and Harriet Whitehead (eds) *Sexual Meanings.* Cambridge University Press: Cambridge, 1-28.

Ottenberg, Simon (1955) 'Improvement Associations among the Afikpo Ibo'. In *Africa*, 25:1, 1-28.

Page, Hilary J. (1986) *Child Bearing Versus Child Rearing: Co-residence of Mothers and Children in Sub-Saharan Africa.* Working Paper 1986-2, Interuniversity Programme in Demography, Brussels.

Page, H. J., Lesthaeghe, R. J. and Shah, I. H. (1982) *Illustrative Analysis: Breastfeeding in Pakistan.* Scientific Reports No. 37. International Statistical Institute, Voorburg, Netherlands.

Pahl, Ray (1984) *Divisions of Labour.* Basil Blackwell, Oxford.

Pakizegi, Behnaz (1978) 'Legal and Social Positions of Iranian Women'. In Lois Beck and Nikki Keddie (eds) *Women in the Muslim World.* Harvard University Press: Cambridge, Massachusetts, 216-26.

Pala, Achola (1976) 'Woman Power in Kenya'. In *Ceres*, 11:6, 43-6.

Palmer, Ingrid (1979) 'New Official Ideas on Women and Development'. In *Bulletin.* Institute of Development Studies, University of Sussex, 10:3, 42-52.

Panos Institute (1988) *Aids and the Third World.* Panos Dossier 1. The Panos Institute, London. Published in association with the Norwegian Red Cross. (Reprinted second edition).

Papanek, Hanna (1976) 'Women in Cities: Problems and Perspectives'. In Irene Tinker, Michèle Bo Bramsen and Mayra Buvinić (eds) *Women and World Development.* Praeger, New York, 54-69.

Papanek, Hanna (1977) 'Development Planning for Women'. In Wellesley Editorial Committee (ed.) *Women and National Development: The Complexities of Change.* University of Chicago, Chicago, 14-21.

Papola, T. S. (1986) 'Women Workers in the Formal Sector of Lucknow, India' In Richard Anker and Catherine Hein (eds) *Sex Inequalities in Urban Employment in the Third World.* Macmillan, Basingstoke, 171-212.

Parry, Jonathan (1980) 'Ghosts, Greed, and Sin: The Occupational Identity of the Benares Funeral Priests'. In *Man*, 15:1, 88-111.

Pasteur, David (1979) *The Management of Squatter Upgrading.* Saxon House: Farnborough.

de la Paz, Trinidad (1984) *The Katiwala: An Experience in Primary Health Care.* Paper presented to a joint UNICEF/WHO consultation on primary health care in urban areas, Guayaquil, Ecuador, 15-19 October, 1984. World Health Organisation, Geneva.

Peake, Linda (1987) 'Government Housing Policy in Guyana and its

Implications for Women'. In Caroline Moser and Linda Peake (eds) *Women, Human Settlements and Housing*. Tavistock, London, 113–38.

Pearson, Maggie (1987) 'Old Wives or Young Midwives? Women as Caretakers of Health: The Case of Nepal'. In Janet Momsen and Janet Townsend (eds) *Geography of Gender in the Third World*. Hutchinson, London, 116–30.

Pearson, Ruth (1986) 'Latin American Women and the New International Division of Labour: A Reassessment'. In *Bulletin of Latin American Research*, 5:2, 67–79.

Peattie, Lisa Redfield (1968) *The View from the Barrio*. Ann Arbor, Michigan.

Pedredo, Mercedes and Rendón, Teresa (1982) 'El Trabajo de la Mujer en México en los Setentas'. In Secretaría de Programación y Presupuesto (SPP) (ed.) *Estudios sobre la Mujer 1: El Empleo y la Mujer. Bases Teóricas, Metodológicas y Evidencia Empírica.* SPP: México DF, 437–58.

Peel, J. D. Y. (1968) *Aladura: A Religious Movement among the Yoruba*. Oxford University Press, London.

Peel, J. D. Y. (1973) 'Cultural Factors in the Contemporary Theory of Development'. In *Archives Européennes de Sociologie*, 14, 183–203.

Peel, J. D. Y. (1983) *Ijeshas and Nigerians*. Cambridge University Press, Cambridge.

Peil, Margaret (1975) 'Female Roles in West African Towns'. In Jack Goody (ed.) *Changing Social Structure in Ghana*. International African Institute, London, 73–90.

Peil, Margaret with Sada, Pius. O. (1984) *African Urban Society*. John Wiley, Chichester.

Pescatello, Ann (1976) *Power and Pawn: The Female in Iberian Families, Societies and Cultures*. Greenwood Press, Westport, Connecticut.

Phillips, Anne (1983) *Hidden Hands: Women and Economic Policies*. Pluto, London.

Phongpaichit, Pasuk (1982) *From Peasant Girls to Bangkok Masseuses*. International Labour Office, Geneva.

Phongpaichit, Pasuk (1984) 'The Bangkok Masseuses: Origins, Status and Prospects'. In Gavin Jones (ed.) *Women in the Urban and Industrial Workforce: Southeast and East Asia*. Development Studies Centre Monograph No. 33. Australian National

University, Canberra, 251-7.

Pico, Isabel (1974) 'The Quest for Race, Sex and Ethnic Equality in Puerto Rico'. Paper read at the Latin American Studies Association, San Francisco, 14-16 November, 1974.

Pine, Frances (1982) 'Family Structure and the Division of Labour: Female Roles in Urban Ghana'. In Hamza Alavi and Teodor Shanin (eds) *Sociology of Developing Societies*. Macmillan, London and Basingstoke, 387-405.

Pittin, Renée (1983) 'Houses of Women: A Focus on Alternative Life-Styles in Katsina City'. In Christine Oppong (ed.) *Female and Male in West Africa*. George Allen and Unwin, London, 291-302.

Pittin, Renée (1984) 'Gender and Class in a Nigerian Industrial Setting'. In *Review of African Political Economy*, 31, 71-81.

Plotnicov, L. (1967) *Strangers to the City: Urban Man in Jos, Nigeria*. University of Pittsburgh Press, Pittsburgh.

Population Information Program (PIP) (1985) *Fertility and Family Planning Surveys: An Update*. Population Reports Series M, No. 8. Johns Hopkins University, Baltimore.

Powell, Dorian (1986) 'Caribbean Women and their Response to Familial Experiences'. In *Social and Economic Studies*, 35:2. Institute of Social and Economic Research. University of the West Indies, 83-130.

Prothero, R. Mansell and Davenport, Jeffrey (1986) 'The Geography of Health in South-East Mexico: A Research Study and Agenda'. In *Social Science and Medicine*, 22:12, 1321-7.

Prothero, R. Mansell (1987) 'Mankind and the Mosquito'. In *World Health*, June 1987, 18-19.

Pryer, Jane and Crook, Nigel (1988) *Cities of Hunger: Urban Malnutrition in Developing Countries*. Oxfam, Oxford.

Pryor, Robin J. (ed.) (1979) *Migration and Development in South-East Asia*. Oxford University Press, Kuala Lumpur.

Qunta, Christine (ed.) (1987) *Woman in Southern Africa*. Allison and Busby, London.

Raczynski, Dagmar (1977) *El Sector Informal Urbano: Controversías e Interrogantes*. Corporación de Investigaciones Económicas para Latinoamerica, Santiago de Chile.

Radcliffe, Sarah (1986) 'Gender Relations, Peasant Livelihood Strategies and Migration: A Case Study from Cuzco, Peru'. In *Bulletin of Latin American Research*, 5:2, 29-47.

Rechini de Lattes, Zulma and Wainermann, Catalina (1986) 'Unreliable Accounts of Women's Work'. In *Signs: Journal of Women in Culture and Society*, 11:4, 740–50.

Rees, Judith and Odell, Peter (eds) (1987) *The International Oil Industry: An Interdisciplinary Perspective*. Macmillan, Basingstoke.

Reich, Michael, Gordon, David and Edwards, Michael (1980) 'A Theory of Labour Market Segmentation'. In Alice Amsden (ed.) *The Economics of Women and Work*. Penguin, Harmondsworth, 232–41.

Resources for Action (1982a) *Women and Shelter in Honduras*. United States Agency for International Development, Office of Housing, Washington DC.

Resources for Action (1982b) *Women and Shelter in Tunisia: A Survey of the Shelter Needs of Women in Low-Income Areas*. United States Agency for International Development, Office of Housing, Washington DC.

Rey, Pierre Philippe (1979) 'Class Contradictions in Lineage Societies'. In *Critique of Anthropology*, 4:13/14, 41–60.

Richards, A. I. (1950) 'Some Types of Family Structure among the Central Bantu'. In A. R. Radcliffe-Brown and Daryll Forde (eds) *African Systems of Kinship and Marriage*. Oxford University Press for International African Institute, London, 207–51.

Rifkin, Susan (1984) *Community Participation in MCH/CP Programmes: An Analysis Based on Case Study Materials*. World Health Organisation, Geneva.

Roberts, Bryan (1978) *Cities of Peasants: The Political Economy of Urbanization in the Third World*. Edward Arnold, London.

Roberts, Pepe (1979) 'The Integration of Women into the Development Process: Some Conceptual Problems'. In *Bulletin,* Institute of Development Studies, University of Sussex, 10:3, 60–6.

Roberts, Pepe (1984) 'Feminism *in* Africa: Feminism *and* Africa'. In *Review of African Political Economy*, 27/28, 175–84.

Roberts, Pepe (n.d.) *Rural Women in Western Nigeria and Hausa Niger: A Comparative Study*. Department of Sociology, University of Liverpool (mimeo).

Robertson, Claire (1976) 'Ga Women and Socioeconomic Change in Accra, Ghana'. In Nancy Hafkin and Edna Bay (eds) *Women in Africa: Studies in Social and Economic Change*. Stanford University Press: Stanford, California, 111–33.

Robertson, Claire (1984a) *Sharing the Same Bowl: A Socioeconomic History of Women and Class in Accra, Ghana*. Indiana University Press, Bloomington.

Robertson, Claire (1984b) 'Women in the Urban Economy'. In Margaret Jean Hay and Sharon Stichter (eds) *African Women South of the Sahara*. Longman, London, 33–49.

Robertson, Claire (1987) 'Developing Economic Awareness: Changing Perspectives in Studies of African Women 1976–85'. In *Feminist Studies*, 13:1, 97–135.

Rochin, Refugio I. (1983) 'Mexico's Agriculture in Crisis: A Study of its Northern States'. In *Mexican Studies*, 1:2, 255–76.

Rocksloh-Papendieck, Barbara (1988) *Frauenarbeit am Strassenrand: Kenkeyküchen in Ghana*. Arbeiten aus dem Institut für Afrika-Kunde No. 55, Hamburg.

Rodney, Walter (1972) *How Europe Underdeveloped Africa*. Bougle-L'Ouverture Publications, London.

Rogers, Barbara (1980) *The Domestication of Women: Discrimination in Developing Societies*. Tavistock, London.

Rogers, Susan Carol (1975) 'Female Forms of Power and the Myth of Male Dominance: A Model of Female/Male Interaction in Peasant Society'. In *American Ethnologist*, 2, 741–54.

Rogers, Susan Carol (1978) 'Woman's Place: A Critical Review of Anthropological Theory'. In *Comparative Studies in Society and History*, 20, 123–62.

Rohrlich-Leavitt, Ruby, Sykes, Barbara and Weatherford, Elizabeth (1975) 'Aboriginal Woman: Male and Female Anthropological Perspectives'. In Rayna R. Reiter (ed.) *Towards an Anthropology of Women*. Monthly Review Press, New York, 115–26.

Ross, Marc Howard (1973) *The Political Integration of Urban Squatters*. Northwestern University Press, Evanston, Illinois.

Ross, Marc Howard (1986) 'Female Political Participation: A Cross-Cultural Explanation'. In *American Anthropologist*, 88, 843–58.

Rostow, W. W. (1960) *The Stages of Economic Growth: A Non-Communist Manifesto*. Cambridge University Press, Cambridge.

Rothstein, Frances (1986) 'Capitalist Industrialisation and the Increasing Cost of Children'. In June Nash and Helen Safa (eds) *Women and Change in Latin America*. Bergin and Garvey, Massachusetts, 37–52.

Rubin-Kurtzman, Jane (1987) *The Socioeconomic Determinants of*

Fertility in Mexico: Changing Perspectives. Monograph Series No. 23. Centre for US–Mexican Studies, University of California, San Diego.

El Saadawi, Nawal (1980) *The Hidden Face of Eve: Women in the Arab World*. Zed, London.

Sacks, Karen (1974) 'Engels Revisited: Women, the Organization of Production, and Private Property'. In Michelle Rosaldo and Louise Lamphere (eds) *Woman, Culture and Society*. Stanford University Press, Stanford, California, 207–22.

Sacks, Karen (1976) 'State Bias and Woman's Status'. In *American Anthropologist*, 78, 565–9.

Sacks, Karen (1979) *Sisters and Wives*. Greenwood Press, Westport, Connecticut.

Safa, Helen (1980) 'Class Consciousness among Working Class Women in Latin America: Puerto Rico'. In June Nash and Helen Safa (eds) *Sex and Class in Latin America*. Bergin, New York, 69–85.

Safa, Helen (1981) 'Runaway Shops and Female Employment: The Search for Cheap Labour'. In *Signs: Journal of Women in Culture and Society*, 7:2, 418–33.

Safa, Helen (ed.) (1982) *Towards a Political Economy of Urbanisation in Developing Countries*. Oxford University Press, New Delhi.

Safa, Helen (1986) Female Employment in the Puerto Rican Working Class. In June Nash and Helen Safa (eds) *Women and Change in Latin America*. Bergin and Garvey, Massachusetts, 84–105.

Saffioti, Heleieth (1986) 'Technological Change in Brazil: Its Effects on Men and Woman in Two Firms'. In June Nash and Helen Safa (eds.) *Women and Change in Latin America*. Bergin and Garvey, Massachusetts, 109–35.

Salman, Magida (1987) 'The Arab Woman'. In Khamsin (ed.) *Women in the Middle East*. Zed, London, 6–11.

Sanday, Peggy Reeves (1981) *Female Power and Male Dominance*. Cambridge University Press, Cambridge.

Sandbrook, Richard and Cohen, Robin (eds) (1975) *The Development of an African Working Class: Studies in Class Formation and Action*. Longman, London.

Sanjek, Roger (1976) 'New Perspectives on African Women'. In *Reviews in Anthropology*, 3:2, 115–34.

Sanjek, Roger (1983) 'Female and Male Domestic Cycles in Urban Africa: The Adabraka Case'. In Christine Oppong (ed.) *Female and Male in West Africa*. George Allen and Unwin, London, 330–43.

Sarin, Madhu (1979) 'Urban Planning, Petty Trading and Squatter Settlements in Chandigarh, India'. In Ray Bromley and Chris Gerry (eds) *Casual Work and Poverty in Third World Cities*. John Wiley, Chichester, 133–59.

Sassen-Koob, Saskia (1984) 'From Household to Workplace: Notes on the Incorporation of Third World Women into Wage Labor through Immigration and Offshore Production'. In *International Migration Review*, 18: 4, 1144–67.

Savara, Mira (1983) 'Report of a Workshop on Women, Health and Reproduction'. In Miranda Davies (ed.) *Third World – Second Sex: Women's Struggles and National Liberation*. Zed, London, 220–7.

Schaefer, Kalmann (1976) *São Paulo: Urban Development and Employment*. ILO, Geneva.

Schildkrout, Enid (1978) 'Roles of Children in Urban Kano'. In J. S. La Fontaine (ed.) *Sex and Age as Principles of Social Differentiation*. Association of Social Anthropologists Monograph No. 17, Academic Press, London, 109–38.

Schildkrout, Enid (1983) 'Dependence and Autonomy: The Economic Activities of Secluded Hausa Women in Kano'. In Christine Oppong (ed.) *Female and Male in West Africa*. George Allen and Unwin, London, 107–26.

Schmink, Marianne (1982) *Women in the Urban Economy in Latin America*. Working Paper No. 1. Population Council, New York.

Schmink, Marianne (1984) *The 'Working-Group' Approach to Women and Urban Services*. Mimeo. Centre for Latin American Studies, University of Florida, Gainesville.

Schmink, Marianne (1986) 'Women and Urban Industrial Development in Brazil'. In June Nash and Helen Safa (eds) *Women and Change in Latin America*. Bergin and Garvey, Massachusetts, 136–64.

Scott, Alison MacEwen (1986a) 'Industrialization, Gender Segregation and Stratification Theory'. In Rosemary Crompton and Michael Mann (eds) *Gender and Stratification*. Polity Press, Cambridge, 154–89.

Scott, Alison MacEwen (1986b) 'Women and Industrialisation:

Examining the "Female Marginalisation" Thesis'. In *Journal of Development Studies*, 22:4, 649–80.

Scott, Alison MacEwen (1988) 'Capitalist Development and Woman's Marginalization from Production: Theoretical and Methodological Problems'. In *Gender and Society* (forthcoming).

Seager, Joni and Olson, Ann (1986) *Women in the World: An International Atlas*. Pan, London.

Seccombe, Wally (1980) 'Domestic Labour and the Working Class Household'. In Bonnie Fox (ed.) *Hidden in the Household: Women's Domestic Labour Under Capitalism*. The Women's Press, Toronto, 25–99.

Sen, Gita and Grown, Caren, for Development Alternatives with Women for a New Era (DAWN) (1988). *Development, Crises and Alternative Visions: Third World Women's Perspectives*. Earthscan Publications, London.

Shapiro, Judith (1980). 'Sexual Hierarchy among the Yanomama'. In June Nash and Helen Safa (eds) *Sex and Class in Latin America*. Bergin, New York, 86–101.

Sharma, Ursula (1978) 'Segregation and its Consequences in India'. In Patricia Caplan and Janet Bujra (eds.) *Women United, Woman Divided*. Tavistock, London, 259–82.

Sharma, Ursula (1984) 'Dowry in North India: Its Consequences for Women'. In Renée Hirschon (ed.) *Women and Property – Women as Property*. Croom Helm, London: St. Martins, New York, 62–74.

Sharma, Ursula (1986) *Women's Work, Class and the Urban Household: A Study of Shimla, North India*. Tavistock, London.

Shields, Nwanganga (1980) *Women in Urban Labor Markets in Africa: The Case of Tanzania*. Staff Working Paper No. 380, World Bank, Washington DC.

Simon, David (1984) 'Responding to Third World Urban Poverty: Women and Men in the "Informal" Sector in Windhoek, Namibia'. In Janet Momsen and Janet Townsend (eds) *Women's Role in Changing the Face of the Developing World*. Papers, Women and Geography Study Group Session, Annual Conference of the Institute of British Geographers, Durham, January 1984, 95–130.

Sinclair, Stuart (1978) *Urbanization and Labour Markets in Developing Countries*. Croom Helm, London.

Singh, Andrea Menefee (1980) *Women in Cities: An Invisible Factor in Urban Planning in India*. The Population Council, New York.

Singh, Jyoti Shankar (ed.) (1979) *World Population Policies*. Praeger: New York, in cooperation with the United Nations Fund for Population Activities (UNFPA).

Singh, Susheela and Ferry, Benôit (1984) *Biological and Traditional Factors that Influence Fertility: Results from the WFS Surveys*. Comparative Studies No. 40, International Statistical Institute, Voorburg, Netherlands.

Singhanetra-Renard, Anchalee (1984) 'Effect of Female Labour Force Participation on Fertility: The Case of Construction Workers in Chiang Mai City'. In Gavin Jones (ed.) *Women in the Urban and Industrial Labour Force: Southeast and East Asia*. Development Studies Centre Monograph No. 33. Australian National University, Canberra, 325–35.

Siraj, Mehrun (1984) 'Islamic Attitudes to Female Employment in Industrializing Countries: Some Notes from Malaysia'. In Gavin Jones (ed.) *Women in the Urban and Industrial Workforce: Southeast and East Asia*. Development Studies Centre Monograph No. 33, Australian National University, Canberra, 163–73.

Skinner, Elliott (1974) *African Urban Life: The Transformation of Ouagadougou*. Princeton University Press: Princeton, NJ.

Skinner, Reinhard (1983) 'Community Participation: Its Scope and Organisation'. In Reinhard Skinner and Mike Rodell (eds) *People, Poverty and Shelter: Problems of Self-Help Housing in the Third World*. Methuen, London, 125–50.

Smith, M. G. (1962) *West Indian Family Structure*. American Ethnological Society Monographs. University of Washington Press, Seattle.

Smith, Margo L. (1978) 'The Female Domestic Servant and Social Change, Lima, Peru'. In Richard Schaedel and Jorge Hardoy (eds) *Urbanisation in the Americas from its Beginnings to the Present*. Mouton, The Hague and Paris, 569–86.

Smith, Mary F. (1954) *Baba of Karo*. Faber and Faber, London.

Smith, Raymond T. (1956) *The Negro Family in British Guiana*. Routledge and Kegan Paul, London.

Smith, Stanley (1981) 'Determinants of Female Labour Force Participation and Family Size in Mexico City'. In *Economic Development and Cultural Change*, 30:1, 129–52.

Solien de Gonzales, Nancie (1965) 'The Consanguineal Family and Matrifocality'. In *American Anthropologist*, 67, 1541–9.

Solien de Gonzales, Nancie (1969) *Black Carib Household Struc-*

ture: A Study of Migration and Modernization. University of Washington Press, Seattle.

Spiro, Heather (1987) 'Women Farmers and Traders in Oyo State, Nigeria: A Case Study of their Changing Roles'. In Janet Momsen and Janet Townsend (eds) *Geography of Gender in the Third World*. Hutchinson, London, 173-91.

Standing, Hilary (1985) 'Resources, Wages and Power: The Impact of Women's Employment on the Urban Bengali Household'. In Haleh Afshar (ed.) *Women, Work and Ideology in the Third World*. Tavistock, London, 232-57.

Steady, Filomina Chioma (1981) 'The Black Woman Cross-Culturally: An Overview'. In Filomina Chioma Steady (ed.) *The Black Woman Cross-Culturally*. Schenkmann Publishing Company, Cambridge, Massachusetts, 7-41.

Stevens, Evelyn (1973) 'Marianismo: The Other Face of Machismo in Latin America'. In Ann Pescatello (ed.) *Female and Male in Latin America*. University of Pittsburgh Press, Pittsburgh, 89-102.

Stewart, Frances (1985) *Planning to Meet Basic Needs*. Macmillan, London.

Stivens, Maila (1985) 'The Fate of Women's Land Rights: Gender, Matriliny and Capitalism in Rembau, Negeri Sembilan, Malaysia'. In Haleh Afshar (ed.) *Women, Work and Ideology in the Third World*. Tavistock, London, 3-36.

Stivens, Maila (1987) 'Family and State in Malaysian Industrialisation: The Case of Rembau, Negeri Sembilan, Malaysia'. In Haleh Afshar (ed.) *Women, State and Ideology: Studies from Africa and Asia*. Macmillan, Basingstoke, 89-110.

Stone, Elizabeth (ed.) (1981) *Women and the Cuban Revolution*. Pathfinder Press, New York.

Stretton, Huw (1978) *Urban Planning in Rich and Poor Countries*. Oxford University Press, Oxford.

Sudarkasa, Niara (1973) *Where Women Work: A Study of Yoruba Women in the Marketplace and in the Home*. Ann Arbor, Michigan.

Sudarkasa, Niara (1977) 'Women and Migration in Contemporary West Africa'. In Wellesley Editorial Committee (ed.) *Women in National Development: The Complexities of Change*. University of Chicago Press, Chicago, 178-89.

Terray, Emmanuel (1972) *Marxism and 'Primitive Societies'*.

Monthly Review Press, New York.

Terray, Emmanuel (1975) 'Class and Class Consciousness in the Abron Kingdom of Gyaman'. In M. Bloch (ed.) *Marxist Analyses and Social Anthropology*. Malaby Press, London, 85–135.

Terray, Emmanuel (1979) 'On Exploitation: Elements of an Autocritique'. In *Critique of Anthropology*, 4:13/14, 29–39.

Tessler, Mark with Rogers, Janet and Schneider, Daniel (1978) 'Women's Emancipation in Tunisia'. In Lois Beck and Nikki Keddie (eds) *Women in the Muslim World*. Harvard University Press, Cambridge, Massachusetts, 141–58.

Thiam, Awa (1986) *Black Sisters Speak Out: Feminism and Oppression in Black Africa*. Pluto, London.

Thitsa, Khin (1980) *Providence and Prostitution: Image and Reality for Women in Buddhist Thailand*. CHANGE International Reports on Women and Society, London.

Thomson, Marilyn (1986) *Women of El Salvador: The Price of Freedom*. Zed, London.

Tienda, Marta and Ortega, Sylvia (1982) 'Las Familias Encabezadas por Mujeres y la Formación de Nucleos Extensos: Una Referencia a Peru'. In Secretaría de Programación y Presupuesto (SPP) (ed.) *Estudios Sobre la Mujer 1. El Empleo y la Mujer. Bases Teóricas, Metodológicas y Evidencia Empírica*. SPP, México DF, 319–44.

Tipple, A. Graham and Hellen, J. A. (1986) *Priorities for Public Utilities and Housing Improvements in Kumasi, Ghana: An Empirical Assessment Based on Six Variables*. Seminar Paper No. 44, Department of Geography, University of Newcastle upon Tyne.

Townsend, Janet (1987) 'Rural Change: Progress for Whom?' In David Preston (ed.) *Latin American Development: Geographical Perspectives*. Longman, Harlow, 199–228.

Townsend, Janet and Momsen, Janet (1987) 'Towards a Geography of Gender in the Third World'. In Janet Momsen and Janet Townsend (eds) *Geography of Gender in the Third World*. Hutchinson, London, 27–81.

Turner, Victor W. (1957) *Schism and Continuity in an African Society*. Manchester University Press, Manchester.

Ul Haq, Mahbub and Burki, Shahid (1980) *Meeting Basic Needs: An Overview*. World Bank, Washington.

United Nations (UN) (1977) *The Social Impact of Housing*. UN,

New York.

United Nations (UN) (1981) *World Population Prospects as Assessed in 1980*. Department of International Economic and Social Affairs, Population Studies No. 78, United Nations, New York.

United Nations Centre for Human Settlements (UNCHS) (1985) *Women and Human Settlements*. UNCHS (HABITAT), Nairobi.

United Nations Children's Fund (UNICEF) (1983) *Urban Examples for Basic Services in Cities, UE-4*. UNICEF, New York.

United Nations Children's Fund (UNICEF) (1984) *Reaching Children and Women of the Urban Poor*. Occasional Papers Series No. 3. UNICEF, New York.

Van Allen, Judith (1976) '"Aba Riots" or Igbo "Women's War?" Ideology, Stratification and the Invisibility of Women'. In Nancy Hafkin and Edna Bay (eds) *Women in Africa*. Stanford University Press, Stanford, 59–86.

Vance, Irene (1985) *Women's Participation in Self-Help Housing: The San Judas Barrio Project, Managua, Nicaragua*. Gender and Planning Working Paper No. 4. Development Planning Unit, University College, London.

Vellenga, Dorothy Dee (1983) 'Who is a Wife? Legal Expressions of Heterosexual Conflicts in Ghana'. In Christine Oppong (ed.) *Female and Male in West Africa*. George Allen and Unwin, London, 144–55.

van Velsen, J. (1961) 'Labour Migration as a Positive Factor in the Continuity of Tonga Tribal Society'. In A. Southall (ed.) *Social Change in Modern Africa*. Oxford University Press, London, 230–41.

Verdon, Michel (1979) 'African Apprentice Workshops: A Case of Ethnocentric Reductionism'. In *American Ethnologist*, 6:3, 531–42.

Verdon, Michel (1983) *The Abutia Ewe of West Africa*. Mouton, Berlin.

Wall, Richard in collaboration with Robin, Jean and Laslett, Peter (eds) (1983) *Family Forms in Historic Europe*. Cambridge University Press, Cambridge.

Ward, Peter (1986) *Welfare Politics in Mexico: Papering over the Cracks*. Allen and Unwin, London.

Ward, Peter (1987) 'Reproduction of Social Inequality: Access to

Health Services in Mexico City'. In *Health Policy and Planning*, 2:1, 44–57.

Ward, Peter and Chant, Sylvia (1987) 'Community Leadership and Self-Help Housing'. In *Progress in Planning*, Vol. 27, Part 2, 69–136.

Ware, Helen (1983) 'Female and Male Life-Cycles'. In Christine Oppong (ed.) *Female and Male in West Africa*. George Allen and Unwin, London, 6–31.

Webster, Andrew (1984) *Introduction to the Sociology of Development*. Macmillan, Basingstoke and London.

Wegelin, Emiel (1977) *Urban Low-Income Housing and Development*. Martinus Nijhoff, The Hague.

Weiner, Annette (1976) *Women of Value, Men of Renown*. University of Texas Press, Austin.

Weiner, Annette (1979) 'Trobriand Kinship from Another View: The Reproductive Power of Women and Men'. In *Man*, 14, 328–48.

Weiss, Ruth (1986) *The Women of Zimbabwe*. Kesho Publications, London.

Wells, Troth and Sim, Foo Gaik (1987) *Till They Have Faces: Women as Consumers*. International Organization of Consumer Unions, Regional Office for Asia and the Pacific/ISIS International, Penang/Rome.

Westwood, Sallie (1984) '"Fear Woman": Property and Modes of Production in Urban Ghana'. In Renée Hirschon (ed.) *Women and Property – Women as Property*. Croom Helm, London: St. Martins, New York, 140–57.

White, Christine (1981) 'Women's Employment and the Family: Report on a Colloquium Comparing the Women's Movement and Government Legislation in Britain and Vietnam'. In *Bulletin*, 15:1. Institute of Development Studies, University of Sussex, 57–61.

White, Douglas R., Burton, Michael and Dow, Malcolm (1981) 'Sexual Division of Labour in African Agriculture: A Network Autocorrelation Analysis'. In *American Anthropologist*, 83, 824–49.

Whyte, Martin King (1978) *The Status of Women in Pre-Industrial Societies*. Princeton University Press, Princeton, NJ.

Whyte, Robert Orr and Whyte, Pauline (1978) *Rural Asian Women: Status and Environment*. Notes and Discussion Papers No. 9,

Institute of Southeast Asian Studies, Singapore.

Wikan, Unni (1980) *Life among the Poor in Cairo*. Tavistock, London.

Wilkinson, Clive (1987) 'Women, Work and Migration in Lesotho'. In Janet Momsen and Janet Townsend (eds) *Geography of Gender in the Third World*. Hutchinson, London, 225–39.

Williams, Cheryl (1986) 'The Role of Women in Caribbean Culture'. In Pat Ellis (ed.) *Women of the Caribbean*. Zed, London, 109–14.

Wilson, Adrian (1985) *Family*. Tavistock, London.

Wolf, Eric (1959) *Sons of the Shaking Earth*. University of Chicago, Chicago.

Wong, Aline (1981) 'Planned Development, Social Stratification and the Sexual Division of Labor in Singapore'. In *Signs: Journal of Women in Culture and Society*, 7:2, 434–52.

Woodburn, James (1968) 'An Introduction to Hadza Ecology'. In Richard B. Lee and Irven DeVore (eds) *Man the Hunter*. Aldine, Chicago, 49–55.

World Bank (1980) *World Bank Research Programme*. World Bank, Washington DC.

World Bank (1987) *The World Bank Annual Report 1987*. World Bank, Washington DC.

World Health Organisation (WHO) (1979) *Traditional Practices Affecting the Health of Women and Children*. WHO/EMRO Publication No. 2. WHO, Regional Office of the Eastern Mediterranean, Alexandria.

Young, Kate (1978) 'Modes of Appropriation and the Sexual Division of Labour: A Case Study from Oaxaca, Mexico'. In Annette Kuhn and Anne Marie Wolpe (eds) *Feminism and Materialism*. Routledge and Kegan Paul, London, 124–54.

Young, Mei Ling and Salih, Kamal (1987) 'The Malay Family: Structural Change and Transformation – A Research Proposal? In Janet Momsen and Janet Townsend (eds) *Geography of Gender in the Third World*. Hutchinson, London, 348–54.

Youssef, Nadia (1972) 'Differential Labour Force Participation of Women in Latin American and Middle Eastern Countries'. In *Social Forces*, 51, 135–53.

Youssef, Nadia and Hetler, Carol (1983) 'Establishing the Economic Condition of Women-Headed Households in the Third World: A New Approach'. In Mayra Buvinić, Margaret Lycette and William McGreevey (eds.) *Women and Poverty in the Third World*. Johns Hopkins, Baltimore, 216–43.

Zabaleta, Marta (1986) 'Research on Latin American Women: In Search of Our Political Independence'. In *Bulletin of Latin American Research*, 5:2, 97–103.

Zack-Williams, A. B. (1985) 'Female Urban Employment'. In Editorial Committee Women in Nigeria (WIN) (eds.) *Women in Nigeria*. Zed Press, London, 104–13.

Zaman, Wasim (1980) 'The World Population Situation'. In *Third World Quarterly*, II:3, 546–54.

Zeidenstein, Sondra (ed.) (1979) *Learning about Rural Women*. Special issue of *Studies in Family Planning*, 10:11/12 Nov./Dec. 1979.

Zosa-Feranil, Imelda (1984) 'Female Employment and the Family: A Case Study of the Bataan Export Processing Zone'. In Gavin Jones (ed.) *Women in the Urban and Industrial Labour Force: Southeast and East Asia*. Development Studies Centre Monograph No. 33. Australian National University, Canberra, 387–403.

Author Index

297

Place Name Index

Subject Index

Abaya (garment, Iraq) 29
abortion 197, 198
  See also birth control
Action Aid 112
Adi-Dravida (low-caste women,
    India) 148, 178
adultery
  consequences for men 20
  consequences for women 20, 32
  as grounds for divorce 36
  See also Family Code; fidelity
African Co-operative Savings and
    Credit Association (ACOSCA)
    223
African Regional Health Education
    Centre (ARHEC) 230
African women 125, 126, 127,
    147–8, 158, 164, 199, 202, 205
  fertility 36–7
  labour force participation 34, 35,
    73, 74, 164, 166, 168, 173, 178
  life expectancy 35
  and marriage 36
  status/position of 33, 35–8, 179
age 155, 233
  and female labour force partici-
    pation 153–4, 171, 174–5,
    180–1
  see also developmental cycle; life
    cycle; marriage; migrant char-
    acteristics
agrarian reform *see* land
agriculture 16, 25, 34, 35, 39, 42,
    115, 116, 146, 162, 229
  intensification of 76–7
  peasant 34, 72
  plantation 22, 91
  subsistence 12, 63, 69, 105, 108,
    123

as mode of production 77
women as percentage of agricul-
    tural labour force, 34, 69, 73,
    75, 92, 125
women's work in 81–2, 83, 84,
    85
See also cash crops; farming
    system; HYV; livestock;
    mechanization; pastoralism;
    shifting cultivation
AIDS 128, 212n
aid, foreign
  for development projects 191
  for population control 191–2
aid agencies *see* development orga-
    nizations
Akan (people) 90, 150
Allah 26
  See also Islam
AMNLAE (Asociación de Mujeres
    Nicaraguenses Luisa Amanda
    Espinosa) 116, 185
anaemia 193, 202
  See also health; maternal health;
    pregnancy
Anglicanism 23
  See also Christianity
Animation Feminine 98
apprentices (as members of house-
    hold) 137–8
apprenticeships 165, 166, 187n
  See also informal sector
art *see* crafts
Arusha Declaration (Tanzania) 115
Asante (people) 50, 51, 137
Asia Partnership for Human Deve-
    lopment (APHD) 220, 231
ascariasis 208
assembly plants *see* export-process-

women's role in managing 68n, 216
See also infrastructure; services
wealth flows 195, 200
weaving *see* crafts; textiles
welfare
expenditure on 188–9
role of extended family in provision of 141
state provision of 189, 192
Western Kingston Women's Construction Collective 220
wheat 87, 88
witchcraft 120n
witches 111, 119
widows 40, 55, 83, 119, 148, 181
remarriage of 40
status of 40, 42, 119
See also household head; pollution; *sati*; women-headed households
Women and Geography Study Group (of IBG) 103, 115
Women and National Development (WAND, Caribbean) 244
Women in the Caribbean Project (WICP) 73, 101, 107
Women in Development International Loan Fund (WID Inc.) 223
women household heads *see* household heads
women-headed households 19, 22, 23, 24
definitions of 45, 135–6
discrimination against (in projects) 103, 215, 216, 228
factors in formation of 22, 24, 36, 54–5, 128–9, 145–51
frequency in rural areas 54, 56, 146
frequency in urban areas 56, 146–8, 213
problems faced by 149–50, 226–7
as target group in development

projects 218, 224, 236
See also culture; household heads
women-only agencies/institutions 223–4, 233–4
See also development organizations
women-only projects *see* projects
Women's Self-Help Construction Project (Panama) 228, 236
Women's Union of Vietnam 116
women's war (Igbo) 68n
Women's World Banking 222, 223
work *see* domestic labour; employment; labour force participation; production; reproduction; underestimation
World Bank (IBRD) 94, 112, 209
world capitalist system 4, 48, 53, 63, 92, 94, 118, 123
World Health Organization (WHO) 205
world market factories 43, 44
women as labour force in 43, 171–2, 186
World Plan of Action 243
See also United Nations, Decade for Women
world religions 63, 66, 94
See also Buddhism, Christianity, Catholicism, Hinduism, Islam

yams 63, 83, 85
Yanomamo (people) 51
Yin-Yang 43
Yoruba (people) 79, 85ff, 93, 177

zenana (women's quarters, Islamic societies) 87
Zimbabwean African National Union (ZANU) 37
Zimbabwean African People's Union (ZAPU) 37
Zionism 243